Reforming College Composition

Recent Titles in
Contributions to the Study of Education

Moral Development Theories–Secular and Religious: A Comparative Study
R. Murray Thomas

An Integrated Theory of Moral Development
R. Murray Thomas

The Condition of English: Literary Studies in a Changing Culture
Avrom Fleishman

Resource Allocation and Productivity in Education: Theory and Practice
William T. Hartman and William Lowe Boyd, editors

The Educational System of Israel
Yaacov Iram and Mirjam Schmida

Writing Centers and Writing Across the Curriculum Programs: Building Interdisciplinary
Partnerships
Robert W. Barnett and Jacob S Blumner, editors

Country School Memories: An Oral History of One-Room Schooling
Robert L. Leight and Alice Duffy Rinehart

Education of Teachers in Russia
Delbert H. Long and Roberta A. Long

Eminent Educators: Studies in Intellectual Influence
Maurice R. Berube

Private Prometheus: Private Higher Education and Development in the 21st Century
Philip G. Altbach, editor

The Bright Boys: A History of Townsend Harris High School
Eileen F. Lebow

Célestin Freinet
Victor Acker

Reforming College Composition

Writing the Wrongs

Edited by
Ray Wallace, Alan Jackson,
and Susan Lewis Wallace

Contributions to the Study of Education, Number 79

Greenwood Press
Westport, Connecticut • London

Library of Congress Cataloging-in-Publication Data

Reforming college composition : writing the wrongs / edited by Ray Wallace, Alan Jackson, and Susan Lewis Wallace.
    p. cm.—(Contributions to the study of education, ISSN 0196–707X ; no. 79)
    Includes bibliographical references and index.
    ISBN 0–313–31093–9 (alk. paper)
    1. English language—Rhetoric—Study and teaching.   2. Report writing—Study and teaching (Higher)   3. Educational change.   I. Wallace, Ray.   II. Jackson, Alan, 1957–   III. Wallace, Susan Lewis.   IV. Series.
PE1404.R383   2000
808′.042—dc21   99–054456

British Library Cataloguing in Publication Data is available.

Library of Congress Catalog Card Number: 99–054456
ISBN: 0–313–31093–9
ISSN: 0196–707X

First published in 2000

Greenwood Press, 88 Post Road West, Westport, CT 06881
An imprint of Greenwood Publishing Group, Inc.
www.greenwood.com

Printed in the United States of America

The paper used in this book complies with the Permanent Paper Standard issued by the National Information Standards Organization (Z39.48–1984).

10 9 8 7 6 5 4 3 2 1

To the Practitioners

Contents

§

Introduction

Ray Wallace, Alan Jackson and Susan Wallace

Reforming College Composition: Writing the Wrongs presents nineteen essays written by leading writing professionals, professors of English in leading colleges and universities throughout the country, educational theorists, teachers "in the trenches," and curriculum designers, all who have one common goal. All these writers are concerned with their own failure as writing specialists to improve their own students' writing skills. These writers examine why entering college students still write poorly, and why our various attempts to redress such poor writing skills have failed for the most part; they compare the "promise" of previously touted new methods, paradigm shifts, and curricular innovations with the "reality" of little change or improvement; they describe what their students can and cannot do in the writing classroom, even after twelve years of primary and secondary education; and they, in several different key ways, address what they see as needed reforms in the whole idea of college composition, especially for the first-year college student.

A book for any academic reader interested in why our students' writing skills have not improved as we had expected them to, and how we are going to, more realistically this time, improve on this state of affairs, *Reforming College Composition: Writing the Wrongs*, begins with the confession that we, as writing teachers, have not achieved as much as we thought we would in the last twenty-five years. With the realization that colleges and universities would be faced with huge increases in student populations, given both the demographics of the baby boom period combined with open admissions policies and the rise of community colleges, teachers of college writing have been aware for a very long time that they would be responsible for bringing a tremendously heterogeneous group of students, varying in age, class, gender, and educational background, to the requisite level of literacy to perform in their respective college careers. We accepted the fact that colleges and universities were no longer homogenous havens for a particular class and/or gender; in fact most writing professionals entered the field precisely because many new populations had finally been granted access to higher education. With these new populations came new employment opportunities.

In the past twenty-five years, we have attempted to persuade each other, and more important perhaps, the paying public, that we know how to improve our nation's writing levels. In the past quarter century we have offered the process movement, writing across the curriculum, critical thinking, English for academic purposes, whole language, grammar instruction, lack of grammar instruction, freewriting, imitation, computer-assisted composition, writing labs, writing groups, MOOs and MUDs (to name just a few). We, as a profession, flit about these "new and proven" techniques with little or no real introspection as to what we are actually producing. We are sailors in search of the wind; practitioners in search of the next movement. And yet, as we drift aimlessly from innovation to innovation that we practice on each year's crop of students, we, in fact, take little reckoning of what works and what does not. We cannot, with any certainty, point to one method that can be replicated with success, and we still rely for the most part on anecdotal "evidence" to persuade others that we have found the "cure for the common writing woe" present in our classrooms.

So, here we are about to enter another millennium. Our literacy levels are falling, our admissions standards are almost nonexistent, and each year the same composition instructors who deal initially with ineffective first-year writers are busy finally sending out first-year teachers trained with the same level of vagueness of purpose and method. It is little wonder we are faced with the recurring problem of entering college students with poor writing and reading skills; we produce the teachers who instruct them. This collection admits our mistakes. Through three distinct sections: Writing the Wrongs: Voices of Concern; Righting the Wrongs: Voices from the Trenches; and, Writing and Righting the Future: Preparing New Voices, the contributors are taking this opportunity to design our profession for the next millennium. They have been asked to write our wrongs, and, then, to right our wrongs.

WRITING THE WRONGS: VOICES OF CONCERN

In "First the Bad News, Then the Good News: Where Writing Research Has Taken Us and Where We Need to Take It Now," Wendy Bishop suggests that for the last twenty years, it has been a strong tenet of composition writing classrooms that instruction should start where the student is–that it should engage students and encourage them to view themselves as literate citizens while developing their literacy skills. While a great deal of composition research was completed to understand how writers compose, how writing students respond to teacher-commentary on their work, and so on, far less research has provided context-based insights into the general classroom experiences of first-year writing students, asking whether and how theory has been put into practice, if students feel engaged in or even well served by contemporary writing curriculums, and if and how they view themselves as developing writers and literate citizens.

Bishop's conversational style, with the reader and herself, offers an appropriate questioning ploy for the focus of this chapter. Indeed, Bishop notes that when researchers have asked such questions, they've uncovered perplexing issues. For instance, Jennie Nelson found students evaluating assignments far more pragmatically than their professors assumed, Susan Wyche-Smith found writing classrooms playing a minor role in complicated student lives, and Susan Miller and five student-researchers uncovered strongly conflicting views of literacy among college professors across the curriculum and among the student-researchers she worked with. Bishop consequently reconsiders the students' repeatedly documented isolation, even from their classmates, and the distancing strategies, humor, and anger they found to naturalize it.

While composition professionals have rightly and usefully looked at curriculum and program design and institutional politics, composing processes and workplace practices—all with the goal of improving classroom instruction—they have, perhaps, overlooked the more difficult to study arena of college composition students' experiences. Bishop explores the ways composition research has focused more on the needs of teachers and programs than on the results of instruction and experiences of student writers in classroom contexts. Bishop calls for a refocusing of our research that might lead us to insights into why–with the best of intentions–some of our classroom practices are having less than stellar success.

Kelly Lowe's chapter "Composition and the End of Everything; or The Bravery of Being Out of Range: What's Wrong with a Postmodern Composition Theory?" takes the reader on an interesting journey from graduate student full of wonder to compositionist full of reality. Here we see the evolution of writing teacher, and this chapter "unpacks" this evolution with startling frankness. Postmodernism is noted as a wonderful theoretical exercise (but not without a few jabs along the way), but when the realities of composition classes (note plural) come to bear, this theoretical construct holds little water. Simply stated, once Lowe enters the world of full-time employment in composition and meets students who have already articulated much for themselves, postmodernity hits a giant academic and philosophical roadblock.

Lowe asks our theorists to think again—to attempt a more realistic approach to his students—and again he points to postmodern composition's failure to reach his students. Through a compelling, no-holds-barred, chapter, Lowe has written frankly and clearly about what it means to "grow up" in the composition classroom. His chapter offers the beginning compositionist hands-on experience and reaction to the implementation of theory (at least postmodern theory) in the composition classroom. The author explores what it means to put theory into practice at the grassroots; his picture makes interesting reading for those on both sides of this fence.

In "Expressivisms as 'Vernacular Theories' of Composing: Recovering the Pragmatic Roots of Writing Instruction," Don Bushman notes that over the course of the last fifteen years, certain methods of composition instruction have fallen into "disrepute," mainly, he suggests in this chapter, because of the "philosophization" of composition studies. When critics like James Berlin and Lester Faigley began to seek out the epistemological roots of various pedagogical methods, they were certainly performing valuable critiques of established pedagogies, but they may also have persuaded many of us to turn our backs on effective pedagogies–among them those that have been classified as "expressivisms." Bushman continues that although recent apologists for expressivism (e.g., Burnham, Gradin) have claimed that expressivist rhetorics have been misread and misrepresented as they've been critiqued, those claims both are and are not justified, that expressivist works often mirror a less-rigid epistemological framework than we have come to expect from a "theory" of composing. The early expressivists, Bushman argues, are not really "theorists" in the same sense that, say, Linda Flower and John R. Hayes are considered "cognitive theorists" of composition. These expressivists are instead "vernacular theorists" of composition. The term "vernacular theory" has been popularized in Thomas McLaughlin's book *Street Smarts and Critical Theory* (U Wisconsin P, 1996), wherein he defines "theory in the vernacular mode" as theories that are undertaken by those "who do not come out of the tradition of philosophical critique" and that "arise out of intensely local issues." He goes on to say that while vernacular theories often "fail to transcend ideologies," they "manage in spite of their complicity [with those ideologies] to ask fundamental questions about culture" (5-6). In this chapter, Bushman proposes that the theories of early expressivist compositionists (such as Macrorie, Coles, and Elbow) are "vernacular theories" and that the criticisms against them are indeed often valid: expressivist rhetorics are often complicit in a foundationalist/essentialist worldview. But he also argues that their often-contradictory epistemological stances in no way impinge upon their pedagogical effectiveness in certain local contexts, and, in the process, he addresses the positive and negative consequences of the "philosophization" of college writing instruction.

In "The Post-Process Movement in Composition Studies," Bruce McComiskey argues that after John Trimbur described the "post-process" movement in composition studies as the result of a crisis within the process paradigm and a growing disillusion with its limits and pressures, the term "post-process" recently enjoyed some currency in composition studies. McComiskey continues that its meaning remains unclear because in each idiomatic usage of the term this "post" means something different, ranging anywhere from a radical rejection to a complex extension of what came before. In this chapter, McComiskey argues that the most fruitful meaning for the "post" in post-process is extension, not rejection, and he offers social-process rhetorical inquiry as a method for extending our present view of the composing process into the social world of discourse.

First, Thomas Kent uses the term "post-process theory" to signify his radical break with modernist writing process pedagogies. Kent argues against "systemic rhetorics" that treat the production and analysis of language as a codifiable process. Language is inherently unstable, contradictory, chaotic, Kent argues; and writing thus cannot be reduced to a system or taught as a process. McComiskey argues, however, that while pedagogical strategies for invention and revision may indeed constitute a systemic "metalanguage," they comprise no more a metalanguage than paralogy and dialogue, the keywords Kent uses most to describe post-process theory. Further, the very word "theory" implies a systemic view of the thing that Kent argues has no system. Without a certain degree of systemic rhetoric, Kent would neither be able to compose arguments against process pedagogy nor even be able to conceive of post-process as a "theory."

McComiskey further notes that the critique of expressivist ideologies from social perspectives in composition scholarship has resulted in the incorrect perception that with this social critique comes a necessary rejection of the composing process, but this is simply not the case. As James Berlin, Lester Faigley, and Karen Burke LeFevre have all pointed out, social approaches to writing instruction view composing as a social (not individual) process. Thus, "the writing process" is not the sole province of expressivism, and the "social turn" in composition studies, which Trimbur labels "post-process," does not constitute, in practice or theory, a radical rejection of the process movement, but rather its extension into the social world of discourse.

McComiskey concludes that social-process rhetorical inquiry, a specific pedagogical methodology that responds to the exigencies of the post-process social turn in composition studies, begins with a cyclical model of writing (the production, distribution, and consumption of discourse) that accounts for both the composing strategies of writers and the socio-discursive lives of texts. Invention heuristics based on this cycle encourage students to understand language and culture as constructive forces conditioned by contexts and negotiated by critical subjectivities who then use their negotiated readings of existing texts to produce new texts, and so on. McComiskey concludes that students who engage in detailed exploration of all three moments in this cycle develop the sense that culture itself is a constantly changing process and that their own writing can influence some of the changes that cultures undergo, and social-process rhetorical inquiry brings these "post" processes of rhetorical intervention consciously to bear on students' own critical writing.

Gina Claywell, in "Finding 'The Writer's Way': What We Expected and How We've Erred," cites Mina Shaughnessy's *Errors and Expectations*, written in 1977, as a response to the basic writing problems created by open admissions, and notes that this work is now canonical in rhetoric and composition, not only for its recognition of the patterns of errors students write but also for its empathy regarding the difficulties that students have with writing and that teachers have with teaching writing. In the twenty years since its publication, the field of rhetoric and composition has blossomed, and its members have zealously examined new trends in related fields, applying a plethora of methods and theories to the teaching of writing as they went. Still, none of us seem quite satisfied with our programs or our individual instruction. Claywell notes that only now are we beginning to understand that Shaughnessy's concern with "the writer's way" implies a multitude of writing processes, not one way of writing shared by all writers. And, though we give lip service to the recommendations Shaughnessy made lo those many years ago and despite the technology that makes writing much less onerous than ever, we still have much more to accomplish in areas such as writing across the curriculum, student writing conditions, the social independence of classrooms, and the content of composition courses themselves. Claywell's chapter examines these areas, comparing the predictions and hopes Shaughnessy revealed to the current status of composition programs at four schools in three states. It draws on past experiences of the author at these sites, but is further supported by incidences cited in current literature and by readily available data on the Internet. The chapter concludes with a discussion of the ways real changes can be made—most of which include the need for English programs to consolidate their political muscle but not before they reach consensus about what they really value.

Christina Murphy and Joe Law's chapter, "The Writing Center and the Politics of Separation: The Writing Process Movement's Dubious Legacy," notes an important development in composition related to the world of writing centers and their place in the composition discipline itself. Famously hailed by Maxine Hairston as a "paradigm shift" on the order of the revolution in science, the writing process movement is closely associated with a curious development in writing centers—a tendency to separate themselves not only from English departments but from the rest of the academy as well. A key moment in this development is Stephen M. North's "The Idea of a Writing Center" (1984), an essay that crystallized the attitudes of many writing center practitioners at that time and that has since been widely regarded as a writing center manifesto. Asserting that English departments do not understand the work of writing centers, North goes on to affirm that this work focuses on writers rather than on their writing, and his description of writing center practice firmly links it to the "paradigm shift" that had occurred in composition.

Murphy and Law do not want to suggest that North's essay is itself the cause of subsequent developments in writing center discussions; however, his frequently cited work seems typical of what has followed. Two principal strands in "The Idea of a Writing Center"—the distinction between the writing center and the rest of the academy and the emphasis on the writer as an individual to be improvedhave dominated much writing center scholarship over the past fifteen years. The classroom and writing center are often treated as though they are in competition. At other times, the sense of conflict escalates to take on the academy as a whole.

Murphy and Law report several unfortunate consequences from these strands. They report that first, although the emphasis on the individual student would seem to be a good thing, published writing center scholarship has tended to center on the affective level of the writing center's work rather than on its effectiveness as pedagogy. That focus includes the current debate about the "ethics" of tutoring. Though interesting in their own right, these side issues do not address the more pressing questions of assessing our pedagogical effectiveness, an issue crucial to the future of writing programs in general. If the public in general—and legislators in particular—continue to perceive problems in higher education, questions of who owns the text will become irrelevant. The authors further note that this larger aspect of "institutional politics" has largely been ignored. Much of the writing on the topic has been of the sort that represents the writing center professional as a martyr to marginalization without looking at the role of the writing center in the institutional context. Such posturing can only alienate the administrators who make crucial decisions about the writing center and justify their tendency to make those decisions without consulting writing center personnel.

Murphy and Law argue that writing center professionals need to examine pularly as the academy as a whole faces unprecedented challenges. With support for higher education dwindling rapidly, schools are increasingly likelier to turn to private enterprises to provide cost-effective instruction that can produce quantifiable results. In this context, Murphy and Law conclude that writing centers can no longer cast themselves as maverick, anti-establishment enterprises but must look much more realistically at the political and economic conditions in which they exist.

RIGHTING THE WRONGS: VOICES FROM THE TRENCHES

Ray Wallace and Susan Lewis Wallace in "Readerless Writers: College Composition's Misreading and Misteaching of Entering Students" note that composition theorists don't seem to be writing theory for the same types of students they teach. They note that several decades ago Walter Ong claimed in a landmark essay that a writer's audience was always a fiction, and in many ways these words have become more prophetic and, alas, ironic in college composition classrooms concluding this century. Ong's essay, of course, dealt with audience considerations, and the supposition that writers had to invent an audience for their writing, had to imagine an audience responding to their writing, and had to understand what this fictional audience would and would not comprehend from their writing; consequently, a writer's drafting and revising strategies would gradually clarify these areas for this audience. Implicit in this compelling argument was, of course, an awareness of what an audience was. Unfortunately, Wallace and Lewis Wallace note that today, their composition classrooms are full of many functional academic illiterates who have not the first idea of what it takes to be considered a reader, let alone think about how another reader (fictional or not) might respond to their attempts at written communication.

They preface their discussion by noting that not all their students fall into this category—many students have already discovered the joy and importance of reading, many read daily newspapers and have subscriptions to several weekly and monthly magazines and other periodicals, many have used the public library and high school library regularly, and many view a visit to a bookstore as both entertaining and elucidating. However, their chapter discusses what for them is an alarming increase in the number of students who are functionally and culturally illiterate and how these students impact both our composition pedagogy and our expectations for their success. They deal with a sizable population who even after twelve years of primary and secondary education still cannot: read eighth-grade materials at the most basic comprehension levels, form sentences correctly, and still have no clear idea about how (or why) to construct an essay (or even a letter). Many of these same students demonstrate an alarming lack of basic factual knowledge about their local, state, regional, national, or international environment. Many of their students have never read a novel, and have never read a newspaper or magazine. Many of their students watch five and six hours of television a day, never attend a cultural event (unless forced to), and have never been exposed to the joy of learning and had the importance of this learning explained to them. Many of their students have in fact seen those without much formal "book-learning" succeed in employment opportunities. Many of their students have no idea how many states there are in this country, cannot accurately talk about their own culture's history, or cannot even find their own locations on a map. The authors note that we are now teaching a group of nonreaders, and, unfortunately, composition pedagogy has not responded to this situation very well.

This chapter first describes in detail this population of nonreaders. Second, the authors discuss how such students affect composition curricula. Third, the authors discuss and offer solutions to the problem of composition's place in the academy. They note that "only when we understand the types of students we are actually dealing with in college composition can we begin to develop appropriate curricula for these students. Until then, composition theorists (i.e., infamous for not having the time to teach the courses on which they theorize; those who preach, but do not practice) are simply burying their heads in the pedagogical sand, while those of us in the trenches (i.e., those of us who actually teach composition, semester in and semester out) will be pounding this same sand in vain."

In the chapter "Peer Review and Response: A Failure of the Process Paradigm as Viewed from the Trenches," Lynne Belcher notes that twenty-six years ago when Donald Murray argued that writing should be taught as a process not a product, he foresaw many implications for teaching the process rather than the product. The first implication Murray lists in his essay "Teach Writing as a Process not Product" is "The text of the writing course is the student's own writing. Students examine their own evolving writing and that of their classmates, so that they study writing while it is still a matter of choice, word by word." Ten years later, Maxine Hairston argued for a paradigm shift in the teaching of writing in her "The Winds of Change: Thomas Kuhn and the Revolution in the Teaching of Writing." She argued that the new paradigm should focus on the readers in students' writing during that process. Belcher notes that she also argued that students benefit "far more from small group meetings with each other than from the exhausting one-to-one conferences that the teachers hold." Clearly, the process method of teaching writing involves reader intervention by students in the writing of their classmates. But how successful has that intervention been in the writing students produce? Since this part of the paradigm is so important to teaching writing as a process, we need to have some idea as to how well it has worked.

A careful examination of what happens as student readers intervene in the writing process of their classmates will show how this part of the process paradigm has failed. Students, for the most part, have not, as Murray argued, "examined their own evolving writing and that of their classmates . . . word by word." Nor has small group work been a greater benefit to student writers than the "exhaustive one-to-one conferences" between teacher and student writer, as Hairston argued sixteen years ago. What seems to be an essential part of the process paradigm has been a failure. In this chapter, Belcher examines what happens when students intervene in the writing of their classmates to see what the failures have been and to speculate as to why these failures have occurred. This chapter reports on a very interesting survey of writing teachers, and gives a real view from the frontlines.

Kerri Morris, in her chapter, "The Service Myth: Why Freshman Composition Doesn't Serve 'Us' or 'Them'," notes that whether or not we have said so explicitly, we have implicitly stated to the academic community that freshman composition is both a service to and a necessary part of an undergraduate education. This largely unexamined assumption has allowed composition specialists the opportunity to remain marketable in a barren hiring climate and has enabled funding for graduate programs across the United States. Additionally, it has been the coat rack upon which our disciplinary authenticity has been hung. The myth is pervasive and widely embraced by administrators, colleagues across the disciplines, and even, grudgingly, by most students. Upon the coattails of freshman composition, English Departments and, increasingly, composition specialists have become powerful forces in colleges and universities.

Morris continues that freshman composition has been our discipline's calling card, our entrance ticket into the academy. It has afforded us institutional power and departmental respect because it claims to do what the rest of the academy doesn't really want to do: teach students to write. However, if freshman composition serves to teach students to write science reports and historical research papers and philosophical speculations and psychological abstracts and to do so without errors and in an organized fashion, then it is not clear that we succeed in teaching students to "write." In fact, no one could accomplish this goal in one course or a two-course sequence. Morris's main concern is that freshman composition exists as a service course both in our minds and in our curricula, that it serves as the foundation for our discipline, and that a service model is an inadequate foundation for a discipline.

In this chapter, Morris examines the role of freshman composition in the academy and in the discipline. She argues that this course is no more or less important than any other introductory course in the curriculum, and she argues that viewing freshman composition as a service course harms students, our role in the academy as specialists, and our discipline.

Don Samson's chapter "Preparing Composition Students for Writing in Their Careers," offers some practical, concrete advice from an academic and a professional technical writer and editor. Samson comments that writing teachers only occasionally hear complaints from faculty in other departments about the quality of writing our students do, but the consensus seems to be that students write poorly, both before and after they take first-year composition. However, the failure of writing courses and programs to develop students' writing skills adequately is seen most clearly in the writing they do after they graduate. Samson explains that employers complain more often (and loudly) about graduates' writing skills, but as these complaints are rarely focused on a particular writing program or instructor, academics can often dismiss them with the customary rebuttal: "What do people in business know about good writing, anyway?"

Samson disagrees with these composition theorists. He states that many professionals in business and government do write well and recognize good writing, and writing instructors, especially teachers of first-year composition, need to pay attention to what they have to say. He explains that we too often do not solicit from our graduates' employers suggestions for our writing programs and instruction. To reform our teaching of composition—and if we are to enjoy outside support from business as funds for education dwindle—Samson thinks we need to consider not how to prepare students for academic, reflective, writer-centered writing, but for the writing they will do in their careers in business and government, writing very different from academic prose.

He notes that professional writing is reader-centered, not writer-centered, and readers in professional settings are very different from academic readers. They usually know less about the subject discussed than does the writer, but we continue to teach students to write for a professor who knows more than the student does about the subject or the approach. Also, in professional writing there is a great difference in purpose: professional writing is designed to communicate information and inform that less-knowledgeable audience, rather than demonstrate the writer's knowledge or ability.

Further, Samson claims, to produce graduates with good writing skills, we need to recognize that most college students will not take an advanced or applied writing course after they finish first-year composition. We need to make at least the second semester (or third quarter) of that course an experience that will prepare them for successful writing in their careers, where they will not write critical analyses of literature, reflective essays, personal narratives, or (especially) research papers. No one gets paid in professional settings to write such documents. We should not waste the precious time we have in composition classes teaching students how to write them when there is so much we can do to prepare them to write what they really will have to write in their work.

Samson's chapter examines the types of descriptive, narrative, and analytical writing that professionals have to do in most fields, and it suggests concrete ways that composition instructors might better prepare students for the writing they will do in their careers, rather than for academic writing.

James C. McDonald, in his chapter titled "Coming to Terms with the Freshman Term Paper," discusses this traditional writing component of the college composition sequence. McDonald agrees that there is a long tradition of complaint about the freshman research paper going back almost as long as the assignment itself, yet the assignment and its pedagogy have not changed significantly since the first *English Journal* article on the freshman research paper in 1930, beyond more emphasis on revising. He argues that the problems with the research paper cannot be separated from the problems of the first-year composition course, problems that the composition movement has yet to solve. Complaints and arguments about the freshman research paper generally reflect tensions between the service nature of the course to provide most of the instruction that students require for academic writing, English departments' definition of their mission primarily as one to teach students to read and appreciate literature, and the competition between composition and literature faculty about the first-year course.

McDonald continues by noting that learning the research methodologies of a field and the discourse conventions of a discipline's academic article takes years. A curriculum that prepares students to write and conduct research requires a thoughtful sequence of instruction in writing, reading, and research that extends beyond the freshman composition course. To expect students to learn to write the research article by the end of their first year of college, only to hone their skills in later research paper assignments, places unrealistic demands on the first-year course and has led to an oversimplification of the reading and research processes involved in composing an academic article. At the same time, the freshman research paper has often been treated as ancillary to the main agenda of the composition course, especially when the course focuses on writing about personal experience or writing about literature.

McDonald claims that answers to the questions of why students should engage "in research" at this stage in their academic careers and what this research instruction should prepare them for generally have not been addressed adequately in the long debate about the freshman research paper. Why first-year college students need to learn to write the academic article, a genre that only a few will write seriously in their careers, is seldom discussed at all. Although some students learn to engage in "independent learning" with the traditional research paper, the assignment does not show students how research can serve their needs and desires and tends to discourage students from regarding research as a necessary component in composing other genres. McDonald cites David Russell's work on the history of writing across the curriculum, to demonstrate that when the research paper replaced the declamation as the dominant genre of a student's college education, instead of writing and speaking to general audiences about important social and political questions, students were asked to write to specialized academic audiences and to address the narrower, often more arcane questions of an academic discipline. The service nature of the freshman research paper (and the high school research paper), to prepare students for research papers that they will have to write in later courses, has distracted attention away from considering what purposes research skills can serve inexperienced students now and what uses they may put their research skills to in their careers and future lives.

McDonald notes that the biggest problem with the freshman research paper has been a failure to treat this assignment, normally taught as a library paper, as a reading-to-write assignment that requires instruction in critical reading strategies of sources. He states that literature faculty are educated in critical reading strategies for literary texts but generally have ignored the problems of reading and critiquing the kinds of texts that students must analyze and argue from in a research paper. Composition faculty, at least until recently, have ignored the importance of reading in writing, often arguing that the only texts in the course should be the students' in fear that faculty trained in literary studies would transform the writing course into another lecture/discussion course about literature. Neither faculty educated in composition studies or literary studies has been educated about reading research and pedagogies. As a result, the reading instruction provided for the research paper in most textbooks and probably most classrooms fails to assume that reading is a recursive, meaning-making process that parallels the writing process, involving planning, drafting, revising, and consulting. Instead reading instruction assumes that language is a transparent window to the writer's thoughts and that reading is a simple process of converting signs to thoughts. Students are encouraged to skim and often discouraged from close reading of texts.

McDonald concludes by recognizing that as the World Wide Web becomes an important source for student research, it will be increasingly difficult to ignore the need to teach students ways of reading sources critically. However, he notes that for any reform to be successful, reading research and pedagogies will have to become an important part of college writing teachers' education, and curricula to provide students with an intelligent sequence of reading, writing, and research instruction will need to be developed.

In "The Bytes Are On, But Nobody's Home: Composition's Wrong Turns into the Computer Age," J. Rocky Colavito begins his chapter by noting that though a relatively new addition to the classroom, the desktop (and now laptop) personal computer has become a focal point for debate surrounding its rightful place in education. The debate is particularly contentious in the camps of Composition Theory and Practice, where the computer is seen as everything from the cure for all writing ills to an obstacle that obscures the students' faces during lectures. Colavito reports that studies have piled up, results have been shared, practices advanced, tested, and discarded, and still the place of the computer in the composition classroom remains under debate. Indeed, he explains, with the ephemeral nature of software packages and Internet publishing, composition teachers are confronted with a brand new set of challenges each day they walk in the classroom. Add to the rapid change a more powerful student body (in the sense that they possess more technical and computing knowledge than their teachers), and we have the makings of a very untenable situation for composition faculty as we slouch toward the millennium.

Colavito asks and answers the question "What got the field to this point?" He posits that it seems to have been a series of figurative, and literal, wrong turns into the "age of information." Rushing headlong into the computer age without regard for instituting measures to ease faculty into the mix is only one of several issues discussed in this chapter. Other wrong turns involve putting too much stock in inconclusive research findings (very few studies of computers and their influence on writing indicate anything more than students writing more and tending to undertake the craft of revising a bit more seriously, but still do little more than surface polishing), getting textbook publishers involved with software production, a seemingly wholesale failure to consider the lot of those students who come to college without computer skills (i.e., the information underclass, the techNOs), a similar disregard for the effects of keyboarding inexperience and cyberphobia in the writing classroom, and many others.

After reviewing the wrong turns, it's time to get out the road map and suggest some ways that Composition can get itself reoriented in the Information Age. Better training for faculty is only a start; the chapter posits some concrete solutions to both the theoretical and practical challenges our willy-nilly slide into the computer classroom has begotten. Colavito's chapter discusses better ways to meld traditional teaching with the use of computers, better ways to construct future studies, and, most significantly, better ways to construct more accommodating computer-supported classrooms so that all who use them, student and teacher alike, can profit from what each element has to offer.

Linda Myers-Breslin continues this discussion in "Technology, Distance, and Collaboration: Where Are These Pedagogies Taking Composition?" She also notes that a little over a decade ago, computers changed the face of composition. Computer-assisted composition instruction became an important subdiscipline within Composition and Rhetoric. Over the last five years, computer-assisted composition instruction has grown and changed considerably due to a shift in network use. Initially, technology allowed pedagogies to focus on revision and editing. Then, pedagogical movement toward collaboration was enabled by local-area discussion software like Daedalus Interchange and stand-alone hypertext programs such as Story-space and Hypercard. More currently, Internet technologies such as e-mail, MOOs and MUDs, Usenet news, interrelay chat, and the World Wide Web allow for larger, more public collaborative ventures. Myers-Breslin notes that when embarking upon such ventures we need to recognize not just the important differences between the LAN-based discussions and the public writing spaces of the Internet, but, regardless of the technologies used, the differences between placing words in the same space and collaboration.

Myers-Breslin also claims that unfortunately, as technology proliferates in composition classrooms and collaborative pedagogies, students spend more time using shared writing spaces to avoid work and sharing valuable, on-task ideas than they do actually using the space to their advantage by sharing ideas to complete the assigned task. Thus, we must ask ourselves several questions: Is the collaborative use of electronic writing spaces helping our students write well and continually improve their composition skills or is the technology distracting students from writing well and hindering their improvement?

Myers-Breslin responds to those of us looking for new ways to spice up our CAI pedagogy and those new to computers-assisted writing instruction, the Internet appears as a big public writing space, a larger version of our LAN-based writing spaces. As we move students from private to public audience, it makes sense to place students into the Net, to ask them to write in a space where anyone and everyone can read their words, to have them exchange ideas in a more real-world setting, with those out there in the real world. Through World Wide Web pages, newsgroup threads and chat rooms, and MOO discussions all have a space in which to place their words.

Naturally, the author claims that we would like this to mean that there is an instant writing community. We hope that students read what others have to say and convey their own ideas. But, Myers-Breslin asks, "Is this what is really happening?" She thinks not, and she claims that networked writing does not constitute community or even collaboration. To collaborate means more than to read what another writes and to place one's own thoughts. This constitutes brainstorming. Collaboration is a concerted pedagogical effort toward the creation of an end product. It is more than conversation. Finally, Myers-Breslin suggests that composition's application of the terms community, collaboration, and conversation to the Internet needs to be thought through more carefully than has been done by most up to this point.

In the final chapter in this section, "Linguistics and Composition," Sara Kimball explains that linguistics has long enriched the theory and practice of composition. In the 1950s and 1960s insights from linguistic theory into the systematic nature of language helped composition free itself from the bonds of prescriptive usage. Historically, linguistics has also inspired composition practice (e.g., transformational grammar and sentence combining), and it has been a source of useful metaphors both on the theoretical level (e.g., "recursion" in process accounts) and on the level of practice (e.g., Christensen's generative rhetoric). But the optimism of assessments of the potential value of linguistics to composition from the 1950s and 1960s contrasts strikingly with the more circumscribed tone of later assessments, such as Sharon Crowley's or Frank Parker and Kim Sydow Campbell's.

In this chapter, Kimball argues that some of the dissonance between the fields of composition and linguistics results from limited definitions of linguistics. She claims that the emergence of theoretical syntax as the dominant paradigm in linguistics and the creation of independent linguistics departments in the 1960s and 1970s tended to isolate linguistics from composition, since these changes took the focus of linguistics out of English and other language departments. Although linguists continue to study and teach in English departments, theoretical syntax is the face linguistics as a discipline presents to the public, and it is an aspect of linguistics that is unlikely to be congenial to the more humanistically oriented elements within composition and English studies. Kimball suggests that a wider view of linguistics as a multidisciplinary field, however, encompassing not only theoretical syntax, pragmatics, and discourse analysis, but also sociolinguistics and applied linguistics, leads to a more positive assessment of the historical influence of linguistics on composition and a more optimistic assessment of possibilities for the future.

She concludes by describing how composition might be better informed by linguistics. Although teaching undergraduates linguistic terminology is helpful in providing a common vocabulary for talk about language, it is even more important to educate writing teachers themselves. Parker and Campbell's call for cross-training graduate students is a step in the right direction, but it ignores the institutional reality that many composition instructors pursue literary and cultural studies rather than rhetoric and composition. She argues, therefore, that linguistics should remain a vital part of the curriculum of graduate programs in English studies, where it would also benefit students of literature. In this chapter, she offers suggestions about the topics within linguistics that a useful course might cover, including, for example, sociolinguistic variation, text linguistics, discourse analysis, linguistics and cognition, and studies of linguistic features of spoken and written language.

WRITING AND RIGHTING THE FUTURE: PREPARING NEW VOICES

The section begins with Janice Witherspoon Neuleib and Maurice Scharton's chapter titled "Many a Slip Twixt the Cup and the Lip: Teaching and Learning with Graduate Instructors," and these two veteran compositionists explain that senior faculty in charge of writing programs can easily assume that rigorous training and patient support of graduate instructors will ensure consistently successful instruction throughout a program. In the case of a large department, such an assumption can lead to exciting and sometimes frustrating results.

Their chapter includes a profile of facts about students at Illinois State University, including a report on Placement Test distribution for incoming freshmen students (4,500 freshmen per year), and an analysis of interview and observational data gleaned from studies of graduate instructors who teach writing in the program. The department has collected data in the form of classroom observation summaries, student evaluations, and self-reporting, all of which will enrich the interview methodology that will inform the study. All graduate instructors in this large department (served by 150 graduate instructors and a small number—less than 10—adjunct instructors) do receive extensive orientation and ongoing support and supervision during their teaching careers. For the most part, the authors explain, these graduate instructors do teach within the guidelines of the department; in fact, the department has consistently been singled out for its expertise in teaching and teacher training.

However, both Neulieb and Scharton note that despite a complex and theoretically informed program, instructors can vary from the standard supposed by the ideals and theories of the graduate professors in charge of graduate instructor training and support. In fact, these graduate instructors often construct pedagogies quite different from those discussed and recommended in graduate classes. The authors investigate the many positive methods outlined in course goal statements, including student-centered classrooms and state-of-the-art computer classrooms, and instructional techniques of classroom instructors. They also investigate how and why these variations occur, what types of teaching result in classrooms, what gaps exist between theoretically ideal approaches and actual instruction, and how undesirable pedagogies affect student performance, as well as recommend solutions to improve teaching and learning.

Moving into more discussion of training of future teachers, Stuart C. Brown's chapter, "Obscured Agendas and Hidden Failures: Teaching Assistants, Graduate Education, and First-Year Writing Courses," examines a number of the implications related to graduate education in English studies as it has bearing on the teaching of composition. He explores the key problematic areas including that the training of graduate students in teaching composition is done primarily at research universities where student populations often do not mirror the students these future teachers actually encounter; that many graduate students rarely receive training beyond an introductory course (at best) or a several day orientation before entering the classroom; that evaluation (and corrective disciplinary action) of graduate teaching assistants in the classroom is particularly difficult; that programs rely on a majority of graduate student teachers who are not pursuing studies in the teaching of writing, but primarily view this teaching as subsidy for their studies; that writing program directors have little say in who teaches in their programs as students are "awarded" teaching assistantships by disciplinary emphasis; that many graduate students either fail to see themselves as writers or fail to provide this insight to their students; that the graduate students themselves may be poorly prepared writers; that trained compositionists, even as graduate students, are likely to spend more professional time as administrators rather than as teachers; and that there is an increasing disjuncture among theorists, practitioners, and historians of writing that is reflected in the graduate education writing specialists receive.

Brown also notes that there are, of course, broader issues that affect writing programs such as the use and abuse of part-time instructors and adjuncts, the difficulties of many entry-level composition faculty in getting tenure recognition for teaching "service" level courses, and the failure of the academy to justify, or at least explain, its use of resources.

It is clear that Brown's intention here is not to anger, although the discussion within questions some of the fundamental assumptions underlying graduate education not only in English studies at large, but in the discipline of rhetoric and composition. Instead, in this chapter he helps initiate a discussion of how graduate studies is formulated, the costs of that formulation to beginning college writers, and some considerations for rectifying the problems.

From the other side of the desk comes Beth Maxfield's "The Preparation of Graduate Writing Teachers: Creating Substance Out of Shadows" offers a fresh perspective on graduate writing teacher preparation. She notes that a cursory literature review of the recent history of composition studies will reveal that much has been written about the writing competence (or the lack thereof) of freshmen, and even more has been written about the best ways to teach freshman composition. Maxfield claims that those of us who have devoted our professional lives to researching and teaching composition have articulated our diverse views with increasing vigor and conspicuity. However, our theories about writing instruction have not reached the right audience to the extent that they might be practiced by the vast majority of freshman composition teachers—graduate teaching assistants. Furthermore, too little of our time—both as practitioners and as theoreticians—has been dedicated to preparing these future teachers of writing for the realities of teaching such a subjective and personal course as is the writing course. She agrees with others in this collection that a part of this problem rests with the derisive attitude toward teaching of writing within the microcosm of the English department (i.e., the literature specialists) and within the academic community in general; however, a more disturbing aspect is the blasé attitude toward freshman composition teaching by composition teachers themselves. She claims this combination of these attitudes creates a no-win situation for the new TA as well as the freshman writer.

Maxfield continues by noting that despite the rising visibility of composition as a discipline and increasing political pressure to substantiate effectiveness, the practice of placing ill-prepared (and, often, uninterested) graduate teaching assistants in freshman composition classes continues; in fact, at some schools, the only writing teachers freshmen writers see are TAs. While we have professed, through orientation workshops, course requirements, mentorships, practica, and the like, to prepare TAs to enter the freshman composition classroom, we have been doing nothing so much as casting a smokescreen; the training most often provided for TAs is much more abstract and theoretical than it is concrete and practical. She is quick to note that while these new teachers need a philosophical grounding, their more pressing need is practical: how to apply theory in the classroom.

Professor Maxfield, herself not long graduated from a composition program, notes that if we aim to produce better writers, we must first produce better writing teachers. She suggests that in order to do so, we must alter our own attitudes toward the teaching of freshman composition; our enthusiastic teaching of it is necessary for us to teach others how to teach it. We must also be willing to make changes in the status quo and in the process step on some academic toes; some of the changes may be perceived as territorial invasion by members of other disciplines. In her chapter, she explores the merits and faults of some current practices in TA training as seen in survey results; her goal in this chapter is to broach this subject as an opening of discussion and an impetus for initiating action among my fellow composition specialists.

Alan Jackson broaches a different subject, cognition, but with the same goal, to show others its importance to teaching writing, and to initiate discussion and action. In his chapter, "Cognition and Culture: Addressing the Needs of Student-Writers," Jackson considers the failure of composition studies to address the growing diversity of age and experience, a failure that reflects composition's abandonment of cognitive theories. He discusses advances in cognitive science, especially the idea of emergents, that can lead to better, more individualized, college composition teaching methods and classroom dynamics that incorporate the distinct needs and cognitive levels of students. He discusses how most readers are promoted as introducing students to the world around them, which ignores the nontraditional student who lives and works in that world, who has gone past issues of personal growth and awareness thought common to the traditional first-year composition student.

Furthermore, he discusses other areas where this gulf can create problems if not recognized and incorporated in the college composition classroom. For example, most incoming first-year college students are full-time and quickly acculturate to college life, and they also are comfortable with the academic standards and expectations inherent in many classrooms. However, for many other students, college life is not their primary culture and they have lost contact with academic norms. But cognitive and cultural differences also require attention in assigning group work and in handling class discussions, among other activities. Jackson claims that composition professionals need to recognize that many student-writers have gained, from work and life experiences, a broader range of skills and knowledge, as well as a different way of approaching learning. In addition, these students have a greater need for the immediate assistance in adapting their writing to the workplace. Jackson notes our fascination with academic discourse, but also reminds us that for his type of student, the concern is not in developing skills relevant to a future work environment, but in possessing skills for immediate workplace success.

As a framing technique, Jackson examines the current state of cognitive theory as it is reflected in composition journals, a state that has seen little advancement since the work of Linda Flowers. He contends that new developments in cognitive science, of cutting-edge researchers such as Duane Rumbaugh and Michael Cole, will force composition professionals to rethink their understanding of learning. In addition, he explores how these developments might lead to changes in the way we teach writing to individual student-writers: first, by recognizing that cognitive differences require instructional differences and; second, by understanding how experience alters one's cognitive capacity for learning.

In the final essay in this section, "Breaking the Learning Monopoly: Acknowledging and Accommodating Students' Diverse Learning Styles," Eric H. Hobson continues Jackson's premise on the need for individuality in instruction when reports that the past decade has been particularly boisterous within composition studies as any number of "correctives" to the traditional paradigm of the first-year writing program have been championed. Proponents of cultural studies have argued that writing courses benefit from having a critical center. This position links their corrective plan to similar calls for reform that would have first-year writing courses center around critical thinking/problem-solving foci. Responding to writing-across-the-curriculum's success, others see a remedy to the traditional paradigm in a distinctly disciplinary writing sequence, often spread over several years of study. Other remedies would have the first-year writing sequence focus on such issues as race, power, and economics.

He notes that regardless of the extent to which each of these proposals rests on logical, even meritorious, foundations consistent with the best intentions of the liberal arts, they all exhibit a fundamental flaw, one seemingly endemic to American higher education. These reform models are linked to an uncritical and unrealistic understanding of their clientele—ironically, so too is the traditional paradigm they would replace. For the most part, the correctives presented in the past decade paint students taking the first-year writing sequence with a too broad brush; these plans fail to consider the variety of learning styles and preferences that students bring to the composition classroom, learning algorithms through which students make sense both of the world at large and of immediate classroom instruction.

Hobson, drawing from a number of disparate studies of learning styles/preferences found in school populations, suggests that for any fix-it plan to successfully reform the first-year writing sequence, it must make a fundamental, even paradigmatic shift in perspective from viewing students as composite groups—often assumed to share their instructors' learning preferences—to viewing these students on a more individualized basis, recognizing the variety and diversity of learning systems on which students rely in any given classroom. Hobson claims that this recognition, however, although intuitively appealing, is not without profound implications—many of them hard to champion in an era of budget slashing for direct instruction. As such, this chapter not only presents data on the learning styles among the students taking the typical first-year writing course, it compares this data to similar data on instructor learning styles and the teaching practices they employ. The dissimilarities apparent in this comparison raise any number of disturbing issues, including the possibility that the very structure of the course, as it reflects the instructor's biases about what learning style are academically valuable, may, in large part, determine levels of student success in the course.

As editors of this collection, we feel quite fortunate in how this volume has developed. The contributors did not exchange their chapters as they prepared them for this collection, yet in final form they share some important common threads. Consider how many of the authors comment on our theoretical excesses in composition. Consider how many of them question our students' reading skills, and our inability as professionals to integrate reading instruction into writing classrooms. Consider how many suggest that we step back for a moment to revise our vision of the discipline of composition and its boundaries. Consider how many comment on our "place" in the academy, and how we have been underappreciated by our colleagues in other areas of English. Consider how many comment on the need for more individualized instructional methods that explore and acknowledge students' learning styles. Consider how many ask for more concrete evidence as to the successes of our own approaches. Consider how many comment on the problem of composition theorists who don't teach composition.

Of course there are areas in which the authors disagree, but it is these common threads that perhaps offer more hope for the future of our discipline. It has been said that confession is good for the soul, and this is our hope for this volume. By writing our wrongs, we are beginning to draw some of the initial boundaries for our revised discipline. We are coming together here to say that not everything we have tried or claimed has worked, but we have come together here to explore these promises and claims in order not to repeat them. Our failures are acknowledged and seeds for the reconciliation between the discipline as it stands now and the discipline we hope for have been planted in this volume.

We must thank several people who have helped bring this book to completion. Obviously without contributors, a volume such as this is a nonstarter from the onset. Our contributors have been wonderful to work with and continue much of our discussion through e-mail. George Butler and Heidi Straight of Greenwood were with us at all stages of the publication process, and their professional guidance and advice have helped us grow as editors.

Finally, we cannot speak highly enough of the talents that Lesa R. Thompson has demonstrated throughtout this project. Ms. Thompson, Northwestern State University's desktop publishing expert, typesetter, and copyeditor in the Department of Language and Communication, has single-handedly brought the final copy to fruition. We could not have completed this work without her many hours of hard work and her endless dedication.

Reforming College Composition

———— I ————

WRITING THE WRONGS: VOICES OF CONCERN

First the Bad News, Then the Good News: Where Writing Research Has Taken Us and Where We Need to Take It Now

Wendy Bishop

For the last twenty years, it has been a strong tenant of composition writing classrooms that instruction should start where the student is–that it should engage students and encourage them to view themselves as literate citizens while developing their literacy skills. While a great deal of composition research was completed to understand how writers compose, how writing students respond to teacher-commentary on their work, and so on, far less research has provided context-based insights into the general classroom experiences of first-year writing students, asking:

1. Whether and how theory has been put into practice.

2. If students feel engaged in or even well served by contemporary writing curricula.

3. If and how they view themselves as developing writers and literate citizens.

When researchers have asked such questions, they've uncovered perplexing issues. For instance, Jennie Nelson found students evaluating assignments far more pragmatically than their professors might have assumed they were doing; Susan Wyche-Smith found writing classrooms playing a minor role in complicated student lives; and Susan Miller and five student-researchers uncovered strongly conflicting views of literacy, among college professors across the curriculum and among the student/researchers who visited those professors' classrooms:

I consequently also need to reconsider the students' repeatedly documented isolation, even from their classmates, and the distancing strategies, humor, and anger they found to naturalize it. It took no special training in psychology to realize that our frequent group discussions of how often each one fell asleep in class and while studying, Alycia's legalistic view of attendance, Worth's calculated visits to professors, and John's assessment of what he pays professors to do were all expressions of admittedly WASP students, stinging and stung by a system they fully expect to join. (Anderson 31)

Although composition professionals have rightly and usefully looked at curriculum and program design and institutional politics, composing processes and workplace practices—all with the goal of improving instruction in the classroom—they have, perhaps, overlooked the more difficult to study arena of college composition students' experiences.

This chapter will explore the ways composition research, at least recently, has focused more on the needs of professionalization in composition and on writing programs than on the results of instruction and experiences of student writers in classroom contexts. A refocusing of our research could lead us to insights into why—despite the best of intentions—some of our classroom practices are having less than stellar success.

And in fact, as I continue on I'd point out how much I'm part of the problem.

What you've just read is my academic voice. My write-a-prospectus-and-aim-it-from-one-professional-to-another-professional voice. What gets lost between these lines is an examination of what research really is at its simplest, most bedrock, most engaging, and most productive levels. Is the answer to, why would anyone do something that so often feels—as I explained again last fall to students in my research methods course—like making the obvious certifiably obvious? Why are the final results of our research as reported often so much like ... "duh"? Why do we appear to be seemingly just confirming common sense or general experience?

So, a forewarning. This parenthetical wandering you're now entangled in is more actually me, the me as writer of the last five to ten years, which is a me as thinker as I write, the me as active researcher.

To explain why I'm perturbed about composition research, I want to think of what research has most informed my teaching over the fourteen years I've officially been a compositionist, dating from my enrollment in graduate school to achieve that end. I also want to think about what my personal definition of research is and what that means for my teaching. Essayist rather than scholar that

I choose to be here, I want to see if these intuitive strands lead to any insight into this topic—what has been right but not right enough in this area of our field and what now could be made better?

Okay, honestly. What, if any, composition research has changed me as a teacher, informed my classrooms, illuminated my understandings of students-as-writers and as individuals I might help to write more proficiently?

Well, really a lot of it—but it all was part of my research into who I was and would be as a teacher of writing. I certainly benefited by reading the cognitivists and linguists I was assigned to read in the late 1980s and the cultural and critical theorists I read in the early 1990s, but I always was reading them to find out about life in my own petri dishes: what was cooking in my classrooms or in my own writing projects. That is, active researchers search for research that will inform and illuminate their own concerns as they undertake exploratory and explanatory journeys. And then later, learning to naturalistic research methods gave me a vocabulary and an identifiable set of practices for active research as I'm attempting to define it in this chapter.

For instance, after being "taught" about the Daly-Miller Writing Apprehension Survey (and reading across the other essays in *When a Writer Can't Write: Studies in Writer's Block and Other Composing Problems*, edited by Mike Rose), I took that information immediately to my writing classroom in the mid 1980s. I was not a highly apprehensive writer but my students seemingly were—at the time many were basic writers, Native American, and/or rural white Alaskans coming as first-time college students or as older, re-entry adults to the university in Fairbanks where I was teaching. And once I found many of the students scoring as highly apprehensive writers on the surveys I administered, this data led me into a search for research that would help me understand how to intervene in (or at least more fully understand) the writing processes of writers whose text-making experiences were so different from my own. And as most writing teachers know, text-making experiences in a classroom of twenty-five writers are similar to some degree and different to twenty-five degrees.

However, to talk via publications to other teachers about what I was finding out required that I switch from my classroom voice to the voice that opens this chapter, losing touch, to some degree with the very constituencies I was trying to share my work with: working teachers and their writing students. Thus, to enter my disciplinary community of fellow researchers, I did my academic scholarly job and reported what I learned, seeking always to place those reports in more and more prestigious journals as I had been trained to do. At the same time, I was removing my voice from the classroom. (And I need to another time examine the urge to do that—the potlatch sharing urge of an engaged research versus the institution-driven sharing of a tenure-line faculty, both of which I've been and will continue to be.) Mary Louise Pratt once pointed to a similar problem among anthropologists in a way I'd echo here when she wondered why so many interesting people with interesting projects in her field could write them up in such dull ways.

Too often we've agreed to dull ourselves. Isn't it ironic, as Alanis Morissette sings?

So, research is as important as we let it be and as we make it. It is as important as our institutions make it. Those two importances are often very different in degree, creating, in the first, research to understand and exhilarate, to inform and complicate. In the second, creating research for the research community and the researcher's sake (and if we're lucky, also to inform and complicate).

The movement from research primarily as informing educators to research as performing professionally was part, I suspect, of what led Sheryl Fontaine and Susan Hunter to solicit essays for a collection titled *Writing Ourselves into the Story: Unheard Voices from Composition Studies*. Just as "the research paper" was deadened when institutionalized in English classes around the nation, thereby obscuring the true and exciting research processes all learners need to undertake, so too "academic research" can become wooden, an albatross of a category, too often done for the worst reasons and under less than inspired conditions.

In *Writing Ourselves into the Story*, I argued that often we're researching at or on students when we could simply ask them and find out as much, or more; how, say, procrastination is a huge part of their writing process. I've still not seen any substantive research on procrastination, silence in writing, students who actively choose not to write or read and why they do so. Information is sparse on students' views of writing teachers and classrooms and where school fits in their lives and world views (see "Students' Stories").

To explore these issues would of course entail that we redefine research and/or deploy research in very different ways. It might mean we ask very different literacy questions—the types Mina Shaughnessey was asking in her still often cited *Errors and Expectations*, the kind asked in *Language Stories and Literacy Lessons*. The types Deborah Brandt is asking when she interviews a cross section of Americans to understand who sponsored their literacy, who helped them to become the readers and writers they are (no matter what the proficiency level they have attained (see "Remembering," "Accumulating").

When we ask why and what writing students aren't learning and why and what they are learning; how children learn to read; how we grade papers and what feelings of being graded affect a student's next composing experience; what students' writing processes really look like; what writers actually do and feel like (and feel like not doing) when asked to write in ways, in locations, and under conditions they would rather not be in; and how do nonacademics learn to read and write—we're asking them to speak to their own experience and address crucial classroom issues.

The fact that I generally have to seek these discussions out speaks to the problems we may be experiencing as a field. These issues are not in the forefront of journal discussions today that are much taken up with institutional pressures and conditions of teachers' and composition scholars' lives. Such is the bad news. There are reasons, of course. Current market forces, a population of teachers striving to turn scholars and encouraged to do so in our proliferating Ph.D. programs, immediately come to mind.

Still, the fact that I can name any research of this sort speaks to our good intentions and potentials. Such is the good news. It is possible to stay tuned into and attuned to our writing classrooms, to view and practice research as a process and part of our everyday practice.

To do this, we will need to continue to struggle to reconsider and reconceptualize research as part of the active life of teaching: posing and gaining insight into problems; theorizing and trying out answers and reporting those results in different venues. Consider, for instance, what it would mean if we saw innovative composition textbooks—and argued for them within evaluating department committees—as valid, perhaps even the preferred genre for research reports?

Dear reader, when was the last time you asked yourself: what do I really want to know? What do I think writing research can tell me, do for my classroom conditions and for students' literacy learning? What are the crucial questions, the fun questions, the silly and the sublime questions that could and should be explored?

Ask yourself: When I look out across the desks and into the eyes of these co-learners, when standing at the chalkboard or before a computer monitor that holds my teaching outline for the day, when I go home and avoid a stack of papers but still stay engaged with the class's work, what do I speculate on, wonder—idly and intelligently, facetiously or not?

Here's something that I've come up with that might strike a reader of this chapter as frivolous, but I'll use it throughout to test out the ideas I'm raising here.

Simply put—of all the things that confuse me in writing classrooms still—and many things do, and I use confuse in the positive sense of perplex, intrigue, make me think about my work when I'm not working, when I'm jogging or walking the dog—one odd but recurrent one is the issue of names.

Contemporary spellings of names are getting wild. The other day I found myself saying to a store clerk filling out a form and asking for my name: "It's Wendy with a y." I was trying to forestall the question about Wendi, Wendie, or Wendy, and maybe even Wendee. I've noticed in my years on earth that my name has moved from unusual to usual to complicated vowelings of independence. But I realized too at this moment that "It's Wendy with a y" was no longer sufficient. The clerk had paused, so I spelled: W E N D Y. Realizing he was wondering: Wynde, or Wyndy.

When I call roll in first-year writing—I could be concerned with (but I'm not) the elision of *a lot* to *alot* or the switch from his/her to their or the loss of whom to who. No, I spend far more time speculating on why I seem every year to see names spelled ever more inventively: Katina and Katrina in one class. Indee, Jadee (pronounced Judy), and Taquisha (aka Tiki) in another. [Should I investigate why women's names are most inventively spelled—the vowels and diminutive endings rife?] Jenni not Jenny. Alys or Alice. Andree, Lysa. Current best-selling singer, CD: *The Miseducation of Lauryn Hill*. Why do I misspell it and my students don't? What does it mean for me to inhabit their world as I order a copy on Amazon.com? Who is reading and writing what and what for and how well? And how does, how can composition research(ers) help?

I know some of this inventive spelling provides a strong and healthy cross-cultural infusion of dialect and dazzle (the desire to keep naming similar/family and original/my way). But . . . the writing teacher in me wonders if there's a clue in all this to general literacy issues—how students view language conventions, authorship, individuality, and conformity. I'd like to know more—to talk to other teachers about it as I know I will tonight when a local rhetoric reading group meets in Tallahassee, and I'll inevitably share current work-in-progress that is always thinking-in-progress.

I've already suggested one form of research we seem to neglect—that of simply asking students. That's where I might begin. What happens when I hold a classroom discussion on this naming issue? I'm continuously surprised by students' significant (to my teaching) answers to informal classroom questioning. Reading a graduate student's master's thesis draft last week, I noted how strongly the students in her study responded when asked how they felt about the first-year writing teacher whose class was being observed, and about that teacher's practices of sharing or not sharing personal information with them. One interviewee said boldly: "She is not needed to give any credentials, or background to the student. We are not here for her—she is here for us . . . I think she should be more concerned about what we have inside of us, instead of us knowing what she has inside of her." And, as happens when I read research that intrigues me, I mused for the rest of the afternoon on writing students' beliefs, asking myself, not for the first time, what I really knew about how they perceived teachers and what and where those perceptions impacted effective instruction?

Mulling over the student's interview response, I recognized how deflating this calm assessment and this claim would be to my teaching persona if he were my student. I also thought: this is my student. My students have strong opinions that I so often don't elicit. The have strong beliefs and long-inculcated practices that are often underlying and contributing causes to our classroom successes or problems. Nowadays, I believe, I'm simply not reading much about such tacit, undercover, unasked things because composition research, in general does not seem to be doing this type of asking.

Susan Peck MacDonald critiques the line I'm following here—she feels that my focus on researching into student-writers-as-people-who-write assumes that researchers like myself don't care as well *how well* students write: "Writing proficiency has dropped from view as a key purpose. There might be little role for research on student writing if writing proficiency is not the key purpose of the writing classroom" (117).

I'll focus on her use of "might" and insist that there is much to be studied when we consider writers as people, since it is the very humanity of the student I quoted above that accelerates, interferes with, impedes, or enhances his writing proficiency. I believe that as writers our worldviews are intricately entwined with our in-the-world performances in general. And I argue that composition research was on the threshold of considering these complicated interweavings when it took an abrupt (and sometimes but not always necessary) turn toward studying the material conditions of writing programs, writing teachers, and the relationships—often theoretical—between English literature faculty and English composition faculty. A turn that has absorbed us in the 1990s when such work has been prominent in our journals and often completed with an eye toward our tenure reviews.

So, this is more of the bad news—right when cognitive research and classroom-based naturalistic research were about to intersect, we moved away from asking the questions that might have allowed us to join in seeking to understand person-linked-to-personal-performance, in real contexts.

In the same volume, *Under Construction*, edited by Christine Farris and Chris Anson, that presents Susan Peck MacDonald's critique, we find a counterargument to the same that functions also as one explanation for what has happened. Basically, the professionalization of composition has created a class of scholar-researchers —rhetoricians or compositionists as you might name them, as I often name myself—and proletariat teachers who have been excluded from production yet continue to man and woman our classrooms and are even expected to consume the compositionist's often very dry and nearly irrelevant research product. Peter Vandenberg argues:

The reorientation of some compositionists and rhetoricians from "hapless bottom feeders" (Connors, 1991, 72) to endowed chairs has come about, in part, by the privileging of research, a signifier vacated of specific meaning for the purpose of establishing its necessity and, therefore, the necessity of those who produce it. (23)

To see this ever more plainly, ask the institutional researcher if he or she is interested in my classroom musing—why are invented spelling names gaining hold and do those unconventional spelling practices say anything to our students about literacy and/or speak for their attitudes toward learning standard English? Not a likely question of interest, though I continue to insist on how much it interests me.

As researchers, we also don't seem to be considering our work in another light.

What changes, I propose to ask now, if we view research as a type of active (sometimes activist) reading? The kind of reading searching teachers do, students do, theorists do, and testers of hypotheses do. But they all do their searching with different degrees of fluency, and self-consciousness, and for different goals and purposes.

This is my last point for the space I have here. We have cut off the search for information from the site of using at the exact historical moment when we're participating in the largest changes in information-accessing technology—the World Wide Web—that most of us will experience in our lifetimes. Certainly for me, as a writing teacher, the way I teach, the way I research, the way I write has been vastly changed and rapidly altered.

Consider the process of composing this chapter: e-mail proposal submission, on-line searching of the ERIC database to find any missing citations, checking Amazon.com for the spelling of Alanis Morissette because it's faster than walking into the back room and finding the CD. Think about the difference between finding a citation on-line and going to my shelf to look through the journal to walking into my classroom and—because I'm thinking of my "research" question—reading that classroom in a new light. All this information, all these ways of readings. Consider now re-reading the classroom as forum for intelligent hypothesis and doing the same for a student-teacher writing conference later that day. What I like best about my profession is this intense cognitive and contextual interactivity, intertextuality—something the availability of information on the web has actually accentuated.

I can e-mail my editor to ask for more writing time, I can query a colleague or student to gain preliminary answers to my "what is this spelling thing and have you noticed it too" question.

I can check my word processor for writing-about-naming exercises I've done in classes and think forward to how I might embody whatever I learn in this as yet inchoate "research" phase into future classrooms, or into an essay or a textbook exercise/discussion.

In all this, I'm reading my professional world for the good of my professional life.

Teaching the research paper as set of steps doesn't teach my writing students how to think like researchers. Neither does conducting writing research primarily for credentialing committees (though I have ultimately no problem with research functioning that way in an *and* capacity). Understanding composition research as part of my teaching process keeps me alive in the profession. And I'm finding this critical since many of my best buddies, my teaching cronies, my composition colleagues, are producing much talk about burnout—whether day-to-day classroom burnout or tired-of-the-elitist academy burnout, or both. Burnout comes from repetitive, wearing, unimaginative often-conflicted action. From policing and producing without speculating and renewing. It comes from divorcing research from practice (and assuming theory doesn't live here either).

So thanks for the pep talk, you may be saying, if you're still here at all. We should like our jobs. Research our classrooms. Seek to understand the intellectual, material, social conditions under which our students write and which keep them from writing more ably. We should renew and network, ask silly and sublime research questions. But how? Who and what will reward us? When and where can that work take place in our very busy lives?

No easy answers. But small suggestions.

Foremost among them. When you come upon interesting problems—honor them with a teacher's journal entry. When you're writing collegial e-mails, enliven them with those questions (every teacher likes to be asked teaching questions if the conditions are right). When you're wasting time on the web (face it—these days most all of us do), try out some of those questions on ERIC or other databases. Give yourself a reading (research) holiday and read an essay or article or book that you "assign" yourself—not for profit but for feeding your professional mind. If you don't value these activities first, no other person will—not a student, not a fellow teacher, department chair, funding agency, editorial review board.

Don't be afraid of research. If you integrate questioning into your teaching life processes there's no good or bad research, there's no guinea pig. There's the classroom as intellectual scene. There's the teacher as co-learner.

Likewise—I'm not arguing for anti-intellectualism. Do read published research, but recast it to aid you in your own search for answers. Critique it as you would a play a poem an essay a film. Reformulate the question and make it your own. Better yet—or is this and/also—co-research with your writing students. Just as you write with them. Pose classroom questions to them and get the immediate relief their often insightful (though not necessarily intentionally so) answers can provide. And then push to continue exploring—double-check. Of course they are not always the best experts to ask, but they do have some expertise and we in composition have so often overlooked what is there. I agree with the big claim, made by Peter Vandenberg:

If the working conditions of writing teachers—not the disciplinary status of rhetoric, composition studies, or whatever one chooses to call the privileged institutional arrangement built on the backs of writing teachers—are to change,they will change as a result of physical and symbolic action outside the order of academic publishing. (29)

I'm feeling as urgent about making the more modest and yet equally imperative claims: If you want to know more about students as writers and if you want to feel more integrated, more fully involved in your own work, think about how to make composition research—the process of active research—more comfortably your own. This is where we need to take ourselves now.

WORKS CITED

Anderson, Worth, Cynthia Best, Alycia Black, John Hurst, Brandt Miller, and Susan
Miller. "Cross Curricular Underlife: A Collaborative Report on Ways with Academic

Words." *College Composition and Communication* 41 (1990): 11-36.

Bishop, Wendy. "Students' Stories and the Variable Gaze of Composition Research." *Writing Ourselves into the Story: Unheard Voices from Composition Studies*. Ed. Sheryl I. Fontaine and Susan Hunter. Carbondale: Southern Illinois UP, 1993.

Brandt, Deborah. "Accumulating Literacy: Writing and Learning to Write in the Twentieth Century." *College English* 47.6 (Oct. 1995): 649-68.

———. "Remembering Writing, Remembering Reading." *College Composition and Communication* 45.4 (Dec. 1994): 59-79.

Harste, Jerome C., Virginia A. Woodward, and Carolyn L. Burke. *Language Stories and Literacy Lessons*. Portsmouth, NH: Heinemann, 1984.

MacDonald, Susan Peck. "Voices of Research: Methodological Choices of a Disciplinary Community." In Farris, Christine and Chris M. Anson, eds. *Under Construction: Working at the Intersections of Composition Theory, Research, and Practice*, 111-23. Logan: Utah State UP, 1998.

Nelson, Jenny. "This Was an Easy Assignment: Examining How Students Interpret Academic Writing Tasks." *Research in the Teaching of English* 24 (1990): 362-96.

Rose, Mike, ed. *When a Writer Can't Write: Studies in Writer's Block and Other Composing Problems*. New York: Guilford P, 1984.

Shaughnessy, Mina P. *Errors and Expectations: A Guide for the Teacher of Basic Writing*. New York: Oxford UP, 1977.

Vandenberg, Peter. "Composing Composition Studies: Scholarly Publication and the Practice of Discipline." In Farris, Christine and Chris M. Anson, eds. *Under Construction: Working at the Intersections of Composition Theory, Research, and Practice*, 19-29. Logan: Utah State UP, 1998.

Wyche-Smith, Susan. "Time, Tools, and Talismans." *The Subject Is Writing: Essays by Teachers and Students on Writing*. Ed. Wendy Bishop. 2 Ed. Portsmouth, NH: Boynton/Cook.

Composition at the End of Everything; or, The Bravery of Being Out of Range: What's Wrong with a Postmodern Composition Theory?

Kelly Lowe

I would like to argue that our students–our teaching mission–offer us a way of bypassing the tangle of theoretical disagreements and gluing the fragmented pieces of our discipline back together again not into a once-and-for-all rigidity of either structure or orthodoxy, but at least into a shape, into an enterprise that can define its primary aims.

—Marshall Gregory
"The Discipline of English and the 'Empty Center' of the Field's Sense of Itself"

GIVE THE (TEACHER) WHAT S/HE WANTS: THE PROBLEMATIC CONSTRUCTION OF THE POSTMODERN/STUDENT-CENTERED CLASSROOM

I must admit that I truly enjoy reading postmodern theory and literature, and feel that much of it presents a valid critique of the social, cultural, economic, and/or political situation(s) in late twentieth-century America—especially as they plague our students. I say this despite the inability of even the most thorough and/or sublime of postmodernists to "define" what it is they are discussing and therefore presenting much of postmodernism as a through-the-looking-glass construct.[1] Be that as it may, I find the pieces in *College Composition & Communication, College English, JAC: A Journal of Composition Theory* (as well as in "noncomposition" journals like *Critical Inquiry*) and in book-length works ranging from Faigley's *Fragments of Rationality* and Berlin's *Rhetorics, Poetics, and Cultures* to collections like *Contending with Words* to be great fun—much, I submit, like playing chess, attempting to reason with a six-year-old, eating acid, or attempting to come to grips with Mahler can be—a terrific, sometimes mind-expanding experience—but one that leaves me wondering what I've just done and why on earth I've done it.

But what, I submit, does postmodernism as a composition theory do for students and teachers who don't have the time, the energy, the desire, or indeed, the institutional mandate or mission to use the typical introductory composition course to "bring about more democratic and personally humane economic, social, and political arrangements" (Berlin 116)?

The idea that a postmodern composition theory looks good on paper but leaves a lot to be desired in the classroom is what I would like to argue here. The old conservative charge, that writing teachers are simply using the classroom as a forum for their own political agenda, while also interesting, will not be addressed in this chapter.[2] On a political level, I am very sympathetic toward the liberal progressive postmodern agenda and in my personal life I work toward social justice and a politics of inclusion.

My worry about taking politics and making them the forefront of the composition classroom comes about not because of my own politics, but from a sense that the classroom shouldn't be about me and/or my political agenda.

The idea that recurs throughout much postmodern composition theory, that students ought to be taught to "resist" things—whether it is the dominant State ideology/discourse/hegemony, television, *The Wall Street Journal* editorial page, or their own desires—seems a difficult/complex pedagogical move; indeed, how, I wonder, do we "teach" students to "resist" things in discreet box A all the while not having them resist the things in discreet box B (in other words, what do I do with the student who feels that it is necessary to "resist" things like attendance policies, due dates, speeding laws, or, in a far more serious vein, sexual harassment policies or the civil rights of his/her fellow students)?[3] And how do we "help" them resist those items/ideologies in discreet box A without "giving" them pre-formed value judgment about the things in discreet box B?

James Sosnoski, in a brave attempt to put into practice what others have theorized, runs head-on into this student-teacher conceptual gap. Sosnoski writes that

It is one thing to treat students fairly, to attend to their painful problems, to encourage their resistance to the system, to listen between the lines of their inarticulateness, and quite another to make their interests the main concerns of the class. (209)

The question, and I don't think it can be asked enough, is simple: Who benefits when the conflict between student and teacher desire/interest is "subverted" or "resisted" to the point where it magically ends up in/at the place the teacher wants it to be? Let me try a concrete example.

Most of the students at Mount Union College are very interested in sports—partly because of our location (northeast Ohio, where, I am constantly reminded, professional football was, well, professionalized) and partly because of the wild success of our athletic programs (four division III football championships in six years, as well as division titles in basketball, wrestling, track, swimming, soccer . . . well, one gets the picture—and these are not only men's teams; the swimming, soccer, basketball, and track teams were women's' teams).[4] Many of the students in our first-year writing courses would be, undoubtedly, happy to discuss sports at every class meeting. What happens to these students, as happens to be the case more often than not, when the only person in the room not interested in sports is the teacher? What, in other words, is so "democratic" about the teacher subverting the class into a critique of sports when that is the last thing the students want?[5] To claim, as some will, that students "wanting" to talk unreflexively about sports is simply a reflection of the students' desire to enter the dominant hegemony, and to posit such desire as "bad" or "ignorant" or "naive" strikes me as the height of both arrogance and elitism. Did somebody say resistance?

I realize the rather simplistic nature of my example, so let me unpack it a bit. Under no circumstances do I advocate the use of the composition classroom to discuss the latest trades or who won and who lost the big game last night. Nor (and this, I think, is what many of the more politically minded fear most) does this classroom "worship" the athlete as a model of manliness and thus abrogate any sort of social responsibility for the student-athlete who abuses his/her power (in the classroom, bedroom, or locker room). My argument is simply that if an instructor is truly interested, as Sosnoski and others claim to be, in making the class center on the students' lives, then it would seem only logical to really become interested in what the students are interested in, and not some sort of projection of what they should be interested in.[6]

Indeed, let me posit a more local example—one that uses and builds upon the students' interests—one that moves from theory to practice so to speak. In his framework for a possible first-year composition course, Berlin writes that "This course focuses on reading and writing the daily experiences of culture, with culture considered in its broadest formulation" (116). Berlin goes on to note that this class would

start with the personal experience of the students, with emphasis on the position of this experience within its formative context. Our [the teachers of the course] main concern is the relation of current signifying practices to the structuring of subjectivities—of race, class, sexual orientation, age, ethnic, and gender formations, for example, in our students and ourselves. (116)

For the past five years, the Cleveland Indians have been either in the playoffs or the World Series. Needless to say, the attention paid to the team in the local media and the rabid and vocal fan support is, in this part of the state, nearly omnipresent. Each semester in my college writing courses, I have had the students read and write about the Indians, specifically, the students are asked to encounter, from a variety of perspectives, the horrifyingly racist symbol/mascot of the team, "Chief Wahoo." During this time, we read and discuss Ward Churchill's excellent essay "Indians R US? Let's Spread the 'Fun' Around: The Issue of Sports Team Names and Mascots," as well as Michael Dorris's "For The Indians, No Thanksgiving." I try to "balance" or "juxtapose" (choose your pedagogical weapon) these essays with press releases from the Indians organization, editorials and columns from local newspapers, and excerpts from Charles Alexander's *Our Game: An American Baseball History.*[7] We have wonderfully rancorous class discussions, most (and this still never ceases to amaze me) revolving around the perceived opportunism of the Native-American protesters ("Where were they," the question always goes, "when the Indians were losing"?). Such questions, I will admit, leave me stymied by the deeply held feelings of identity and privilege and ownership that the students have about the Indians mascot (and the utter unwillingness to even recognize the racist nature of the symbol). If these feelings were the result of a discussion about slavery or welfare or affirmative action or gay rights, the students would meet with stiff social and potentially even administrative resistance—yet for Chief Wahoo, there is broad social and administrative support; thus, to ask students to "resist" the racist symbol of the Cleveland Indians is to ask them to work counter to the local culture, the school administration, and nearly all of their daily life. And while this unit can lead to some interesting discussion(s) about the rights of groups to forge their own identities and the power associated with naming things, students simply don't want to hear it. The power of sports in the lives of these college students is stunning.[8]

This, of course, could be a problem for the classroom that Berlin envisions in *Rhetorics, Poetics, and Cultures.* Donald Jones, among others (and here he is borrowing from Patricia Bizzell), argues very effectively that

Resistance against presumably oppressive discursive practices requires most students to doubt too much of their previous knowledge. They are unwilling to submit to this pervasive skepticism because postmodern instructors offer few specific alternatives to their present beliefs or even a way to develop such options. (86)[9]

In other words, what often passes for a "critique" of sports in a postmodern classroom becomes, in reality, an indictment of students who like sports, wear athletic apparel, play on athletic teams, or want to write papers related, in some way, to sports.[10] Why would a student want to be in a class like this, and why (and this is even more important) would a student do anything but "shut down" intellectually when it became apparent that her/his values, beliefs, dreams, etc. are simply, in the eyes of their instructor, mindless "perpetuation[s] of the dominant discourses" (86)? The postmodern binary at work here is the idea that students can't be "thoughtful" and also believe in things their instructor doesn't. [11]

WHERE'S THE WRITING? WHEN POSTMODERN COMPOSITION THEORY OMITS COMPOSITION.

I have, in the bottom right-hand drawer of the desk in my office, a neatly bound dissertation chock full of optimistic theory about what a postmodern writing class, inside a postmodern writing program, with/in a postmodern world would look like. I came to this dissertation by way of a failed attempt at literary scholarship and the discovery along the way that I really liked teaching composition. The excitement of discovery of ideas from the likes of James Berlin, John Schilb, Sharon Crowley, Lester Faigley, Henry Giroux, etc. made a great deal of sense to me at the time. My move from the stolid center of literary studies to the outer fringe of composition studies gave me energy and passion. Then I got a job.

Currently I am the only person in our eight-person English department with a degree in rhetoric and composition. I direct the writing center, the writing across the curriculum program, summer placement and assessment, as well as teach a good cross section of rhetoric, composition, and cultural studies courses.

I talk, in my capacity as administrator, on a near daily basis, with many of the stakeholders in our campus writing program—students, teachers, administrators. Coming to grips with the way people write in their disciplines has been as revelatory to me as any piece of theory ever has been. I have worked closely with mathematicians, biologists, sociologists, historians, and musicians toward improving the writing that goes on in their classes, and in many instances, their own work as academics. Many of my preconceived ideas about writing and the purpose of a freshman writing course were influenced by what I see as an intense humanities/rhetoric/composition bias toward one kind of writing/process (for the lack of anything better to call it, academic expository discourse seems adequate) and one kind of result/product (the move toward agency/resistance in the general "discovery" type essay). The postmodern classroom doesn't really seem to fit within the larger relationship between the composition class and the college. The idea that the composition might just be a skills course for students who enter college inadequately prepared, while anathema to some, is the cold reality of our program. To ask, as we do, instructors from across the disciplines to teach writing in their courses, and not to prepare students to receive such instruction is, as I mentioned above, arrogant.

In the essay "Writing in a Post-Berlinian Landscape," Michelle Sidler and Richard Morris offer one potential for what kinds of writing might go on in a postmodern writing course. Sidler and Morris write that their intention in their composition course(s) is "to implode the rhetorical divisions of invention and post-invention, interpretation and composing, or 'brainstorming' and organizing" (278). How does one do this? They give the following example:

For example, a student who critiques the lyrics of a rock group might find that she/he wants to communicate this message to the group's fans who have web sites. The student might choose to construct a web page or might decide to send an e-mail message to site owners who list their addresses. He/she may even compose lyrics and music that stand as an alternate text to the song. (285)

This, of course, despite a well-reasoned rationalization for what students might gain from this activity, begs the question: How is this helping the students with their writing? Although this assignment might help them to become a citizen/agent in late twentieth-century America, how does it help them with the kinds of writing they will have to do outside of the writing classroom? How, I wonder, are students going to be able to operate with/in current political and economic conditions—get and maintain a fulfilling job, be part of a family or other social network, have hobbies, and so on—if they can't work with/in the current expectations of capitalism? Having students rewrite song lyrics or create web pages,[12] while fun and entertaining and certainly far easier to respond to than student papers, seems largely counterproductive to a composition course in a writing program that has any sort of institutional mission beyond the theory/practice issues of its instructors. The postmodern writing course, at least as Berlin, Sosnoski, and Sidler and Morris have fashioned it, means very little beyond itself. I would argue that a first-year composition course and the writing program that it is housed in has a responsibility to something beyond the ephemeral ideal that students can, in fifteen weeks, confront their own racist, sexist, classist, imperialist, and capitalist ideological preconceptions while at the same time learn the skills to help them eventually become better writers of lab reports, art history essays, business letters, case studies, essay exams, newspaper articles, and advertisements, to name only some of the writing they'll be expected to do in college and after they leave. Oh yes, and students are expected, in freshman composition, to become social critics of others' writing, as well as of television, film, music/lyrics, and the ever ubiquitous advertisements.[13]

I hear the argument loud and clear that students can't/shouldn't be taught the dominant discourse because it's (potentially) damaging to them because they will never have access to the dominant culture/class. The argument, for instance, that a student shouldn't be taught how to write good memos because they'll never be in a position to write one is, on the surface, a powerful one. Of course, this seems to deny two particular impulses—the first one is simply that students want to learn the dominant discourse and who are teachers to deny them that? The driving impulse for most college students is that college is a gateway to the dominant culture. [14]

The second impulse seems more complex—that teaching students to resist the dominant hegemony can, and often does, run counter to the mission of the college and/or the mission of writing as a part of the larger college community. Let me offer an example.

The mission statement of Mount Union College, arrived at after several years of committee meetings, attempts to account for the whole four-year experience at college. It reads, in part, as follows: *The College affirms the importance of reason, open inquiry, living faith, and individual worth. Mount Union's mission is to prepare students for meaningful work, fulfilling lives, and responsible citizenship.* In other words, I do not doubt that the reading and writing (and/or even the subtle deconstructing) of rock lyrics is fun, nor do I doubt that it serves a larger, some might say better, political purpose;[15] but I do not see how, in my institution's case, the previously mentioned assignment would help students in any discernible fashion. As one of only three universal requirements (Speech and an introductory religion/philosophy course are the other two), freshman composition has a responsibility to do something beyond an individual instructor's desire to resist the dominant hegemony.

KEEP THE FAITH: COMPOSITION ISN'T IN TROUBLE, DESPITE WHAT PEOPLE MIGHT SAY

All outward appearance to the contrary, composition theory/studies isn't in much trouble. In fact it's a thriving discipline filled with dedicated practitioners and theorists who are working to keep the discipline one of rigor and compassion. I have faith in the knowledge that students are slowly but surely learning how to write and that teachers are constantly searching for new and better ways to teach (while retaining the pedagogies that have worked in the past). Postmodernism doesn't really account for faith at all except for the faith that if students only understood the social codes and semiotic structures of late capitalism, they would finally become well-developed human beings.[16]

So what might be done in a composition classroom to assure not only that students are becoming better students and critics, but that composition, especially the required composition course, is living up to its institutional responsibility to produce good thinkers and writers? In the words of Patricia Bizzell, one way is to "work collectively toward achieving consensus on a pluralistic grouping of ways to do academic discourse" (663). As I mention above, I have learned as much about writing and the teaching of writing from my peers and colleagues outside of the English department as I have learned from my brothers and sisters within. Despite the postmodern pretense to the contrary, "We may wish to do away with an oppressive academic discourse, but we cannot do without any academic discourse at all" (663). And although this may sound, to some, like a half-hearted Clintonian/Fallwellian call for "standards," it is apparent that many different groups have very particular "standards" or "expectations" about writing, and to not teach students how to work with/in those standards and expectations is irresponsible.

One of the most eloquent statements addressing this very issue comes from Edward P. J. Corbett and Robert Connors, who write that "It must be emphasized . . . that the disposition of one's material is not an indifferent matter" (259). This means, of course, that others (i.e., the audience) have a great say in what student (and professional) writing ultimately does. The most compelling argument for studying, mastering, and only then, perhaps, subverting, the dominant discourse, for students, comes again from Corbett and Connors when they tell us that "a writer must be in command of a variety of styles, in order to draw on the style that is most appropriate to the situation. *This is not to say that these several styles will differ radically from one another*" (338 italics mine). And this is my point—writing is all about the dominant discourse, and most radical derivations or subversions are simply reinventions of the wheel—indeed, much of the so-called radical subversions that go on in the contemporary writing classroom are the same sort of poorly reasoned quasi-academic fluff that caused us to question current-traditional composition pedagogy in the first place.

A contemporary composition classroom is more than likely one that is, no matter what the teacher desires, steeped in the dominant discourse. The composition classroom needs to question the reading-response-writing-revision-reading hermeneutic that developed as a result of current-traditional rhetorical strategies and look at the kind of writing that is going on (or that is going to be going on) in the students' lives. (Of course, composition also needs to leave open the idea that, once questioned, it could prove to be true that read-draft-write-revise is a good methodology/pedagogy—stranger things have been known to happen.) The argument that having students work toward mastery of professional or technical discourse is making students unthinking tools of the capitalist society is, as I argued above and will argue again below, as irresponsible as it is silly.

No less radical an educator as Henry Giroux persuasively calls upon educators to [acknowledge] the importance of those diverse educational sites through which a generation of youth are being shaped within a postmodern culture where information and its channels of circulation demand new forms of understanding, literacy, and pedagogical practice. (197)

By "diverse educational sites," Giroux cites "videos, films, music, television, radio, computers" as far more important than the traditional (composition) classroom tools of/for responding to essays (197). And he is right. But it is also true that outside of the composition classroom, in other classes, traditional, text-based teaching and learning are going on. And perhaps, more important than in school, once someone is outside of the classroom, the dissemination of information is still (and will be far into the future) text-based; the ability to create and produce this kind of discourse is the most important thing we can help our students achieve.

Philosopher Richard Rorty reminds us that "it is the vocabulary of practise [sic] rather than of theory, of action rather than contemplation, in which one can say something useful about truth" (162). I read Rorty's statement as meaning that we need to have students write from a position of what is, not what might be, and work at becoming better writers and thinkers using the kinds of writing that they will actually have to do as students, workers, and citizens—professional writing, scientific writing, technical writing, and legal writing are a few of the dominant professional genres. Rorty's argument that "the pattern of all inquiry—scientific as well as moral—is deliberation concerning the relative attractions of various concrete alternatives" (164) is compelling here. The idea that the freshman writing class deal with "various concrete alternatives" is far more interesting and responsible than the more postmodern idea that a composition course be grounded in the subjective/personal essay of discovery, even when this kind of writing is merely "a baby step on the road to wisdom" (Schilb, *Between* 172).

The area that Rorty is working can be the area where postmodern theory and a new pragmatic might come together. I could see, for instance, the creation of a web page not as a tool for socio-cultural critique (although it could be used for that) but as a way of working toward HTML or VRML or Java literacy where the student would have a marketable post-collegiate skill.[17] The creation of a flow chart and a sketch (draft) version of the web site, the idea of useability and feasability testing, the process of feedback and subsequent revision strike me as distinctly similar to the idea of draft, write, revise that is with us today.

Although sketchy at best, the idea of a new pragmatics of composition theory is exciting. Composition teachers who are truly committed to making the classroom about their students would need to find writing projects that reflect this relationship between the students' lives and the world in which they are going to inhabit. A middle ground between the severe anti-foundationalism of postmodernism and the pseudo-objectivism of current-traditional theories is not only necessary, but entirely possible.

In fact, Ed White speaks to this directly when he writes in "Response: Assessment as a Site of Contention" that "the first question that is likely to occur to readers looking for new directions . . . is Why do the new directions seem so old" (301)? And in a way, what I'm saying, that the "answer" is to have students work with new and emerging technologies is nothing new at all. But I have never found "newness" to equate with "goodness" or "soundness." White writes, in a different essay in the same collection, that teachers of composition will never be solely allowed to set the national agenda for writing, much like medical doctors will never be solely responsible for any sort of national health care policy ("Power" 15) The stakeholding groups are too varied. For teachers, whether they are postmodern, current-traditional, or any other conveniently labeled group, it is imperative to understand that we work within a large social structure that demands things like accountability and standards, and to deny that this is a reason to look at what we do in the classroom and ask if we are best serving our constituencies is to fiddle while Rome burns.

NOTES

I would like to thank my wife and colleague Lori Van Houten for her sensitive and insightful reading of this chapter. My colleague in the History Department Dr. John Recchiuti, was very generous in helping me shape my conclusions and helping me clarify my reading of Richard Rorty.

1. John Schilb speaks volumes when, in an attempt to "define" postmodernism in his book *Between the Lines*, he writes, "Here I will follow an increasingly standard practice and suggest that in general 'postmodernism' refers to (1) a certain critique of epistemology, (2) certain academic practices, and (3) certain developments in global practices" (82). The very idea that the grand theory about the death/lack/demise of metanarratives has a rote metanarrative of definition is, at the least, a swell irony.

2. As far as I'm concerned, this issue has been put to rest by the likes of Berlin, Schilb, Harkin, and especially John Trimbur.

3. This is akin, of course, to Richard Rorty's discussion of "the occasional cooperative freshman" who is a committed and unreflexive relativist (116). But my point, nonetheless, that students will "resist" in many different directions, remains valid.

4. Indeed, as I was reminded last year, the percentage of our student body that belongs to an athletic team is astronomically high—at or close to 20 percent.

5. Please note that I am not saying it is "wrong" to critique sports (and, as my example below shows, it can happen as a natural discussion of nearly any sporting event). What I worry about is that there seems to be no space in the postmodern classroom for those who love sports.

6. In this case, I am talking largely about a course (first-year composition) that is required by a great many schools. My assumption (although I could be wrong) is that students have less space to worry about democratic course construction elsewhere.

7. Specifically, where Alexander discusses the history of race in baseball.

8. I would posit that sports is an even more powerful cultural and societal presence in students' lives than film, music, or television—the holy trinity of cultural studies. I am constantly amazed at how few students are watching television or going to the movies or buying music—I'll bring up television shows like *Friends, E.R.,* or *NYPD Blue,* and the students will stare blankly at me as if I'm discussing the latest rage in macrobiotic gardening.

9. See also Patricia Bizzell. "Beyond Anti-Foundationalism to Rhetorical Authority: Problems Defining 'Cultural Literacy.'" *College English* 52 (1990): 661-75.

10. Lad Tobin's shockingly honest (and perhaps ironic) comments about male students who wear baseball caps or write about winning the big football game seem emblematic of how willing some scholars are to reduce people to their lowest common denominators. (159; 161).

11. Although there isn't time to delve into it here, the alternative critique that a postmodern composition theory actually works to exclude those at the margins is devastating in its simplicity. In "An Afrocentric Multicultural Writing Project," Henry L. Evans writes that postmodernism is troubling because "Western academics have advanced theories of deconstruction and decentering of the self that make the advancement of emancipatory self-identity theories problematic" (274). It has been my sneaking suspicion for a while now that postmodernism is the last gasp of the tired old white theorists, and Evan's devastating critique only makes my belief stronger.

12. Of course, I understand that a working knowledge of web page design is poten-

tially helpful for a student's future, but is it the best way to spend one's time in a composition course?

13. It goes without saying that the students are also falling in love, learning to do laundry, getting used to a syllabus, etc.

14. Alexander Astin, in *What Matters in College*, does a far better job than I can explaining why/how this has happened.

15. For instance, it way well be "reason, open inquiry, and . . . responsible citizenship," but is it preparing them for work that they will do elsewhere in college and in the world?

16. There is also the delicious irony that Derrida has pointed out to us on the pages of *The New York Review of Books* that a deconstructionist can have great faith in one's own idea.

17. I'll leave it to someone else to deal with the challenge that college is not supposed or required to help students gain marketable skills.

WORKS CITED

Alexander, Charles C. *Our Game: An American Baseball History*. New York: MJF Books, 1991.

Astin, Alexander. *What Matters in College? Four Critical Years Revisited*. San Francisco: Jossey-Bass, 1993.

Berlin, James. *Rhetorics, Poetics, and Cultures: Refiguring College English Studies*. Urbana: NCTE, 1996.

Bizzell, Patricia. "Beyond Anti-Foundationalism to Rhetorical Authority: Problems Defining 'Cultural Literacy.'" *College English* 52.6 (Oct. 1990): 661-75.

Churchill, Ward. "Indians R US? Let's Spread the 'Fun' Around: The Issue of Team Names and Mascots." *Race, Class, and Gender in a Diverse Society: A Text-Reader*. Ed. Diana Kendall. Boston: Allyn and Bacon, 1997. 218-22.

Corbett, Edward P. J. and Robert Connors. *Classical Rhetoric for the Modern Student*. 4th ed. New York: Oxford UP, 1999.

Dorris, Michael. "For The Indians, No Thanksgiving." *Crossing Cultures: Readings for Composition*. Eds. Henry and Myrna Knepler, New York: Macmillian, 1991. 199-202.

Evans, Henry L. "An Afrocentric Multicultural Writing Project." *Writing in Multicultural Settings*. Eds. Carol Severino, Juan Guerra and Johnnella Butler. New York: MLA, 1997. 273-86.

Faigley, Lester. *Fragments of Rationality: Postmodernity and the Subject of Composition*. Pittsburgh: U of Pittsburgh P, 1992.

Giroux, Henry. "Where Have All the Public Intellectuals Gone? Racial Politics, Pedagogy, and Disposable Youth." *JAC* 17.2 (Spring 1997): 191-205.

Gregory, Marshall. "The Many-Headed Hydra of Theory Vs. The Unifying Mission of Teaching." *College English* 59.1 (Jan. 1997): 41-58.

Harkin, Patricia and John Schilb, eds. *Contending with Words: Composition and Rhetoric in a Postmodern Age*. New York: MLA, 1991.

Jones, Donald C. "Beyond the Postmodern Impasse of Agency: The Resounding Relevance of John Dewey's Tacit Tradition." *JAC* 16.1 (Spring 1996): 81-102.

Rorty, Richard. *Consequences of Pragmatism*. Minneapolis: U of Minnesota P, 1982.

Schilb, John. Between the Lines: *Relating Composition Theory and Literary Theory*. Portsmouth: Boynton/Cook, 1996.

———. "Cultural Studies, Postmodernism, and Composition." *Contending with Words: Composition and Rhetoric in a Postmodern Age*. Eds. Patricia Harkin and John Schilb. New York: MLA, 1991. 173-88.

Sidle, Michelle and Richard Morris. "Writing in a Post-Berlinian Landscape: Cultural Composition in the Classroom." *JAC* 18.2 (Spring 1998): 275-91.

Sosnoski, James. "Postmodern Teachers in Their Postmodern Classrooms: Socrates Begone!" *Contending With Words: Composition and Rhetoric in a Postmodern Age*. Eds. Patricia Harkin and John Schilb. New York: MLA, 1991. 198-219.

Tobin, Lad. "Car Wrecks, Baseball Caps, and Man-to-Man Defense: The Personal Narratives of Adolescent Males." *College English* 58.2 (Feb. 1996): 158-75.

Trimbur, John. "Response to Maxine Hairston, 'Diversity, Ideology and the Teaching of Writing'." *College Composition and Communication* 44.2 (May 1993): 248-49.

White, Edward. "Power and Agenda Setting in Writing Assessment." *Assessment of Writing: Politics, Policies, Practices*. Eds. Edward White, William Lutz, and Sandra Kamusikiri. New York: MLA, 1996. 9-24.

———. "Response: Assessment as a Site of Contention." *Assessment of Writing: Politics, Policies, Practices*. Eds. Edward White, William Lutz, and Sandra Kamusikiri. New York: MLA, 1996. 301-4.

3

Expressivisms as "Vernacular Theories" of Composing: Recovering the Pragmatic Roots of Writing Instruction

Don Bushman

In his essay, "The Recovery of Practical Philosophy," Stephen Toulmin explains that the contemporary interest in practical philosophy is related to the fact that the most pressing issues of the past half of the century–things like nuclear war, medical technology, and the environment—are such that they cannot be adequately addressed "without bringing back to the surface questions of the significance of human life" (343). In short, they're issues that make us aware of potential perils to human existence and hence demand that we address them with respect to human experience. Practical debates over these sorts of issues, Toulmin insists, "are no longer 'applied philosophy': they are philosophy itself" (345). And within such a pragmatic philosophical milieu, experience holds a central place: "Set everyday practical experience beside the 'sense experiences' of perceptual theory . . . and 'sense data' surely appear to be fictious, dreamed up after the event, to make good the missing links between epistemological theory and practical life" (346). Toulmin sees practical or pragmatic philosophy, then, as a central "contribution to the reflective resolution of quandaries that face us in enterprises with high stakes—even [issues of] life and death"(352).

To writing instructors like William Coles, Peter Elbow, and Ken Macrorie, the world of higher education in the 1960s and 1970s was a high stakes enterprise. When, for example, a failing student could find himself kicked out of college one day and ordered to the draft office the next, it was important that teachers find methods to help students succeed. These so-called expressivist teachers sought to address these quandaries by bringing their own classroom experiences to bear on them. Coles, for instance, says that he wrote *The Plural I* because, despite the proliferation of "how to" material on writing instruction, "there is surprisingly little . . . on the actual doing, on how a given theory of rhetoric or approach to the teaching of writing feels as an action" (3-4). So rather than offer a book applying a static theory of writing—a theory disconnected from an actual classroom context—his purpose in *The Plural I* is to

offer . . . a presentation of my situation as a teacher at a certain time and in a certain place, which can serve as an illuminating metaphor for all the situations of all teachers in all classrooms dealing with writing as a creative process—whatever . . . techniques or approaches a particular teacher happens to be using. My intention, in other words, is to illuminate what is involved in the teaching (and learning) of writing however one approaches it, in hopes that this will enable other teachers to take a fresh hold on whatever they choose to do. (2)

In the tradition of the pragmatists, Coles rejects what might disparagingly be referred to as a "spectator theory"—a sort of "God's-eye view" of reality that purports to show things "as they really are" (Rorty 3). Instead, Coles sets out to analyze his own experience in his local setting, doing so with a clear sense of the limits to the conclusions he has drawn. Toulmin would thus find praiseworthy in Coles's approach that which he praises in the essays of Montaigne and Bacon: their foregrounding of "individual self-examination" and their offering the account of that self-examination as a possible "method" for others to address the issue at question:[1] "They viewed themselves as 'sample' humans," Toulmin explains, and they intended their self-theorizing to be germane to others in the same way it was germane to themselves (350). Likewise, Coles views himself as a sort of sample teacher: "[T]his book is a way of offering other teachers of writing something similar to the best I think I have to offer to my students: a style performed in such a way as to enable others to make for themselves, or to make better, styles of their own" (1-2).

To many, the theorizing of personal experience seems almost to be a contradiction in terms. Indeed, as Thomas McLaughlin notes, the more popular sense of "theorizing" is "the act of distancing [or] abstracting the mind away from lived experience and personal engagement" (163). As I have suggested above, though, personal experience is central to pragmatic theorizing; hence, the experience-centered works of expressivists like Coles, Macrorie, Elbow, and others can be illuminated by considering them in relationship to pragmatist philosophy. I will develop the associations between expressivism and pragmatism more completely in the course of this chapter, and in doing so I will argue the importance of composition studies' return to the pragmatist mindset that is reflected in the works of expressivists. First, however, I will consider expressivist theories through the lens of McLaughlin's discussion of "vernacular theory" as a way of further explaining the pragmatic nature of expressivists theories, the nature of the criticisms waged against them, and the importance of the pragmatic mindset—a concern for the specific contexts and personal experiences in our theorizing about writing—to the future of composition studies.

EXPRESSIVISMS AS "VERNACULAR THEORIES"

Apologists for expressivism, such as Christopher Burnham and Thomas O'Donnell, have pointed out that expressivist theories are often worked out in less academically rigid fashions than other theories of composing, and that expressivisms are sometimes developed in works intended for wider, sometimes nonacademic, audiences. Thomas McLaughlin would say of expressivist theories that their departure from typical scholarly forms and forums make them instances of "theory in the vernacular mode." In *Street Smarts and Critical Theory: Listening to the Vernacular*, McLaughlin explains that vernacular theories "arise out of intensely local issues" and are undertaken by individuals "who do not come out of the tradition of philosophical critique" (5-6). As examples of such informal theorizing, McLaughlin explores texts from the world of advertising, the writings of a Christian anti-pornography activist, and a variety of independently published 'zines addressing popular culture issues. He explains that while these forms of theorizing often fail to "transcend ideologies," they "manage in spite of their complicity [with those ideologies] to ask fundamental questions about culture" (5). McLaughlin argues that the practice of vernacular theory "is widespread in the culture," that it "does not differ in kind from academic theory," and that, since theorizing is a commonplace phenomenon, we should see academic theory "not as an elitist and totalizing activity, but as a rigorous and scholarly version of a widely practiced analytical strategy" (6). In other words, theoretical practice can be seen as existing on a continuum, from the not-so-scholarly to the exceedingly scholarly, and the way we must distinguish one form of theoretical practice from another is with reference to the "status and style and scholarly rigor" of a practice, not to its "goals and strategies" (6).

Few would argue that the rigorous, scholarly theorizing and taxonomizing done by James Berlin and others helped to enhance the disciplinary respectability of composition studies over the course of the last twenty years. As a result of this theorizing, though, a hierarchy has developed within the discipline of composition studies, and an undeniable dismissiveness has been directed toward expressivist theories, primarily because of their lack of compliance with the meticulous standards of academic theorizing. Some of the now-familiar criticisms waged against expressivisms are that such views of writing and pedagogy hold an unsound "commitment to an epistemology that locates all truth within a personal construct arising from one's unique selfhood" (Berlin 153) and that by committing to such an epistemology we and our students are engaged in a form of self delusion (Bartholomae 128-29). During the early 1980s when the field of composition was finding its place in the academy, these are the sorts of critiques, with their insistence on the rigorous union of rhetorical theories and epistemological assumptions, that succeeded in diminishing the importance of expressivist works. O'Donnell believes these criticisms were influential because expressivist "practitioners seem (and perhaps are) unconcerned about the task of articulating a theory of knowledge and meaning, and even when they have done so, their efforts are ignored" (432). It is O'Donnell's contention that these attacks were made on "caricatured expressivist epistemologies" rather than on fair-minded representations of expressivisms (432; see also Gradin 91-124; Fishman and McCarthy).

From the perspective of someone like McLaughlin, however, it is less important to ask whether or not expressivist theories measure up to a certain standard of theoretical consistency as it is to ask whether or not those theories actually "raise important questions about the premises that guide cultural practice" (5). Remembering Toulmin's assertion about the reasons for the dominance of practical philosophy, we might imagine McLaughlin making a similar assertion: that theorizing about epistemological matters in the context of a discussion about writing instruction makes far less sense than considering practical issues that will enable students to produce better writing. Within the academy, though—especially within a discipline that was just cutting its theoretical teeth—the sort of criticisms Berlin, Faigley, and others posed served as a way of making our discipline hold itself accountable to a rigorous set of standards. An unfortunate result of this attachment to epistemological theorizing, though, has been a reification of many people's views regarding certain theories and pedagogies. We would do well to heed McLaughlin's warning about our attachment to any single theoretical conviction: "No theoretical system should be taught . . . as an orthodoxy," he warns; rather, "[t]he goal of academic theory is to keep inquiry open, not to provide . . . machines of interpretation that will produce epistemological closure" (159). Defenders of expressivist theories have helped us to reconsider a number of faulty interpretations and critiques, and they have helped to show the ways in which expressivisms question status quo thinking about writing instruction and schooling.

Indeed, a questioning spirit is at the heart of expressivist thinking. Coles, for instance, makes clear that "unless [any] fundamental question is being seen freshly, it isn't being seen as a question at all," noting that we should distrust any "teacher of composition who claimed to know the Answers" to the fundamental questions that we ask about teaching and learning (2-3).[2] The same dissatisfaction with the status quo that McLaughlin says drives any theoretical action can also be said to drive expressivist works. The concern for an awareness of "voice" in writing can be said to constitute one method by which expressivists seek change—both in the classroom and in the world beyond. According to Burnham, "Voice is important for the value system it symbolizes" (168). Burnham compares Elbow and the other expressivists to those involved in feminist and liberatory pedagogies, all of whom are "working to subvert the pedagogical practices and institutional structures that oppress, silence, or appropriate individual voice" (168). This liberatory impulse is apparent in Coles's desire for his students to discontinue the practice of "Themewriting" (19) and the use of "Englishclassese" (23). Macrorie calls this institutional language "Engfish"—the language students use when writing "themes" or any other sort of "teachers' exercises [which are] not really a kind of communication" (*Telling* 1-2). By being critical of "school writing" and "Engfish," Macrorie suggests, we resist the impersonality and hegemony of institutions and reclaim writing for the purposes of real communication. Elbow proposes freewriting activities precisely because of the institutional power school possesses to make us "obsessed with the 'mistakes' we make in writing": "Almost everybody interposes a massive and complicated series of editings between the time words start to be born into consciousness and when they finally come . . . onto the page"; thus we need strategies to help us overcome the impediments that schooling has placed on our abilities to express our thoughts (5). In this way, expressivist pedagogies are like vernacular theories in that they are "survival tactic[s]" aimed at "producing a livable personal and social negotiation with the rules in force" (McLaughlin 164). And since these negotiations are personal, they may appear in as many forms and contexts as there are persons to produce them.

By placing importance on experience and the individual perspective of the person involved in that experience, expressivisms share similarities to pragmatism. According to Hephzibah Roskelly and Kate Ronald, "pragmatic philosophy is constantly on the lookout for new experience to test past conclusions, including in that experience a reexamination of old experience . . . acknowledging that the inquirer is always faced with the possibility not only of being wrong but the certainty of being not completely right" (89). This is the stance toward his subject matter we see in Coles: that his book is an expression of his method and that, while he hopes others find it useful, he knows it won't be completely applicable to every teacher everywhere: "Part of what it means to develop a style as a teacher is to begin to find ways for one's self," he says, adding that "my way of dealing with [Themewriting and Englishclassese] may be only one way of confronting the problem, but it is my way for me" (19). His hope, to be sure, is that others will find his way of use, but no way exists to know for sure.

EXPRESSIVISMS AS PRAGMATIC THEORIES

Pragmatist philosophy's belief in the contingency of knowledge—explained by Roskelly and Ronald above—is an indication of its rejection of a "God's-eye view" of reality. John Dewey describes the pragmatist view of knowledge as

an affair of *making* sure, not of grasping antecedently given sureties. What is already known, what is accepted as truth, is of immense importance; inquiry could not proceed a step without it. But it is held subject to use, and is at the mercy of the discoveries that make it possible. . . . When things are defined as instruments, their value and validity reside in what proceeds from them; consequences, not antecedents supply meaning and verity. (*Experience* 154)

The idea that knowledge "is held subject to use" is key to the pragmatists' way of thinking. Because we use knowledge in order to adapt our environment to our needs, ideas are seen as "instruments" whose "value and validity" are determined by how effectively they may be put to use in the world. For pragmatists, knowledge is not an end in itself, not a thing to be attained, but rather, as Dewey's contemporary George Herbert Mead puts it, "knowledge is an expression of the intelligence by which animals meet the problems with which life surrounds them" (383-84). I would argue that this pragmatic definition of knowledge provides a worthwhile way of viewing the knowledge generated by expressivist theorists. When we read Coles's *The Plural I*, for example (and to a lesser extent, Macrorie's *Uptaught*), we see the author "making sure": he invites us to experience his interactions with his students, meeting the problems that surround him and his students, and through his reflections on those experiences, we are able to see the circumstances that lead to his discoveries about those students and those classroom practices. Coles's rejection of the "how to" book form reveals his pragmatic intent.

The vision of the classroom provided by expressivists such as Coles and Macrorie is that of an active teacher and active students engaged in the process of discovery. Such classrooms are informed by the same sense of discovery as those advocated by Dewey, whose own "laboratory school" at the University of Chicago is considered the birthplace of an active pedagogy based on the experimental or scientific method. The aim of Dewey's progressive pedagogy, according to Darnell Rucker, was to promote knowledge "by leading the child into scientific inquiry, in the sense that 'scientific' is opposed to authoritarian" (99). This same dissatisfaction with traditional, teacher-centered instruction motivates expressivists like Macrorie, who describes his "Third Way" of teaching in contrast to the accepted methods of his day:

In the First Way the teacher hands out a package of information and tests to see whether students can remember its content . . . . In the Second Way, the teacher provides complete freedom and no direction at all. . . . In the Third Way, which I stumbled onto, students operate with freedom and discipline. They are given real choices and encouraged to learn the way of experts. (*Uptaught* 27)

Central to Macrorie's Third Way of teaching is what he calls "the here principle," which is how he describes an education that proceeds from students' own experiences. As an example, he suggests that a student in a political science course can better understand the material being discussed in class by relating it to his own daily activities, such as "dorm meetings or committees of some student organization where he observed how real and pseudo power contend with each other. Somewhere in campus life around him . . . lies a here for the student to investigate" (*Uptaught* 168). Here again is a concern for real communicative acts—learning "the way of experts"—rather than non-communicative "themewriting." And Macrorie follows his own "here principle" while writing his texts, essentially engaging in a form of experience-based "I-search" to develop his ideas about the writing classroom. In the end, his texts re-enact for his readers the very same knowledge he discovered in his classroom.

Both the pragmatists and the expressivists subscribe to the notion that the way to learn things that are worthwhile is through *doing* those things. And since the process paradigm has been around, writing teachers have adhered to this pragmatic principle: the understanding has been that students learn to write by writing. Nowhere is this idea expressed more clearly than in expressivist texts. Coles, for instance, claims that neither writing nor teaching writing is something that can be taught; rather, "the most that would seem possible is for someone to enact his notion of what is involved in the activity in such a way as to demand that others respond with an enactment of what for *them* is involved in it" (1). Elbow, too, believes that writing is such a complex of "contrasting but interdependent skills" that "no one yet has succeeded in making" the teaching of writing an "orderly, hierarchical progression that works" (135). Expressivist ideas about writing and the teaching of writing, then, are in line with the pragmatist notion that verifiability "rests in experience, in tested conclusions" (Roskelly and Ronald 86). Pragmatism "is therefore scientific, or technical, in its approach to the possibility of knowledge and truth" (86). Although the popular use of the term "scientific" doesn't provide a fitting description of expressivist texts, the term "experimental" is more apt, since such texts walk us through specific procedures for dealing with student writing problems in the "laboratory" of the classroom. And the authors of these studies are basing their results on many years of experience performing these same sorts of classroom activities.

Both pragmatists and expressivists then can be seen as attempting to employ more humane, student-centered ways of teaching. The teacher illustrated in expressivist texts is less like an institutional authority and more like an interested fellow communicator. Conscious of the oppressive nature of "Engfish" and "Englishclassese," Macrorie and Coles sought to show students that they need not be ruled by these forms of discourse, that they could be linguistic agents instead of victims of Engfish. Getting that message across required treating students differently, breaking from traditional student-teacher hierarchies in a way that mirrored other societal changes of the time. The 1960s and 1970s, when early expressivist texts were written, found America undergoing significant social and political changes; meanwhile, institutions of higher education were adapting to vast new populations of students, to student war protests, and to other such irregularities.[3] Macrorie's actually begins *Uptaught* by telling about a student protest on his campus and his institution's brutal and "irrational" response to it by bringing in "about thirty white-helmeted policemen carrying clubs and marching in tight formation" (2). Such is the social and educational environment within which expressivist theorists were writing. Wary of an institution's ability to trample individuals, Macrorie wanted students to learn to write in ways that didn't mirror the voiceless language of the academy or other faceless institutions. The student who writes "Engfish," he says, attempts to communicate in "a language that prevents him from working toward truths, and [as a result] he tells lies" (4). Good writing must above all else speak to a reader; it must have an *effect* on another (*Telling* 3)—as such it is "instrumental."

Dewey, too, says that communication is "instrumental"; this is so because it "liberat[es] us from the otherwise overwhelming pressure of events and enabl[es] us to live in a world of things that have meaning" (204). In other words, communication helps us get ideas right with ourselves so that we are then able to articulate those ideas to others.[4] Dewey and his fellow pragmatists saw effective communication as just one of the ways humans dealt with the problems they encountered in the world, and in the spirit of the pragmatists, expressivist theorists sought to engage students in real-world communicative acts and to stress the pragmatic necessity of connecting with one's reader. In order to promote this human connection, expressivists embrace group feedback in the classroom. O'Donnell points out that expressivist texts "have always emphasized communal responses to a writer's words and the value of exploring those regions of self-knowledge that call attention to themselves in the rhetorical acts of naming, defining, describing, and adducing, and the interpretive acts of doubting and believing" (436-37). This is another way of saying that expressivists espouse as central to the act of communicating the notions of self-awareness and agency, for when we connect with another in writing it is imperative that we take responsibility for the effects of that connection.

CONCLUSION

When Toulmin noted that the pressing issues of the late twentieth century cannot be adequately addressed "without bringing back to the surface questions of the significance of human life" (343), the comparison of life-and-death issues to writing instruction might seem at first a bit of a stretch. However, put into the context of the social and educational environments that Coles, Macrorie, and other expressivist were confronting—and the resistance to institutional power they were promoting—they certainly were, in a manner of speaking, "bringing back to the surface questions of the significance of human life." As McLaughlin says, "The act of naming power is a potent strategy of active resistance" (162). Expressivist theorists' attempts to overhaul composition instruction begin with a concern for a human voice in writing in an attempt to rescue those mired in Engfish and Englishclassese. And by implementing a pedagogy that involves group feedback, they sought to return a human face to the act of communication. Writing is a subject that is deeply personal, and—thanks to schools and their traditional mania over correctness—it is also anxiety-producing. To do well writers have to feel as though they have a stake in what they're writing. This point is as central to Macrorie's thinking as is to Dewey's, whom Macrorie quotes: "There is all the difference in the world between having something to say and having to say something" (*Uptaught* 118). When one "has something to say," one is a subject with agency in the world. When one "has to say something," one is essentially a victim, being pushed around, ruled by some outside force. Elbow, in fact, developed his texts out of his own frustrations as a writer, having been himself the victim of writer's block brought on by attitudes that stress correctness (viii-ix). He and Macrorie and Coles are embracing agency instead of victimization, McLaughlin would say, by taking up theory, by questioning the status quo and the assumptions upon which common practice is based (162).

McLaughlin says of the vernacular theorists he explores that "[a]ll cultural practices have their self-conscious operators, those who have reflected on the premises that make the practice possible. . . . There are theorists everywhere in our culture . . . [and we] need to know as much about each other's methods as we can" (165). McLaughlin's call for such understanding mirrors the one Stephen North made to the emerging field of Composition twelve years ago in *The Making of Knowledge in Composition*. North believes that "a spirit of methodological egalitarianism" is necessary in order for Composition to become a coherent discipline (372). North also called for "the re-establishment of Practice as inquiry," but an impediment to this way of thinking, North explains, is that practitioners tend to set a different set of priorities than those who exist in the other communities North constructs (e.g., Historians, Philosophers, Formalists, and so forth). That is:

[Practitioners'] first allegiance, rightly, is to their classrooms, their second to their immediate colleagues, and then their third—often a distant third, at that—to their profession . . . . The other communities' traditional response to these different priorities has been to try and strengthen their relationship with Practitioners by creating a dependency: selling a brand of knowledge that Practitioners cannot produce for themselves, and at the same time ignoring or devaluing [Practitioner] lore. (372)

When composition's epistemological theorists of the 1980s spoke to the theoretical shortcomings of the works of expressivist practitioners, that form of academic theory spoke more loudly and persuasively than did the *vernacular* theory of expressivists.

McLaughlin's discussion of vernacular theory, however much it helps to clarify the level of theorizing that inheres in the works of expressivists, confirms that there is, indeed, a difference between academic theory and vernacular theory. And within the walls of academia, certain priorities exist (and will likely continue to exist) that are reflected in, for example, the way scholarship is favored over teaching and service. Yet within the classroom those institutional priorities need not matter, as North suggests they typically don't for practitioners. Working and learning within an institution does not necessitate speaking and writing the voiceless language of an institution. As Thomas Newkirk points out, "the truly subversive move" in Donald Murray's work was "to claim that the professional writer (and not the academician) should be the model for the student" (104). To one degree or another, this subversive move was made by each of the expressivists I have mentioned here. The peer editorial methods of professional writers have continued to be a commonplace pedagogical tool in our classrooms, but too often they are employed in the service of academic papers—not essays that ask a student to attend to his or her voice as an individual in the world addressing a specific topic. Newkirk's recommendation that we assign personal essay topics because of the pragmatic importance of such writing can have in developing writers' lives seems especially important (85). By giving students the opportunity to explore topics of importance to them and their own lives in the process, we are encouraging the sort of self-awareness that both pragmatists and expressivists see as essential to being human. Writing thus becomes an "instrument" for achieving this self-awareness, which is itself an instrument for personal growth and change.

NOTES

1. As Roskelly and Ronald note, the terms "experience" and method are essentially synonymous in a pragmatist mindset (86).

2. Donna Qualley, in her work cited, refers to this questioning spirit as an "essayistic stance."

3. Roskelly and Ronald point out that pragmatism, too, was born out of a spirit of protest against certain social and educational forces, particularly against the rising tide of industrialism, which was often seen "unreflectively . . . as a thoroughgoing benefit to American culture" at the end of the last century (93-94).

4. This idea is central to much of Elbow's work. See especially his "Closing My Eyes as I Speak: An Argument for Ignoring Audience." *College English* 49 (Jan. 1987): 50-69.

WORKS CITED

Bartholomae, David. "A Reply to Stephen North," *PRE/TEXT* 11.1-2 (1990): 122-30.

Berlin, James A. *Rhetoric and Reality: Writing Instruction in American Colleges, 1900-1985*. Carbondale: Southern Illinois UP, 1987.

Burnham, Christopher C. "Expressive Rhetoric: A Source Study." *Defining the New Rhetorics*. Eds. Theresa Enos and Stuart C. Brown. Newbury Park, CA: Sage, 1993. 154-70.

Coles, William E., Jr. *The Plural I: The Teaching of Writing*. New York: Holt, 1978.

Dewey, John. *Experience and Nature*. 1929. New York: Dover, 1958.

Elbow, Peter. *Writing Without Teachers*. New York: Oxford UP, 1973.

Fishman, Stephen M., and Lucille Parkinson McCarthy. "Is Expressivism Dead? Reconsidering Its Romantic Roots and Its Relation to Social Constructionism." *College English* 54 (1992): 647-61.

Gradin, Sherrie. *Romancing Rhetorics: Social Expressivist Perspectives on the Teaching of Writing*. Portsmouth, NH: Boynton/Cook, 1995.

Macrorie, Ken. *Uptaught*. New York: Hayden, 1970.

———. *Telling Writing*. New York: Hayden, 1970.

McLaughlin, Thomas. *Street Smarts and Critical Theory: Listening to the Vernacular*. Madison: U Wisconsin P, 1996.

Mead, George Herbert. *Selected Writings*. Ed. Andrew J. Reck. Chicago: U Chicago P, 1964.

Newkirk, Thomas. *The Performance of Self in Student Writing*. Portsmouth, NH: Heinemann, 1997.

North, Stephen M. *The Making of Knowledge in Composition: Portrait of an Emerging Field*. Portsmouth, NH: Boynton/Cook, 1987.

O'Donnell, Thomas G. "Politics and Ordinary Language: A Defense of Expressivist Rhetorics." *College English* 58 (April 1996): 423-39.

Qualley, Donna. *Turns of Thought: Teaching Composition as Reflexive Inquiry*. Portsmouth, NH: Boynton/Cook, 1997.

Rorty, Richard. "Introduction: Pragmatism as Anti-Representationalism." In John P. Murphy. *Pragmatism: From Peirce to Davidson*. Boulder, CO: Westview, 1990. 1-6.

Roskelly, Hephzibah, and Kate Ronald. *Reason to Believe: Romanticism, Pragmatism, and the Teaching of Writing*. Albany: State U of New York P, 1998.

Rucker, Darnell. *The Chicago Pragmatists*. Minneapolis: U Minnesota P, 1969.

Toulmin, Stephen. "The Recovery of Practical Philosophy." *The American Scholar* 57 (Summer 1988): 337-52.

4

The Post-Process Movement in Composition Studies

Bruce McComiskey

The term *post-process* has recently gained some currency in composition studies, yet its meaning remains unclear. Reactions among writing teachers to the term *post-process* are often as strong as reactions have been among literary theorists to the term *postmodern*. One of the reasons for such reactions to these terms is that in each idiomatic usage the "post" means something different, ranging anywhere from a "radical rejection" to a "complex extension" of what came before. In this chapter, I argue that the most fruitful meaning for the "post" in post-process is "extension," not "rejection" and I offer social-process rhetorical inquiry as a pedagogical method for extending our present view of the composing process into the social world of discourse.

THE WRITING PROCESS MOVEMENT

As Lester Faigley, James Berlin, and others have argued, the 1960s and 1970s ushered in a new historical moment in composition studies, a moment marked by social revolution and educational reform. During these foundational decades, writing teachers as diverse as Peter Elbow, Janet Emig, Linda Flower, Janice Lauer, James Moffett, and many others began to examine carefully and act upon Donald Murray's famous call to educational arms, "Teach Writing as a Process Not Product." Reacting against the rigid rules that governed student writing before the Vietnam War, these disparate scholars all agreed that the best way to teach writing was to throw away mode-based literary and nonfiction readers (which functioned as illusive manifestations of our grading standards) and focus instead on what happens when individuals write, and they defined their own educational space in opposition to the space occupied by current-traditional rhetoric.

During its tenure in college composition studies, the writing process movement shifted from a negative dialectic against the evils of the current-traditional rhetoric to a more positive articulation of its own goals and strategies. And in this shift, the writing process movement became more and more associated with expressivist approaches to teaching composition. Lad Tobin, for example, suggests, "Though there is not a necessary connection between process pedagogy and personal writing . . . the two have often been linked in practice and perception" (6), and Robert Yagelski laments that the terms "process" and "expressivism" are often used synonymously (206). Throughout the 1970s and 1980s, this burgeoning expressivist writing process movement took hold of the college composition studies scene and became the "standard" for effective writing instruction, especially at certain influential institutions such as the University of Massachusetts and the University of New Hampshire. Through a variety of invention strategies (freewriting, clustering, journaling, brainstorming, and so on), students accessed their inner speech, harnessed the multiplicities of meanings that were found within themselves, outside the limiting confines of institutional discourses; and through re-vision, students were encouraged to look and look again at their own identities in a variety of personalized contexts.

This is not to say, of course, that approaches to writing instruction other than expressivism did not exist in the 1970s and 1980s. They did. But many, such as those arising out of cognitive psychology, were co-opted by expressivism, and with very little effort indeed. Most of us would acknowledge that the early rhetoric of cognitive psychology, articulated in landmark studies by Janet Emig and Linda Flower, among others, is "transactional" (to borrow a term from James Berlin's *Rhetoric and Reality*), engaging more than one element in the traditional rhetorical triangle. In this respect cognitivist rhetorics are distinct from mostly subjective rhetorics such as expressivism. Yet these early cognitivist rhetorics, despite having certain transactional qualities, still focused on the "psychology of the individual" (Berlin, *Rhetoric* 159). For example, while Linda Flower recommended that writers convert writer-based prose into reader-based prose (a transactional move), she still encouraged novice students to begin with writer-based prose, a claim Peter Elbow would also make in "Closing My Eyes as I Speak" a few years after Flower's landmark essays on cognitive problem solving. It was easy, really: expressivists simply used Flower's innovative strategies for inventing writer-based prose, and they stopped there.

But all of this has been utterly problematized in the 1990s. In The *Construction of Negotiated Meaning*, for example, Flower articulates a "social-cognitive" approach to literacy and composing, negotiating in the process a position between expressivist and social epistemic rhetoric. Although Flower admits, "I guess I am a bit of a conventionalist, brought up on the language of expressive writing" (293), she nevertheless seeks "an integrated vision of literacy that recognizes that writers need to know discourse conventions as well as strategies, to belong to a community and still take independent journeys of the mind" (292). Also, in *Romancing Rhetorics*, Sherrie Gradin argues for a "social-expressivist" view of composing in which writers are both constructed and free agents. It is not very long ago that the hyphenated adjectives "social-cognitivist" and "social-expressivist" would have been considered oxymorons, yet they have recently become commonplace. These kinds of negotiations articulate an aporia between traditional oppositions such as social versus expressivist and social versus cognitivist approaches to teaching writing. And it is just this sort of impulse to negotiate that I believe forms both the theoretical and pragmatic foundation of a "post-process" composition studies that extends (rather than rejects) its own history.

POST-PROCESS COMPOSITION: REJECTING THE WRITING PROCESS MOVEMENT

Let me begin my discussion of the recent "post" responses to the writing process movement with a conception of post-process composition that I believe has limited value in classroom practice, the idea that the post-process movement constitutes a radical break with the concerns of the writing process movement. Thomas Kent, the foremost advocate of this "anti-process" version of post-process composition, argues against what he calls "systemic rhetoric" that "treats discourse production and discourse analysis as codifiable processes" ("Beyond" 492). In composition studies, Kent describes three different manifestations of systemic rhetoric—expressivist, empirical, and social constructionist—that, though different in some ways, all "assume that discourse production and analysis can be reduced to systemic processes and taught in classrooms in some codified manner" ("Paralogic" 25). Kent argues, however, that "discourse production and analysis refute systematization," and so "we cannot codify our interpretive acts and then arrange them in any sort of systemic metalanguage" (35). Thus, Kent continues, "With this process approach to writing instruction. . . we assume that the writer can discover, in some predictable way, what it is she wants to say and how to say it: we mistakenly assume that a fit, link, or convention exists between the different hermeneutic strategies employed by both the writer and the reader" (36). Writing, then, is not a codified process of discovering ideas but a hermeneutic exploration of different interpretive strategies, and writing teachers, then, become paralogic participants in a classroom dialogue rather than masters of some desired discourse (37).

While I agree with Kent that language is much too unstable to be codified into universal principles for generating discourse, I do not believe that this is what the writing process movement in composition has done. Language, as Kent describes it, is inherently unstable and fraught with contradiction, and on this point we concur. However, invention and revision strategies, as I understand and teach them, do not assume a stable and predictable linguistic system for generating universal meaning; their function is, instead, to harness the polyphonic character of language in communities, to develop rather than constrict a writer's sense of purpose. When I teach my composition students about language, I tell them that it is unstable, that meaning resides in the communication context and in each person's interpretation of the very words we use. But I also tell them that *writing* well transforms this unstable language into discourse that can accomplish real purposes. And while we are not able to predict with absolute certainty the hermeneutic strategies readers might use in the interpretation of a text, the writer of that text can, I believe, invoke in a reader certain hermeneutic strategies over others. Just as an audience might be invoked into particular relational roles by the linguistic qualities of a text, so too can readers be invoked into particular interpretive stances by the linguistic qualities of a text. We have, of course, learned this lesson well from Walter Ong, Douglas Park, Lisa Ede, and Andrea Lunsford, among others.

My most pressing concern with Kent's "anti-process" version of post-process theory, however, is that it constructs for composition studies yet another version of its most common and most destructive binary opposition—theory versus practice. In *Constructing Knowledges*, Sidney Dobrin suggests that Kent's post-process theory "has been intruded upon by composition's pedagogical imperative" (63) in two ways: first, it has been critiqued for its lack of attention to classroom practice, and, second, it has been subjected too soon to the development of pedagogical strategies. Dobrin contends that the "post-process" movement in composition studies should remain, at least for now, a purely *theoretical* enterprise, and it should consequently not yet fall victim to this pedagogical imperative (64). Yet Dobrin's desire to limit the discourse about post-process composition, first, violates the very principles of paralogy upon which this anti-process version of the post-process movement is based, and, second, privileges theoretical "discourse" over pedagogical "strategies," denying that theory and pedagogy both construct knowledges in a dialectical process. Post-process theory, as Dobrin and Kent describe it, received its very generative impulse as a paralogic and oppositional reaction against what is arguably composition studies' most valued pedagogical strategy—teaching the composing process—yet post-process theory offers no pedagogical strategy of its own; regarding actual writing instruction, then, it is purely a negative dialectic.

POST-PROCESS COMPOSITION: EXTENDING THE WRITING PROCESS MOVEMENT

Although I argue in this chapter that the "post" in post-process should not represent a radical break with the composing process movement, this "post" does indeed signify at least a certain degree of anxiety. As I have already indicated, the writing process movement gained prominence in the college composition scene during the 1970s and retained its prominence for nearly two decades, and, according to Faigley, "it was not until the later 1980s that expressions of general disillusionment with writing as process began to be heard" (67-68). Further,

John Trimbur suggests that the recent "social turn" in composition studies is the result of a "crisis within the process paradigm and a growing disillusion with its limits and pressures," and he argues that this disillusionment has generated a "post-process" approach to writing instruction that views "literacy as an ideological arena and composing as a cultural activity by which writers position and reposition themselves in relation to their own and others' subjectivities, discourse, practices, and institutions" (109). Those who have articulated expressions of disillusionment (though not utter despair) have critiqued the writing process movement as an expressivist and cognitivist obsession with the individual writer.

Numerous scholars, including James Berlin, Patricia Bizzell, James Clifford, Lester Faigley, and Susan Miller, among many others, argue that the individualist ideologies associated with expressivist and cognitivist approaches to composing assume a modernist conception of student writers as ultimately sovereign subjects, able to "rise above" the debilitating pressures culture and society place on the production of discourse. Yet these scholars believe that no such social subject exists. Instead, student writers must address rather than ignore, critique rather than dodge, the very social forces that pressure them to behave in certain institutionally advantageous ways, and they must learn to address and critique culture in social and collective ways rather than individual ways.

It is a common perception that with this social critique of the expressivist and cognitivist writing process movement comes a necessary rejection of the composing process in general and of invention in particular, but this is simply not the case. As James Berlin, Lester Faigley, Karen Burke LeFevre, and Robert Yagelski have all pointed out, social approaches to writing instruction view composing as a process (no less than expressivist and cognitivist approaches do), yet the difference is that these approaches define composing as a social (not individual) process. In *Invention as a Social Act*, for example, Karen Burke LeFevre argues that although theories of invention are commonly based on a conception of the creative individual writer, "rhetorical invention is better understood as a social act" (1). Invention methods themselves, in other words, are neither individualistic nor social; according to LeFevre, "what matters is the way the scheme is interpreted and used" (51). Thus, "the writing process," as a rubric for studying and teaching composition, is not the sole province of expressivist and cognitivist rhetorics, and the "social turn" in composition studies, which Trimbur labels "post-process," does not constitute, in practice or theory, a rejection of the process movement, but rather its extension into the social world of discourse.

Yet the problem is more complex than I have represented it so far. With the rejection of expressivist and cognitivist rhetorics from social, post-process perspectives has also come a renewed interest in "written" products, cultural "texts" from a variety of verbal and visual media. While students' own texts remain a focus in post-process composition classes, many post-process teachers believe that *only* using student texts in writing classes neglects fully half of the composing process, the process of *reading* cultural discourse as a form of composing. Doug Brent, for example, argues that reading is generative and forms the exigencies of future texts. M. Jimmie Killingsworth contends that new communication technologies have reintroduced "texts" into the composing process. David Bartholomae suggests, "it is the product and not the plan for writing that locates a writer on the page" (144) and situates a writer within social institutions. And Louise Weatherby Phelps urges compositionists to deconstruct the process/product opposition and reconstruct discourse structure itself as a *process*, an event, a dance. While Brent, Killingsworth, Bartholomae, and Phelps offer very different perspectives on the issue, all agree that a renewed attention to texts in the teaching of writing enhances students' abilities to succeed in both the production and reception of discourse. Whether we call them "discursive practices" (Brodkey) or "signifying practices" (Berlin, *Rhetorics, Poetics*), strategies for both reading and writing cultural texts have become a prominent focus in post-process composition classrooms.

But this renewed interest in texts by no means represents a reassertion of current-traditional ideologies into composition studies. Whereas current-traditional writing teachers introduced ideal texts to their students as models to be imitated, post-process writing teachers, on the other hand, introduce cultural texts to their students as objects of critique, as representations of social values that institutions would impose on their readers, as generative forces that comprise exigencies for writing that has meaning both inside and outside the confines of the composition class. There is little value in imitation-based, current-traditional, "read-this-essay-and-do-what-the-author-did" pedagogical strategies, and the post-process movement in composition studies avoids this simplistic use of texts. Even so, many composition teachers who were involved in the early process versus product wars are reluctant now to acknowledge most potential uses for texts (other than those their students write) in their composition classes. While I agree that a piece of writing is "never finished," I also believe that, finished or not, most writing is read, is intended to be read, so writers must then be able to account for the ways in which texts are not only produced but also distributed and consumed within specific communities. As a means to accomplish these complicated rhetorical tasks with both the processes and products of discourse, I offer social-process rhetorical inquiry.

SOCIAL-PROCESS RHETORICAL INQUIRY

Social-process rhetorical inquiry is a method of invention that usually manifests itself in composition classes as a set of heuristic questions based on the cycle of cultural production, contextual distribution, and critical consumption. First, heuristics based on this cycle direct students' attention to the ways in which texts and their contexts promote cultural and social values, leading readers toward frameworks of judgment that favor certain preferred values over others. Second, these heuristics encourage students to adopt a critical stance toward encoded values, determining from their own perspectives the veracity of the cultural and social values promoted in target texts, and accommodating ethical values, resisting unethical values, and negotiating values that have some worth within certain alternative contexts. Finally, this social-process cycle of rhetorical inquiry is not complete until students produce their own discourses, their own texts, based on the critical knowledge they have gained and in response to the problems they have identified through the inquiry process. While composition studies, I believe, has extensively explored the cognitive and social processes by which discourse is produced, the processes of distribution and consumption (and the entire cyclical process of production, distribution, and consumption) have been largely neglected. The integration of these rhetorical processes is the very function of social-process rhetorical inquiry.

Those who practice social-process rhetorical inquiry understand all communication as "discursive practice," as strategic participation in the "flow" of discourse. Discourse pre-exists the physical act of writing, and writing enters the con/texts of discourse. In order to understand how this "flow" of discourse operates, we need to engage the cycle of production, distribution, and consumption as an analytical and generative heuristic at least twice—first to understand how particular discursive formations operate (how their members produce, distribute, and consume discourse), and second to enter these discursive formations with new rhetorical interventions.

The most common "discursive formations" manifest themselves as "institutions." Norman Fairclough, in *Critical Discourse Analysis: The Critical Study of Language*, suggests that "Social actions tend very much to cluster in terms of institutions; when we witness a social event (e.g., a verbal interaction), we normally have no difficulty identifying it in institutional terms, i.e., as appertaining to the family, the school, the workplace, church, the courts, some department of government, or some other institution" (37). This is because institutions, more than any other communicative contexts, produce and structure social interactions, thereby both enabling and restricting discourse. We must, Fairclough continues, view "the institution as simultaneously facilitating and constraining the social action (here, specifically, verbal interaction) of its members: it provides them with a frame for action, without which they could not act, but it thereby constrains them to act within that frame" (38). Yet this "frame" also has much more profound consequences, for "in the process of acquiring the ways of talking which are normatively associated with [an institutionalized] subject position, one necessarily acquires also its ways of seeing, or ideological norms. And just as one is typically unaware of one's ways of talking unless for some reason they are subjected to conscious scrutiny, so also is one typically unaware of what ways of seeing, what ideological representations, underlie one's talk" (39-40). But institutions are by no means ideological monoliths: while there is often a dominant discourse promoted by high-ranking members of an institution, there are also, just as often, competing discourses that vie for sub(versive)-dominance at lower levels of the hierarchy. Yet these discourses usually remain unknown or suppressed. According to Fairclough, "Naturalization gives to particular ideological representations the status of common sense, and thereby makes them opaque, i.e., no longer visible as ideologies" (42).

It is the purpose of social-process rhetorical inquiry to make visible these opaque institutional ideologies, to de-naturalize ideologies through writing, thereby helping students reconstruct perspectives on institutions that work toward more inclusive ethics. This is not to say, however, that students are completely blind to the workings of institutions, as Joseph Harris points out; most are, for example, keenly aware of the ways in which schooling encourages certain subjectivities over others. Yet social-process rhetorical inquiry can provide for students fresh perspectives from which to observe and critique the inner workings of institutionalized socialization, enhancing the critical powers they already possess.

I prefer to focus my students' rhetorical attention through social-process rhetorical inquiry on the discourses and institutions that most profoundly impact their own lives, institutions like school, work, media, and government. In one particular assignment, my students write about the ways in which specific workplaces promote certain cultural values over others. Appendix A contains the handout students receive that guides them through the critical process of examining the cultural production, contextual distribution, and critical consumption of discourse in a workplace of their choice. It should come as no surprise that students write best about subjects that impact their lives everyday, and work has always been a generative subject for my students, whether they interrogate their own work experience or the experience of someone else in a job they would eventually like to have.

Yet I want my students to understand their (and others') work experiences in critical not personal ways, *discursive* not experiential ways, *institutional* not individual ways. And in order to encourage these critical, discursive, and institutional interpretations of students' work experiences, I provide them with a complex invention heuristic that guides them through the cycle of social-process rhetorical inquiry, and I have reproduced this heuristic in Appendix B. Using the invention heuristic as a guide, students generate material for their critical and practical essays. But the heuristic is only a guide and students should not feel obliged to answer all of the questions in equal depth. Some of the questions are simply not going to be relevant for every workplace and others will yield a great deal of information. For example, I have had some students write several pages of notes on "Employee Relations" and completely ignore "Geographical Layout," whereas others find that "Geographical Layout" is crucial to their understanding of various aspects of their work experience. In the pages that follow, I examine a student's response to the heuristic invention and the resulting critical and practical essay. I hope to demonstrate the important connections among the exploratory invention notes and the eventual essays, and I also hope to demonstrate the importance of encouraging students to move beyond personal narrative to institutional critique.

The following is an excerpt from Kelly Mount's invention notes on her work experience at Gapkids:

Cultural Production: Cultural values at Gapkids include: the ideal sales associate should always be at work on time, greet every customer within three minutes, offer to do anything for the customer, always sell more than one item at a time, say "thank you" and "come again," smile, answer the telephone in a cheerful voice, keep the store clean, follow the dress code.

Contextual Distribution: Methods used to reinforce the cultural values include: you have to wear Gap clothes, sales techniques are reinforced at staff meetings and in company memos, training sessions on the latest selling and display techniques. Sales are important, so we also learned how to make the store appear neat so that the clothes would be more appealing. We often worked long hours after the mall closed, cleaning and straightening the merchandise for the next day's sales.

Critical Consumption: I always followed the dress code and wore the right (Gap) clothes, greeted the customers, and tried to sell lots of items; however, I did not always feel comfortable with these requirements. What I especially hated was walking out to my car after closing. We would usually keep cleaning the store until nobody else was around. It was frightening walking to my car alone at the back of the dark parking lot.

These invention notes (excerpted here) led Kelly to explore her experience working at Gapkids in critical ways, moving beyond her own personal experience with this workplace to an institutional critique of the cultural production, contextual distribution, and critical consumption of cultural values. Under "cultural production," Kelly explores what Gapkids considers to be essential qualities of the ideal sales associate. These qualities/values are written from Gapkids' perspective, not Kelly's, and her goal here is simply to understand and describe Gapkids' ideal worker. Under "contextual distribution," Kelly describes specific ways in which Gapkids encourages its sales associates to strive for these ideals. Company memos, staff meetings, and employee training sessions are just a few of the "distribution" methods Gapkids uses to promote their image of the ideal sales associate. While students' notes under "cultural production" and "contextual distribution" are often brainstorming lists, their notes under "critical consumption" usually begin to acquire a center of gravity. Following her invention process, hard-sell techniques and the dangers of a dark parking lot were two ideas about which Kelly knew she would be able to write well.

Based on these invention notes, Kelly chose a few of the most important cultural values, with their attending modes of distribution and her own critique of these values and modes, and she developed them into a full critical essay. The following is one complete section of Kelly's critical essay in which she critiques the cultural value "The ideal Gapkids employee should keep the store as neat and clean as possible":

Nothing is more irritating than walking into a clothing store with a dirty floor and tables filled with unfolded, disorganized clothes. A store with this appearance does not leave a good first impression on the customer. The store seems overwhelming because you have no idea where to begin looking for a certain size or color. Shopping becomes more like a chore than a pleasurable activity. But Gapkids stores are always immaculate. When I began working at Gapkids, I was extremely surprised at how much time and effort was put into cleaning, folding clothes, and straightening the store. I recall one evening when my manager asked me to fold a stack of button-down shirts and make sure that the buttons were lined up and even. At first, I thought she was just being picky, but I soon learned that every Gapkids store expects attention paid to even the smallest details. I also remember being asked to vacuum the air vents in the ceiling one night after the store and the rest of the mall had already closed. In fact, every night after closing time, we spent an hour or two folding clothes and taking out the trash.

All of this effort put into the appearance of the store paid off economically. It created a great first impression for our customers and helped us show them the right sizes and colors without having to search the sales floor. However, all of this work did have some negative effects. Since we always had to stay for an hour or two each night after the store and mall had closed, we were usually the last people to leave the mall. This was dangerous because we were left to walk to our cars in the dark either alone or with one other worker. I think it would be better if Gapkids employees could come in an hour or two before the store opens and clean from the previous day. This would eliminate the need for sales associates to walk to their cars late at night.

Kelly structured this section of her essay into two paragraphs, each with a distinct rhetorical purpose. In the first paragraph, Kelly describes the values associated with keeping Gapkids stores neat and clean, and she does so largely from Gapkids' perspective.

The ideal sales associate is, of course, charged with this important responsibility (maintaining a proper appearance) and must adopt behaviors consistent with it (vacuuming air vents, lining up buttons, etc.). Kelly plays the role in this paragraph of an advocate, describing a single value (or complex of related values) and its modes of institutional distribution, and explaining its importance in the context of Gapkids. There is no sense, yet, of critique, of evaluation, of the accommodation of worthy values, the resistance to unworthy values, or the negotiation of values that might gain some importance in alternative contexts. These are rhetorical goals that Kelly reserves for the second paragraph where she plays the role of a critic.

In her second paragraph, Kelly begins by describing and accommodating the positive aspects of the values described above (economic success, appealing to customers), and she then describes and resists some problems with these values (walking alone in a dark parking lot). Finally, Kelly negotiates a compromise (cleaning before opening rather than after closing) that retains the cultural values in question (neatness, etc.) and Gapkids' methods for promoting them (memos and meetings). In these two brief paragraphs, Kelly accomplishes a purpose that I believe has powerful significance for improving institutional discursive practices. Negotiation, the process of harnessing competing discourses (in

Kelly's case, Gapkids' economic success versus employees' safety), acknowledges the importance of existing institutional values, yet it introduces other values into the mix and calls for a compromise that maintains both the established and new values. Knee-jerk resistance results in oppositional audience responses and rarely accomplishes real rhetorical purposes. Ambivalent accommodation affirms the status quo. But measured negotiation enables change through compromise.

Thus far in the assignment series, Kelly has explored and critiqued the cultural production, contextual distribution, and critical consumption of institutional values promoted by Gapkids. Exploration and critique are, of course, valuable pursuits, but they should not be rhetorical ends in themselves. Richard Johnson, founding member and former director of the Birmingham Center for Contemporary Cultural Studies, suggests that "Critique involves stealing away the more useful elements and rejecting the rest. From this point of view cultural studies is a process, a kind of alchemy for producing useful knowledge" (38). Through social-process rhetorical inquiry, Kelly has produced useful knowledge regarding some of the institutional practices at Gapkids; however, she has yet to use this knowledge. Thus, following this critical analysis of her work experience at Gapkids, Kelly was faced with a different rhetorical task, a more practical task, that of using her critical knowledge to write a letter that describes and solves a problem in the workplace. Kelly chose to write to the manager of the store she worked in. The following is an excerpt from that letter (which originally also addressed the problem of high-pressure sales tactics):

Dear Ms. Doughton:

I have worked with you at Gapkids for over two years now, and I have really enjoyed my position as a sales associate. But there is something you might not be aware of that puts some of us in danger. Several sales associates and I feel uncomfortable walking to our cars in the empty mall parking lot at 11:30 p.m. every night. I remember last week you said you were also nervous about it. I know how important it is to keep our store looking great, but there may be another way to accomplish the goal. I've been thinking that we could schedule two employees to come in at 8:30 to clean the floors and straighten the clothes for an hour and a half before the customers arrive. This way, everybody working the night shift could leave at 10:00 p.m. when a lot of people are still around the parking lot area. I know you have always been concerned about the welfare of your workers. Please let me know if there is anything else I can do to help you solve this problem. Sincerely,

Kelly Mount

In this letter, Kelly is careful to acknowledge the importance of the cultural values she has observed at Gapkids (e.g., keeping the store "looking great"), yet she also introduces problems that these values cause (e.g., dangerous nighttime walks in the parking lot). While much of her rhetorical efforts until this point were spent engaged in detailed exploration and critique, it is interesting to note that Kelly spends little time in her letter recounting the knowledge she generated during social-process rhetorical inquiry. Kelly knows that such critical pursuits are only appropriate in academic discourse, and the way to accomplish rhetorical goals in workplace settings is to avoid repeating information that is known or assumed and move quickly to the point of negotiation (i.e., cleaning before the store opens). Yet we must remember that this point of negotiation arises out of the critical explorations resulting from social-process rhetorical inquiry.

Throughout this assignment series, Kelly has engaged the entire cycle of cultural production, contextual distribution, and critical consumption, first to explore and critique the cultural values promoted at Gapkids, and second to enter the flow of discourse and enable institutional change. Whether or not students actually send the letters they write is up to them; but even if the letters are not actually sent, even if they are not distributed and consumed in their target communities, students nevertheless learn valuable rhetorical strategies for future situations.

CONCLUSION

Critical writing, by means of social-process rhetorical inquiry, focuses on rhetoric, writing, and culture (all of which are inextricably intertwined) as processes, as means for accomplishing real goals both inside and outside of our classrooms. As such, it does not reject the writing process movement as a whole (though it does reject certain expressivist and cognitivist versions of it); instead, social-process rhetorical inquiry extends the writing process into the social world of discourse, the "dance" (to invoke Phelps again) of processes and products in the cycle of cultural production, contextual distribution, and critical consumption. Established process methodologies (invention strategies, revision techniques, etc.), conceived as "social acts" (LeFevre), are all key components in the cultural production of discourse. Yet social-process rhetorical inquiry extends our understanding of the composing process outward (i.e., out of the individual writer's consciousness) toward institutional processes of socialization. Writing, thus conceived, is both a way of knowing and acting, a way of understanding the world and also changing it.

APPENDIX A

WORK CRITICAL AND PRACTICAL ESSAYS: ASSIGNMENTS

In this essay, you will examine the culture of "work" critically. Most of you have either worked in the past or are currently working, and even more of you will work in the near future. For most of us, activities associated with work will occupy about one half of our adult waking hours (8 hours of work, 8 hours of leisure, 8 hours of sleep), so it is crucial that we fully understand the cultural assumptions prevalent in our particular work situations. When we understand these cultural assumptions, we can then make informed decisions about how to live our working lives. We have the choice of accommodating, resisting, or negotiating these cultural assumptions, and in doing so we open up the potential to change the assumptions that operate against our own beliefs regarding workplace conditions and relationships.

Work Critical Essay

Those of you who have work experience (full or part-time, paid or volunteer) might write an autobiographical account of a single job you have occupied and the company that employed you. Your topic for this essay will center around a job you have (or have had) that requires you to complete a variety of tasks and interact with a number of other employees. You will derive the arguments and specific, concrete details for your work critical essay directly from your own experience in this workplace.

Those of you who have never worked might write an ethnographic description of a particular workplace and its employees. Your topic for this essay will center around a workplace to which you have easy access. You will derive the arguments and specific, concrete details for your work critical essay directly from your own detailed observations of this workplace and from interviews with its employees.

After you have decided on the general approach you would like to take in your essay (autobiographical account or ethnographic description), and you have decided on the specific workplace you would like to examine critically, then complete the invention heuristic provided for this assignment. Answer as many of the questions as you can in as much detail as you can.

After you have completed the invention heuristic, you are ready to begin writing your work critical essay. Your essay should include the following elements:

1. An introduction to the work environment and a preview of your conclusions about it. You might also include any good or bad feelings—biases—you have toward the workplace that might influence your descriptions.

2. Fully developed and well-detailed paragraphs explaining and critiquing a number of cultural values perpetuated in the workplace you are examining critically. Discuss each of these values in terms of their cultural production and contextual distribution by your employers, and your own critical consumption (accommodation, resistance, and negotiation) of the values.

3. A conclusion based on ways you think the work environment might be improved.

Your audience for this critical essay should be people who have work experience in the kind of job or company you are writing about but who have not worked in exactly the same job or company. In other words, assume that your audience has fairly general knowledge of your topic but lacks specific understanding of the particular problems you have faced at work.

Work Practical Essay

Write a formal letter to someone in the workplace (a fellow worker, manager, or owner) who can do something about the problem(s) you describe in your critical essay. This letter should be approximately one single-spaced page in length, your tone in the letter should be appropriate to your audience and purpose, and you should suggest viable solutions.

APPENDIX B

WORK CRITICAL AND PRACTICAL ESSAYS: INVENTION HEURISTIC

Whether you are writing an autobiographical account of a job or an ethnographic description of a workplace, you will need to explore the topic before beginning to write. Answer the following questions in as much detail as you can. Your answers to these questions will generate details and arguments for use in your work critical essay.

Cultural Production

Use the following prompt to generate as many cultural values perpetuated in your workplace as possible: "The ideal X employee should Y." Substitute the company and job you occupy for X and the cultural effects your employers try to create in you for Y. The more cultural values you can generate, the better your selection will be when you begin writing your work critical essay.

Good cultural values are the key to a successful work critical essay. Cultural values answer the question "What kind of people do my employers want me and other employees to be?" Cultural values should be written from the perspective of the company, and they should always express qualities inherent in the ideal employee.

The following examples are several well-written cultural values: the ideal Wayerhaeuser factory worker is always thinking about safety first; the ideal Rayovac receptionist should always be pleasant regardless of the circumstances; the ideal Wal-Mart associate should always be busy. The following examples are poorly written cultural values: the ideal Hardee's cook should cook each hamburger for 2:35; KinderCare pre-school teachers and daycare workers should only be paid minimum wage; Nike employees think they should be promoted according to how long they have been with the company.

Contextual Distribution

Brainstorm methods your employers use to reinforce (i.e., distribute) each cultural value in the workplace: job descriptions, posted policies, orientation workshops, supervision, observation, training sessions, verbal reprimands, productivity awards, staff meetings, and so on. Several others should present themselves as you remember or observe your workplace.

Details regarding a company's product/service output, its employee relations and activities, and its geographical layout also contribute to the distribution of cultural values. Use the following prompts to explore how cultural values are distributed in the workplace you have chosen to critique.

Company Output: What products does the company produce and what services does it offer? What technologies are used in the company? What clientele does the company serve? Who are its target audiences? What geographical regions does the company serve?

Employee Relations: What is the power hierarchy in the company and what is your place in it? Try to draw as detailed a diagram of the company's power hierarchy as you can. What are the social relationships like among employees (workers, managers)? What kinds of interaction are allowed or encouraged among employees?

Employee Activities: What activities are assigned to your position in the company? Are your activities negotiable or strictly assigned? If negotiable, to what extent? What activities are assigned to other positions in the company? Are their activities negotiable or strictly assigned? If negotiable, to what extent?

Geographical Layout: What is the geographical layout of the company "space"? Try to draw a detailed diagram of the company's geographical layout. What "spaces" are better than others and why? Who occupies these better and worse spaces?

Critical Consumption

Describe ways that you and other employees accommodate, resist, and negotiate the cultural values perpetuated in your workplace. We accommodate work cultural values when we accept the ideal images the company places on us and we willingly complete the tasks the job requires. We resist work cultural values when we disagree with the ideal images the company places on us and we find ways to avoid or subvert the tasks the job requires. Most important, we negotiate work cultural values when our opinion of the ideal images the company places on us varies from situation to situation and we sometimes complete the tasks the job requires and other times avoid or subvert the same tasks.

Rhetorical Intervention

Write a letter to a member of the company that you think would be most likely (and best able) to change the workplace for the better.

What members of the company are in the best position to do something about the problems you point out? List two or three as potential audiences and answer the following questions for each of them: (1) How much does the audience know about the problems you describe? (2) What is the audience's attitude toward the problem (would they want to solve it)? (3) What is your rhetorical purpose in this intervention (inform, persuade, etc.)?

Choose one audience and compose a letter stating problems, describing solutions, and using an effective tone for your rhetorical purpose.

WORKS CITED

Bartholomae, David. "Inventing the University." *When a Writer Can't Write: Studies in Writer's Block and Other Composing Process Problems*. Ed. Mike Rose. New York: Guilford, 1985. 134-65.

Berlin, James. *Rhetoric and Reality: Writing Instruction in American Colleges, 1900-1985*. Carbondale: Southern Illinois UP, 1987.

———. *Rhetorics, Poetics, and Cultures: Reforming College English Studies*. Urbana: NCTE, 1996.

Bizzell, Patricia. *Academic Discourse and Critical Consciousness*. Pittsburgh: U of Pittsburgh P, 1992.

Brent, Doug. *Reading as Rhetorical Invention: Knowledge, Persuasion, and the Teaching off Research Based Writing*. Urbana: NCTE, 1992.

Brodkey, Linda. *Writing Permitted in Designated Areas Only*. Minneapolis: U of Minnesota P, 1996.

Clifford, John. "The Subject in Discourse." *Contending with Words: Composition and Rhetoric in a Postmodern Age*. Eds. Patricia Harkin and John Schilb. New York: MLA, 1991. 38-51.

Dobrin, Sidney I. *Constructing Knowledges: The Politics of Theory-Building and Pedagogy in Composition*. New York: State U of New York P, 1997.

Ede, Lisa, and Andrea Lunsford. "Audience Addressed/Audience Invoked: The Role of Audience in Composition Theory and Pedagogy." *College Composition and Communication* 35 (1984): 155-71.

Elbow, Peter. "Closing My Eyes as I Speak: An Argument for Ignoring Audience." *College English* 49 (1987): 50-69.

Emig, Janet. *The Composing Process of Twelfth Graders*. Urbana: NCTE, 1971.

Faigley, Lester. *Fragments of Rationality: Postmodernity and the Subject of Composition*. Pittsburgh: U of Pittsburgh P, 1992.

Fairclough, Norman. *Critical Discourse Analysis: The Critical Study of Language*. London: Longman, 1995.

Flower, Linda. "A Cognitive Process Theory of Writing." College Composition and Communication 32 (1981): 365-87.

———. *The Construction of Negotiated Meaning: A Social Cognitive Theory of Writing*. Carbondale: Southern Illinois UP, 1994.

Gradin, Sherrie. *Romancing Rhetorics: Social Expressivist Perspectives on the*

Teaching of Writing. Portsmouth, NH: Boynton/Cook, 1995.

Harris, Joseph. "The Other Reader." *Composition Theory for the Postmodern Classroom*. Eds. Gary Olson and Sidney I. Dobrin. New York: State U of New York P, 1994. 225-35.

Johnson, Richard. "What Is Cultural Studies Anyway?" *Social Text* 6 (1987): 38-80.

Kent, Thomas. "Beyond System: The Rhetoric of Paralogy." *College English* 51 (1989): 492-503.

————. "Paralogic Hermeneutics and the Possibilities of Rhetoric." *Rhetoric Review* 8 (1989): 24-42.

Killingsworth, M. Jimmie. "Product and Process, Literacy and Orality: An Essay on Composition and Culture." *College Composition and Communication* 44 (1993): 26-39.

LeFevre, Karen Burke. *Invention as a Social Act*. Carbondale: Southern Illinois UP, 1987.

McComiskey, Bruce. "Social-Process Rhetorical Inquiry: Cultural Studies Methodologies for Critical Writing about Advertisements." *Journal of Advanced Composition* 17 (1997): 381-400.

Miller, Susan. *Textual Carnivals: The Politics of Composition*. Carbondale: Southern Illinois UP, 1991.

Murray, Donald. "Teach Writing as a Process Not Product." *The Leaflet* (November 1972): 11-14.

Ong, Walter. "The Writer's Audience Is Always a Fiction." *PMLA* 90 (1975): 9-21.

Park, Douglas. "The Meanings of 'Audience.'" *College English* 44 (1982): 247-57.

Phelps, Louise Wetherbee. "The Dance of Discourse." *Pre/Text: The First Decade*. Ed. Victor Vitanza. Pittsburgh: U of Pittsburgh P, 1993. 31-64.

Tobin, Lad. "How the Writing Process Was Born—And Other Conversion Narratives." *Taking Stock: The Writing Process Movement in the 90's*. Eds. Lad Tobin and Thomas Newkirk. Portsmouth, NH: Boynton/Cook, 1994. 1-16.

Trimbur, John. "Taking the Social Turn: Teaching Writing Post-Process." *College Composition and Communication* 45 (1994): 108-18.

Yagelski, Robert. "Who's Afraid of Subjectivity? The Composing Process and Postmodernism or a Student of Donald Murray Enters the Age of Postmodernism." *Taking Stock: The Writing Process Movement in the 90's*. Eds. Lad Tobin and Thomas Newkirk. Portsmouth, NH: Boynton/Cook, 1994. 203-18.

5

Finding "The Writer's Way": What We Expected and How We've Erred

Gina S. Claywell

A cursory look on the ERIC database or at a bibliographic list in most any composition theory text quickly confirms Mina Shaughnessy's place in the field of rhetoric and composition; just such a list is attached at the conclusion of this chapter. Words such as "legacy," "profound," and "quintessential" frequently appear, a testimony to the power and timeliness of her one major work, *Errors and Expectations: A Guide for the Teacher of Basic Writing*. As most of us know, *Errors and Expectations* reveals the struggles Mina and her Basic Writing students experienced as they negotiated the birthing of the open enrollment movement at City University of New York. She discovered patterns in student errors in her tireless efforts to bring these new, underprepared students—who had always been considered uneducable—to an understanding of academic prose. In the twenty years since its publication, the field of rhetoric and composition has blossomed, although few of us are yet quite satisfied with our programs or our individual instruction. Only now are we beginning to understand that Shaughnessy's concern with "the writer's way" (*Errors* 81) implies a multitude of writing processes, not one way of writing shared by all writers. And, though we give lip service to the recommendations Shaughnessy made lo those many years ago and despite the technology that makes writing much less onerous than ever, we still have much more to accomplish in areas such as the political placement of composition, basic writing instruction, writing across the curriculum, student writing conditions, the social independence of classrooms, and the content of composition courses themselves. Indeed, several interrelated "errors and expectations" exist that composition programs, writing centers, and English programs in general need either to be made aware of or to continue to address into the twenty-first century.

A NEW DEFINITION FOR BASIC WRITING

Shaughnessy's work is often used to train graduate students preparing to tutor or teach developmental or first-year writing. I use the book in such a way chiefly because it painfully reveals to those entering the profession the necessity of balancing the standards required for academic products with an understanding of the difficulties associated with writing processes, especially for students who have read or written very little. At first, graduate students find Shaughnessy's students' writing to be oddly humorous, even appalling. Then, they tutor or teach a student whose work looks hauntingly like the *Errors'* examples, and they find themselves grappling with the same issues Mina herself dealt with two decades ago. Many of these new instructors are encountering this field in a trial-by-fire manner—learning the realities, the theory, the definitions, and the day-to-day business of writing instruction all at once. Their own strong writing and reading skills earned them a general undergraduate degree in English steeped in literary terms and traditions and frequently devoid of the very classes these graduate students are preparing to tutor or teach because they successfully challenged first-year composition as undergraduates.

These beginning teachers often hold, consequently, very contradictory notions of elitism and confusion. "How," they wonder, "could students arrive at college without knowing what a sentence is?" On the other hand, they question their own abilities: "How can I be a graduate student in English and not know the first thing about teaching composition?" They quickly develop strong opinions about the appropriateness of college-level developmental writing courses. Initially, they pooh-pooh the very idea of a university's offering remedial instruction. Gradually, as they get to know their students, they realize the innate intelligence that such Basic Writers have; soon, graduate students develop cynicism that schools, or teachers, or parents, have allowed such bright individuals to arrive at college without a proper introduction to academic reading and writing. Finally, as they begin to distinguish between those Basic Writing students who are merely behind and those who lack basic cognitive abilities that might ever enable them to "get it," the graduate students display outright indignation at administrative and legislative dictates pushing high enrollments and fiscal accountability. Such number-crunching encourages the admission (and fee payment) of severely learning-disabled students at the expense of those students' self-esteem since so few realistically will or actually do matriculate. The new instructors arrive at seemingly jaded conclusions that are neither naive, mean-spirited, nor wrong; indeed, they are shared by experienced mid-level administrators who deal daily with learning-disabled students and basic writers.

One such administrator recently revealed to me his intention of proposing a minimal competency level based on standardized scores in order for students to be admitted to his regional public university. His proposal was based not on insensitivity or on any elitist desire to deny students academic opportunity or close open-door policies; rather, he constantly sees the demands that severely limited students place on the resources of time, money, facilities, and faculty allotted to basic instruction. These students, he asserts, arrive at the university at the insistence of either parents or former high school teachers, counselors, or principals, some of whom admit the students' probable inability to succeed in vocational education programs; thus, the adults encourage college enrollment for lack of a better alternative and, sometimes, in spite of the students' lackadaisical attitudes about being there. While neither this administrator nor I necessarily want our home heating and air conditioning systems wired by someone with substantially reduced cognitive abilities, we are perplexed by what to do with these same students in the academic setting. All students can, of course, benefit from the cultural enrichment and humanistic traditions often associated with general education courses, and it is a moral imperative in this country that we all have the opportunity to pursue an education. And, just because they probably will never complete a degree is not reason enough alone to deny admission despite how it affects university matriculation rates. Still, these students lack some of the "basic" skills that even Mina's Basic Writers possessed. They are indicative of a trend in open enrollment that prevents student support services from assisting those students who have "basic" skills and both the potential and desire to overcome obstacles because such offices are swamped with the overwhelming needs of some students. Someone with Mina's empathy then or now might assert, with due reason, that standardized examinations might be able to measure potential, but they cannot indicate determination and thus should not be used to decide who gets educational services; however, the severity of problems universities are encountering as open enrollment is being extended to those with limited literacy skills is becoming a financial and ethical dilemma.

While this trend of admitting students with diminished intellectual capacity may be an understandable result of a complex interaction of increased rights for the disabled, political correctness and a subsequent fear of litigation, and continued attention to recruitment and retention, among other things, still, problems arise when open enrollment is fully extended—gone haywire until the hinges burst—and thus gives rise to a new definition of "basic."

TRAINING TEACHERS VIA MODELING

My experience at several schools across the Upper South has revealed that many graduate students enter composition theory courses as though they are entering a new country; they struggle to learn both the new language and the new content simultaneously, initially overloaded. Undergraduates, however, rarely have the benefit of such instruction, and, more important, look on pedagogies frequently used in composition classes with disdain or fear because their own backgrounds in English suggest that such instruction—because it is not in a lecture format or focused on the professor's knowledge of a literary figure or era—is not what English is really "about." Perhaps it is due to pervasive and ongoing attitudes such as those revealed by John Schilb in a review of texts in *College English*:

> If many English faculty still scorn composition studies, this is partly because writing specialists see pedagogy as a scholarly concern. To raise the status of teaching and of composition, English departments will have to make material changes. But many of them will also have to change their thinking. For one thing, they will have to historicize pedagogy, recognizing how concepts and practices associated with it have altered over time. (341)

We do not, as a field, adequately distribute our knowledge about how we teach and how we have taught composition over the past century to those outside our community, partly because we ourselves do not have an accurate understanding of those methods. We have histories, of course, but in many cases, that history examines textbooks alone, while ignoring data that might be more representative of what really goes on in the composition classroom materials such as actual student writing, gradebooks, lesson plans, and, eureka!, teacher and student interviews. In fact, such research from the 1930s and 1940s in Kentucky and Tennessee suggests that, despite falling squarely in what was supposed to be the current-traditional paradigm, students at private and public universities spent a lot of time writing and less time doing rote memorization than might be expected. And teachers, lo those many years ago, also spent an inordinate amount of time grading papers! (Claywell).

So, it is important that future teachers be made aware of what really has been tried in the past and what the results of those efforts were just as they need to be introduced to the contemporary notions of composition instruction. Perhaps it is more important that primary and secondary school teachers have such grounding than future college professors since the better prepared our first-year college students are when they enter college, the stronger our composition programs will be. Former colleagues in Oklahoma did such training and went even further by professionalizing all English and English Education students on both the undergraduate and graduate levels—by encouraging participation *and by also participating themselves* in their statewide NCTE affiliate. Former students returned to the annual conference each year with stories of their in-class successes. And, since it was a regional university and most of the students remained as teachers in the area upon graduation, the first-year composition classes were filled with students who had been taught both literature and composition with the most up-to-date techniques by instructors who knew their place in the legacy of teaching writing.

In order to reach these goals for improving teacher education, composition instructors need to TALK—talk, talk, talk, talk, talk—about pedagogy both with their colleagues who teach literature, TESOL, technical writing, etc., and with their students—those in English Education or who plan to pursue graduate coursework in English and perhaps with their first-year students. And, at the expense of perpetuating the "House of Lore" that Stephen North describes as merely practitioner-building (27), one of my biggest concerns in preparing future teachers is that we do not talk about or model good teaching strategies—which composition theorists have so readily adopted—in the other areas of English instruction (and, from my experience in observing college composition instructors, we sometimes forget to model such strategies in our own classes). This mixed message tells novice teachers that those pedagogies that psychologists say most effectively facilitate learning are best used only with writing instruction but that literature and the other courses required for English studies are best presented via lecture.

Future college and high school English teachers must have a firm grounding in the history of composition instruction; they must know contemporary theories about how we write and think; they must be coached and mentored by faculty who model the most effective means of teaching. Otherwise, as Shaughnessy pointed out, "Teachers must do something on Monday morning, and this reality forces them either to do what their teachers did on Monday morning or to invent English composition anew out of their understanding of the craft and their observations of students learning to write" (*Errors* 120). They will, if we do not modify the ways we teach *all* English classes, probably teach exactly as they have been taught, in a teacher-dominated classroom with students who will learn to regurgitate facts, not apply them. Their students will then walk into our college composition classrooms with few critical thinking, collaborative, or even basic reading skills.

DIGGING DEEPER TRENCHES

Just as we need to professionalize graduate students preparing to teach college and English Education majors readying for secondary schools, so do we need to encourage the continued professionalization of adjuncts. As administrators continue to drag their feet concerning hiring tenure-track faculty, the numbers of adjuncts being used to teach composition and other general education courses rise. A November 1995 article in *The Council Chronicle* states that "at the postsecondary level, 38 percent of teaching is done by adjunct faculty" (Cassebaum 5). As this text goes to press, more than 97 percent of the composition courses are being taught by adjuncts and graduate assistants at my university an increase of 53 percent in just four years.

Observations of these teachers show their passion and energy, their dedication and creativity. I empathize with their ongoing struggle to keep computers running, papers graded, and students motivated. Their jobs are not easy. I am amazed at how they do it since many not only teach three courses for us but also teach at other schools.

I am appalled at the response administrators give to the situation. The pay is lousy, the benefits are nonexistent, and even simple considerations are not provided. For instance, invitations to faculty development workshops rarely are extended to adjuncts. Many, of course, would be too busy to attend, but the offer itself would say a lot about the value the university places on them. And, despite the increase in technology that has reduced some of the burdens of teaching composition, few things seem to have changed in composition instruction since the 1930s and 1940s, when adjuncts were called upon at the last minute to teach courses they were not always comfortable with, and they shared heavy teaching loads for little pay. They agonized over student performance, and they spent countless hours grading papers, often with children at their feet or ailing parents in their homes (Claywell). The similarities between their existence and the professional lives of adjuncts today far outweigh their differences.

What are the implications of these similarities? Gender and economic factors are involved, since many of the adjuncts then and now are female with little opportunity for moving into tenure-track positions. It is, as Cassebaum points out, "a labor issue. It's also a feminist issue" (5). Furthermore, despite the relative growth of the field of rhetoric and composition and the professionalization of many of its members, writing is still considered administratively as something easily and readily taught by graduate assistants or adjuncts. I do know many adjuncts and graduate assistants who are fine teachers, but having an extremely high percentage of courses taught by them is an indication that composition instruction has strength primarily in the number of students taught, not in its support from higher administration. Even the numbers are scary, with ever-increasing student-teacher ratios further compounding teaching loads, especially for adjuncts. When the students are basic writers, especially with the severe problems previously mentioned, the problems of high workloads are compounded. Nevertheless, we need to anticipate continued pressure to increase course numbers while diplomatically refusing to increase those numbers despite administrators' demands.

We must incorporate adjuncts into our departments by welcoming them to participate in the democratic decisions that affect composition programs. Then, we should provide them equitable pay for such service they provide beyond classroom instruction. Some schools have formed unions to aid the plight of graduate students and adjuncts, but such measures must be well organized to gain ground and must be supported by composition programs. In general, we must provide adjuncts opportunities to grow and learn, to feel a part of the departmental discourse rather than isolated from it.

PERPETUATING THE LONELY-WRITER-IN-THE-GARRET MYTH

The rise of computer technology has created no less than a revolution in the teaching of writing at the university level and has, admittedly, improved the potential for and ease of revision in student papers. While many instructors have wholeheartedly embraced the technology, many others, not all of whom are old-school, have begun to question the efficacy of the technology in actually creating better writers, as opposed to more prolific writers.

Related technologies such as distance-learning are also being questioned by teachers as perhaps raising more problems than they solve. New technology provides political muscle to university recruitment, so it becomes an administrative imperative to push technology incorporation into the classroom, but the pedagogical implications need to continue to be examined. Chris Anson writes in *College English,*

New technologies introduced with the overriding goal of creating economic efficiencies and generating increased revenues may lead to even greater exploitation in the area of writing instruction, the historically maligned and undernourished servant of the academy. (Anson 263)

Not only do technological advancements make it possible for administrators to push higher student enrollments per class because they are no longer limited to classroom size or other artificial constraints in an electronic environment, but they also open up the possibility of returning us to the myth that writers best produce writing when secluded from the world. Computer monitors in dorm rooms and in high school classrooms miles away from the college composition class are now making it possible for students to get writing credit without actually physically interacting with their peers or instructors. And maybe, if writing really is the goal, this is fine, but it certainly seems to remove some of the social component that has always made the college experience, the human experience, what it is. It removes the face of the audience and replaces it with a text, and it turns teachers into mere text-readers.

Curiously, it is such distancing that might allow instructors to really focus attention on student writing patterns by, for instance, providing students flexible deadlines that allow for their own writing processes. Such personalized attention was Shaughnessy's focus, but, if student numbers continue to rise as a result of the perceived ease of teaching via technology, this potential benefit will be counteracted. Furthermore, as "aliteracy"—the choice not to read or write—becomes an increasing problem in American schools, finding patterns that neatly identify the problems in student writing may be problematic because the global qualities of student writing will continue to deteriorate.

Composition programs must also look carefully at movements many from within English departments—to move the attention of composition classrooms away from a focus on writing per se to writing about literature, service, politics, humanities, and so on, because, just as technology poses political problems, so do such content classes. They threaten to remove a concentration from "writing" as a concrete, measurable subject of study and as a worthy academic enterprise. They also mystify writing style and fluidity so that composition becomes mysterious, inaccessible, or not important at all and thus reaffirm the myth of the lonely writer in the garret.

MAKING THE CHANGES

How can real changes be made? English programs need to consolidate their political muscle but not before they reach consensus internally. English programs must help administrators become aware of the importance of our programs—a goal unreachable until we ourselves come to an agreement about what composition courses mean financially, politically, and theoretically—and then present a united front with administrators about what and how much we do and have been doing for all these years.

We must be proactive in working with university administrators by publicizing successes, strengthening assessments, and developing creative solutions to both fiscal and physical problems. Few administrators realize either the labor intensity of teaching composition or how the addition of two to three students per section compounds that workload. Stronger connections with other departments, specifically education departments, and with the media must be forged. What we do is important, and we should actively seek to get that work acknowledged and understood. The dividend in better public understanding is worth the effort.

As we teach writing, whether it be basic, first-year, or advanced, we need to continually ask ourselves those vital questions Shaughnessy asked in *Errors*:

1. What is the goal of instruction? Is it awareness, improvement, or mastery?

2. What is the best method of instruction? What cognitive strategy, that is, will work best in teaching a particular skill?

3. What is the best mode of instruction, the most effective social organization and the best technology?

4. How do the individual items of instruction relate to one another? Where do they come in a sequence of instruction and how much time can be allowed for each? (286-87)

As we fine-tune our curricula, we need to find ways to incorporate technology without losing humanity. We need to develop more innovative methods for reaching those students who choose to be aliterate, and, unless admissions standards change, we must develop new, efficient ways to present writing skills to those lacking much of the cognitive ability required for literacy. We must, most important, model good teaching and reach out to those who would be teachers.

To accomplish these goals will require a balance between teaching and research; the problems are interrelated and complex, and thus solving them will not be easy. Mina Shaughnessy did not expect change to be easy either. Her 1976 address at the Conference of the CUNY Association of Writing Supervisors in New York entitled, "The Miserable Truth," could be given at a conference today:

1. Our staffs are shrinking and our class size increasing.

2. Talented young teachers who were ready to concentrate their scholarly energies on the

sort of research and teaching we need in basic writing are looking for jobs.

3. Each day brings not just a new decision but rumors of new decisions, palcing us in the predicament of those mice in psychological experiments who must keep shifting their expectations until they are too rattled to function.

4. Our campuses buzz like an Elizabethan court with talk of who is in favor and who is out. And we meet our colleagues from other campuses with relief: "Ah, good," we say (or think to ourselves)—"you're still here."

5. We struggle each day to extract from the Orwellian language that announces new plans and policies some clear sense of what finally is going to become of the students whom the university in more affluent times committed itself to educate. (263-64)

Shaughnessy's words were a discouraging prediction; time has proven that her expectations did not err.

SELECTED WORKS BY AND ABOUT MINA P. SHAUGHNESSY

Bannister, Linda. "Examining Contemporary Women Rhetoricians: Is There a Feminine Rhetoric?" Presented at the 41st Annual Meeting of the Conference on College Composition and Communication, Chicago, 22-24 March 1990. ED 317 996.

Bartholomae, David. "Released into Language: Errors, Expectations, and the Legacy of Mina Shaughnessy." *The Territory of Language*. Ed. Donald A. McQuade. Carbondale: Southern Illinois UP, 1986.

DeMott, Benjamin. "The Age of At Variance." *Change* 22.2 (March-April 1990): 24-29.

———. "Mina Shaughnessy: Meeting Challenges." *The Nation* 9 Dec. 1978: 645-48.

Emig, Janet. "Mina Pendo Shaughnessy." *College Composition and Communication* Feb. 1979: 37-38.

Lu, Min-zhan. "Redefining the Legacy of Mina Shaughnessy: A Critique of the Politics of Linguistic Innocence." *Journal of Basic Writing* 10.2 (Spring 1991): 26-40.

Lyons, Robert. "Mina Shaughnessy." *Traditions of Inquiry*. Ed. John Brereton. New York: Oxford UP, 1985.

Maher, Jane. *Mina P. Shaughnessy: Her Life and Work*. Urbana, IL: NCTE, 1997.

McAlexander, Patricia J. "Mina Shaughnessy in the 1990s: Some Changing Answers in Basic Writing." Presented at the 44th Annual Meeting of the Conference on College Composition and Communication, San Diego, CA, 31 March-3 April, 1993. ED 359362.

Shaughnessy, Mina P. "Basic Writing." *Teaching Composition: Ten Bibliographical Essays*. Ed. Gary Tate. Fort Worth: Texas Christian UP, 1975.

———. "Diving In: An Introduction to Basic Writing." *College Composition and Communication* Oct. 1976: 234-239.

———. "The English Professor's Malady." *Journal of Basic Writing* Spring 1994: 117-24.

————. *Errors and Expectations: A Guide for the Teacher of Basic Writing.* New York: Oxford UP, 1977.

————. Introduction. *Journal of Basic Writing* Fall /Winter 1976: 1.

————. Introduction. *Journal of Basic Writing* Spring 1975: 3.

————. "The Miserable Truth." *The Congressional Record* 9 Sept. 1976: E4955-56. Reprinted in Maher 263-69.

————. "Open Admissions and the Disadvantaged Teacher." *College Composition and Communication* Dec. 1973: 401-4.

————. "Some Needed Research on Writing." *College Composition and Communication* Dec. 1977: 317-20.

————. "Statement on Criteria for Writing Proficiency." *Journal of Basic Writing* Fall/Winter 1980: 115-19.

————. "Teaching Basic Writing." *Journal of Basic Writing* Spring 1994: 103-16.

WORKS CITED

Anson, Chris M. "Distant Voices: Teaching and Writing in a Culture of Technology." *College English* 61 (1999): 261-80.

Cassebaum, Anne. "Attitudes Encountered in the Struggle for Fair Pay and Job Security." *The Council Chronicle* Nov. 1995: 5.

Claywell, Gina. "A Qualitative Approach to First-Year College Composition in the American Upper South from 1930 to 1945." Diss. U of Tennessee, 1996.

North, Stephen M. *The Making of Knowledge in Composition: Portrait of an Emerging Field.* Portsmouth, NH: Boynton/Cook, 1987.

Schilb, John. "Review: Histories of Pedagogy." *College English* 61 (1999): 340-46.

Shaughnessy, Mina P. *Errors and Expectations: A Guide for the Teacher of Basic Writing.* New York: Oxford UP, 1977.

————. "The Miserable Truth." *The Congressional Record* 9 Sept. 1976: E4955-56: Reprinted in Maher 263-69.

6

The Writing Center and the Politics of Separation: The Writing Process Movement's Dubious Legacy

Christina Murphy and Joe Law

In 1984, Stephen M. North's "The Idea of a Writing Center" was the first essay devoted exclusively to writing centers to be published in *College English* and instantly became a manifesto of writing center identity and politics, signaling a new interpretation of the role of the writing center within the academy and within academic politics. In the intervening fifteen years, North's polemical essay has become the single most important and the most quoted essay in writing center scholarship. The essay has had great appeal for writing center scholars both because it asserts the primacy of a student-centered pedagogy and because it chastises English department faculty for possessing a "second layer of ignorance" and "a false sense of knowing" about what the role of a writing center is within the department and the academy (433). As a result of this long tradition of ignorance and indifference, English department faculty have practiced exclusionary and marginalizing politics with regard to writing centers and writing center professionals. The movement of writing centers into the academy—which North dates to around 1930—represents an uneasy alliance of differing traditions and pedagogies that has generated the ongoing rift between writing centers and English departments. Not surprisingly, given the critical tone North's essay takes when its focus turns to the negative view English faculty hold of writing centers, North's conclusion is to assert that writing centers represent their own reason for being because their pedagogical tradition of tutoring and of apprenticeship learning has stood the test of time since Socrates as a "continuous dialectic" that has been centered outside of the academy and in the public realm—what North calls the "marketplace" tradition of Socrates and Athens (446). North argues that writing centers are not to be viewed as an ancillary service: "We are not here to serve, supplement, back up, complement, reinforce, or otherwise be defined by any external curriculum. We are here to talk to writers" (440). His essay, North asserts, is a "declaration of independence" that may sound to some "more like a declaration of war" (441).

While it would be impossible to overestimate the influence of North's essay on the ways writing centers have subsequently described themselves and carried out their work, it is also important to place the essay in its time period and to examine its assumptions in terms of what precedes and what follows in the history of composition studies. It should be noted that, at the time of North's essay, English departments were largely literature departments, and so the rift North discusses was even wider in theory, practice, and emphasis. This was a time in which literature was regarded as an intellectual and humanistic tradition while writing instruction was viewed as a nontheoretical, remedial effort to instill in students the basics of literacy education. It was also a time that gave rise to the "lingering snobbery" that John Schilb describes as "comp-bashing" (341). Thus, it is not surprising, given this history and the negative attitudes literature faculty traditionally have held toward composition studies, that North's essay is both a call for understanding and a call for separation. Nor is it surprising that North's essay replicates many of the ideas presented in a famous essay by Maxine Hairston published in 1982—"The Winds of Change: Thomas Kuhn and the Revolution in the Teaching of Writing." Hairston's major premise was to describe the shift from product-centered to process-centered writing instruction as a "paradigm shift" on the order of the Copernican revolution in science. Sharply distinguishing the work of composition and rhetoric specialists from the work of their predecessors, Hairston describes the new approach in these terms: "We cannot teach students to write by looking only at what they have written. We must also understand how that product came into being, and why it assumed the form that it did. We have to understand what goes on during the act of writing if we want to affect its outcome" (84).

One of Hairston's purposes seems to have been to codify this new model so that it might be passed along as the new mode of instruction, as her final sentence suggests. There she identifies the challenge to "today's community of composition and rhetoric scholars: to refine the new paradigm for teaching composition writing for the nonspecialists who do most of the composition teaching in our colleges and universities" (88). A decade later, from a much more defensive position, Hairston again summarized what she saw as progress in the new field of composition and rhetoric and its concomitant new paradigm for teaching that was "focused on process and on writing as a way of learning." Citing her 1985 address as chair of CCCC, she reminded readers of her earlier call for "psychological and intellectual independence" from English departments run by literary critics, claiming compositionists could not develop their potential and "become fully autonomous scholars and teachers" under those conditions. She also repeated her insistence "that writing courses must not be viewed as service courses. Writing courses, especially required freshman courses, should not be for anything or about anything other than writing itself, and how one uses it to learn and think and communicate" ("Diversity" 179). That her attitude toward independence remained unchanged can be seen in her professed "first response" to the politicized classroom of the 1990s: "You see what happens when we allow writing programs to be run by English departments?" ("Diversity" 183).

Hairston and North represent two writers of the same mind in two important respects—their emphasis on the writer as an individual to be improved through writing instruction and their tendency toward separatist rhetoric. Hairston's and North's essays also manifest the intellectual contours of the process movement that dominated composition studies and writing center practice in the 1980s. In "How the Writing Process Was Born—and Other Conversion Narratives," Lad Tobin claims that the process movement in the 1980s represented a critique of traditional teaching as well as an emphasis on "the [writing] process, student choice and voice, revision, selfexpression" (5). Tobin is also straightforward in asserting that his readers understand "how miserably traditional writing instruction had failed and how desperately the times cried out for change-and for heroes" (3). He goes on to assert:

In the old days, say the mid-80s, those of us who supported writing process pedagogy could tell stories about bad writing classes and bad writing teachers and then prescribe an antidote: change everything. And while we advocated such radical change, we were comforted by the knowledge that we occupied the higher moral ground. After all, we were speaking up against rigidity, legalism, authoritarianism, fuddy-duddyism. We were speaking up for students, freedom, innovation, creativity, and change. As long as we could characterize our opponentsas old fogeys, too tired to change, we were in a pretty comfortable position. (5)

Tobin's essay, written in 1994, affords him a fourteen-year perspective from which to view the writing process movement, and he is quick to assert that, from the perspective of many movements that have followed—including social constructionism and cultural studies—

the writing process founders are seen as terribly *declasse* and outmoded: they are entrepreneurial (for emphasizing the commodification of the individual writer's assets); evangelical (for refusing to provide hard evidence, definitions, research); bourgeois (for treating students as writers or artists or free agents rather than as workers, citizens, and culturally situated beings); and, worst of all for an academic, naive (for not knowing there is no authentic voice, no single-authored text, no self). (6-7)

As Tobin suggests, the intervening years since the zenith of the process movement in the 1980s offer an opportunity to evaluate the central tenets of the process movement and its effects upon composition studies. We would also extend this analysis to writing centers by drawing upon the concepts developed in Tobin's essay and in Hairston's and North's as well. Our purpose is to examine how well the premises and implications of the process movement have served writing centers and the individual writers they work with. Our purpose is also to examine the legacy the process movement has created for the writing center discipline through subsequent philosophies that have influenced the intellectual and practical contours of writing center work within the post-process academy.

For our analysis, the most important ideas we draw from the process movement are these: the emphasis upon the individual writer and his or her creative potential for self-realization; the separatist rhetoric of the process movement that often serves to divide literature, composition studies, and writing centers; the "evangelical" character of the process movement as a revolutionary educational philosophy; and the tendency of the process movement to write the history of composition studies "primarily through the stories we tell" (Tobin 1).

In writing center scholarship, it is easy to see a direct and ongoing connection between the emphasis upon the individual writer and the "evangelical" character of many essays that focus upon writing center practice. One concept underlies the other; that is, if writing centers do embody the revolutionary and the "evangelical" character of the process movement, then the revolution and the evangelism focus upon the individual student as a victim to be saved from an oppressive and unempathic academic system bent on uniformity. The price of uniformity is the stifling of the student's "voice"—a term that often goes undefined but that is as central to process pedagogy as it is to the pedagogies of social constructionism and cultural studies.

The implications of Tobin's assessment are complex for writing center pedagogy and scholarship. For example, although the emphasis on the individual student would seem to be a good thing, the published scholarship has tended to center on the affective level of the writing center's work rather than on its effectiveness as pedagogy. The result is an extensive exploration of the "ethics" of tutoring rather than a sustained analytical exploration of tutoring as an effective pedagogy—one that would draw upon a broad, research-based analysis of modes of cognition and of theories of learning and that would use controlled, empirical studies to assess data. As it is, much of the research and scholarship on writing centers stays on a highly localized and highly emotionalized level. Writing center theorists and practitioners tell narratives of individual students who have been ignored, stifled, or otherwise damaged by traditional academics and yet have prospered in the empathic environment of the writing center. Such powerful tales of redemption and salvation reinforce the "evangelical" character of much writing center scholarship. For example, Nancy Maloney Grimm's CCC essay, "Rearticulating the Work of the Writing Center," focuses upon narratives about and discussions of individual students who have been disadvantaged by their background and are underprepared to cope with the varied demands of academic life. Grimm argues that writing center specialists should use what they learn about the injurious effects of educational discourse to spark political and pedagogical changes that benefit disadvantaged students. As Grimm states:

In this essay, I want to rearticulate the relationship of the writing center to the institution by attempting to address the gap between theorizing about difference in higher education and working with differences in the writing center. I want to situate writing center work with the democratic desire to understand and negotiate difference, to work within heterogeneity rather than to manage to eliminate it. (524)

The "evangelical" approach of Grimm's essay is apparent in its rhetoric and purpose, and the essay is grounded in individual narratives of student failures in academic mainstreaming and successes in the more democratic and empathic environment of a correctly positioned and correctly principled writing center. The political agenda Grimm endorses is one of opposition to "the hierarchical structure of higher education" (529) and a concomitant focus upon counter-hegemony in both the structure and the purpose of writing center practice. Grimm's essay is extensively researched and draws upon scholarship from multiple fields, including literacy theory, feminist theory, literary criticism, and social psychology. In an interesting twist, though, the essay begins with the assertion that

[w]riting center people often gravitate toward practical solutions to these ongoing problems [of marginalization]. They urge one another to get control of their budgets and get out from under the English department. They advise one another to look for the university's five-year plan and make the writing center indispensable by matching its philosophy to that plan. In spite of these practical solutions and perhaps because of them, writing centers on most campuses remain in subordinate service positions. They are marked by social notions of what women provide—refuge, nurturance, emotional support, personal guidance. (524)

Yet despite Grimm's awareness of and reservations about the "social notions" inherent in academics' views of the work of the writing center, Grimm grounds her own essay in the central metaphor of family therapy—a philosophy she uses to emphasize the empathic, emotive, and ultimately redemptive power that can be actualized by radical writing centers that oppose the oppressions of mainstream educational hierarchies and offer refuge, comfort, and hope to students who do not conform to and who are not valued by these hierarchies.

There is an additional historical irony to Grimm's essay that is indicative of what we have deemed "the dubious legacy" of the process movement. The opening of Grimm's 1996 essay echoes many of the same concerns voiced by North in 1984. Like North, Grimm begins her essay by describing the unsatisfactory conditions of writing center work:

Not only are writing center voices infrequently heard in composition scholarship but writing centers also occupy contested positions on their respective campuses. The stories shared among writing center people ring with familiar themes—faculty suspicion about what happens in writing centers, refusal to grant departmental voting rights to writing center professional staff, faculty dismay about the condition of papers that "went through" the writing center (the laundry metaphor), exploitation of part-timers, miffed reactions to undergraduate writing tutors who ask questions about teaching practices, confusion about the status/role of writing center directors. (523)

Grimm's introduction restates the ambiguous and conflicted relationship writing centers and writing center professionals share with English departments that North noted with disappointment and frustration in 1984—this despite the fact that, in the intervening years between North and Grimm, writing centers have come to occupy a central role in the life of the academy with writing centers now on more than 90 percent of the campuses in America (Grimm 523).

Grimm finds it paradoxical and troubling that, despite the long history, diversity, and high numbers of writing centers on American campuses, published scholarship on writing centers generally has not appeared in the major journals and presses but has been confined to professional journals and national and regional conferences within the writing center community (523). Grimm offers one explanation for why this might be so: "The work of the writing center is not integrated theoretically or structurally within the intellectual work of the university. Writing centers are the handmaidens of autonomous literacy—a value-free, culturally neutral notion of literacy—which although extensively challenged theoretically is still strongly at work in the academy" (524). We would like to offer two other explanations, explanations that we trace, once more, to the dubious legacy of the process movement.

For all the apparent newness and contemporaneity of Grimm's essay, which draws upon many postmodern cultural theorists and which demonstrates a broad knowledge of cultural theory, its premises are not far removed from North's process-oriented convictions in his earlier essay. For example, North relies upon the process movement's belief in the value of each student's individual search for self-expression and self-realization to argue that writing centers are safe spaces for students. In writing centers, students find the nurture, support, and encouragement they generally do not find in composition classrooms. The lingering idea that resurfaces in Grimm's essay is that writing centers do nurture by functioning as havens or support centers for students displaced and devalued by traditional mainstream approaches to education. For all the truth and for all the good that may reside in this assertion, nurturing is a difficult concept to integrate "theoretically or structurally within the intellectual work of the university"—as Grimm phrases it (524). Thus, the work of the writing center and the rationale for its success are often best communicated through narratives—the success stories of individual students and of individual writing centers. The narratives manifest the evangelical character of the process movement, "refusing to provide hard evidence, definitions, research" (Tobin 7).

The fact that the history of writing centers, like that of composition studies during the era of process pedagogy, has been "written primarily through the stories we tell" (Tobin 1) points to another vestige of the process movement. Kevin Davis, among other theorists, has noted the difficulty of connecting vignettes, personal histories, and local narratives to theory and to professional direction for an academic discipline in "Life Outside the Boundary: History and Direction in the Writing Center" (1995). Despite this concern, the writing center field continues largely to write its history "primarily through the stories we tell." This tendency also extends to descriptions of writing centers in their setup, operations, institutional relations, and successes or failures. Classic examples of this approach are Joyce Kinkead and Jeanette Harris's edited collection *Writing Centers in Context: Twelve Case Studies* (NCTE 1993), and *Weaving Knowledge Together: Writing Centers and Collaboration*, edited by Carol Peterson Haviland, Maria Notarangelo, Lene Whitley-Putz, and Thia Wolf (NWCA Press 1998). Both texts are collections of narrative essays that focus largely on the personal identities and institutional contexts of individual writing centers. The essays are long on local color, but generally short on a broad or persuasive theoretical framework in which to ground narrative assumptions and conclusions. By grounding their work in narratives, writing center professionals often find it hard to make the case that anecdotal evidence even constitutes evidence, let alone theory. Such a focus does little to address the concerns many academics have about whether there even is a theoretical basis to writing center work and scholarship. The difficulty of integrating the personal and the theoretical in writing center scholarship is one aspect, we contend, of the dubious legacy of the process movement and definitely an area that post-process writing center scholars will need to continue to address.

We do not want to argue, though, that writing center scholarship should simply abandon this portion of the process movement's legacy. It is impossible to deny that many truths reside in and are only found in the personal, and this positive aspect of the influence of the process movement continues to find validation in the writing center discipline. Indeed, the fact that the truths found in the personal may not fit the traditional modes through which scholarship is communicated and rewarded in academics may say more about the need for expanding our sense of the purpose of those traditional modes than it may say about the value of personal truths themselves. Lisa Ede, for example, in "Reading the Writing Process" raises the issue of "the relationship between theory and practice as it has been both textually and materially inscribed in our field" (31). As Ede contends:

Our assumption that theory should inform and guide practice, for instance, reflects the western tradition's positivistic claims for reason. These claims situate the "man of reason" above and beyond the buzzing and blooming multiplicity of everyday life. Like the patriarchal father, the man of reason in his abstract and decontextualized wisdom sees the unvarying and universal "laws" that women and children (and teachers), caught up as they are in the daily and the contingent—or so the familiar western narrativeof reason goes—cannot see. So powerful has this conception of reason (and of theory) been that only now are we beginning to see through its claims to question the rejection of the particular and the situated—of, for instance, the knowledge required to interpret and act upon the "teachable moment"—upon which it depends. (37)

The central principles of Ede's argument actually can be found in Aristotle's discussion in the Nicomachean Ethics of the three categories of knowledge: theoretical (episteme), productive (techne), and practical (phronesis). While episteme or theoretical knowledge deals with necessary truths that cannot be otherwise than they are (151; 6.3.1139b), both phronesis and techne treat "what admits of being otherwise" (152; 6.5.1140a). For Aristotle, ethics falls under the domain of phronesis or practical knowledge, which is "a state of grasping the truth, involving reason, concerned with action about what is good or bad for a human being" (154; 6.5.1140b). We would contend that both Ede and Grimm—and North as well—are arguing for an appreciation of phronetic knowledge in academics, particularly as that knowledge is manifested in composition studies and in writing centers. For North and Ede, the process movement brings this truth home and makes them wish to expand definitions and appreciations of academic knowledge and to persuade their academic colleagues of this value of phrenetic knowledge in relation to theoretical knowledge. For Grimm, the same concepts are found in social constructionism and cultural studies, rather than in the process movement, but the issues remain the same—that there is a domain of knowledge that is practical, that is centered in everyday academic realities, and that embodies ethical choices and implications for real students with real stories to tell that have as much—even more—validity than the hypothetical and theoretical constructs of traditional academic scholarship.

Unfortunately, in writing center scholarship, the argument for an appreciation of phronetic knowledge is often made within a context that ignores, or seeks to ignore, institutional politics. Part of this difficulty resides in naive views of the difference between an intellectual idea and an academic movement—and even more naive assumptions about how ideas and movements play out within institutional settings. It is interesting, for example, that North titled his essay "The Idea of a Writing Center" and emphasized and favored the idea or the ideal over the realities of his own unsympathetic and condemnatory institutional setting. This is an important point, for as George Dennis O'Brien writes in *All the Essential Half—Truths about Higher Education*, "The university is not an idea; it is an institution" (3). To forget this distinction can have important consequences:

discussions of higher education are anywhere from misplaced to mistaken because they address the idea of higher education, not the institution of higher education. . . . Failure to address institution is subtly distorting. An idea that has absolute validity in its own right becomes subtly changed when it becomes institutionalized. . . . an absolute truth becomes a half-truth. (xviii-xix)

Part of the legacy of the process movement for writing centers has been a tendency, in the midst of revolutionary and anti-institutional fervor, to advocate ideas without fully appreciating the significance of the institutions in which such ideas are to be implemented. The "evangelical" character that defines the process movement, according to Tobin and others, has also shaped the writing center movement. Writing center practitioners who believe their role is to offer students an alternative to the oppression and pigeonholing of mainstream academics will resist being identified with or shaped by the mainstream academy itself, for, if this occurs, the identity of the writing center as a revolutionary and anti-establishment space is lost. As a consequence, writing center professionals often advocate a maverick view of the writing center and argue that, to be faithful to the writing center legacy, they must maintain their identities as "renegades, outsiders, boundary dwellers, subversives" (Davis 7).

If that identity as an outlander is lost, often the result is an essay devoted to grief for the loss and nostalgia for the good old days—as "Erika and the Fish Lamps: Writing and Reading the Local Scene" demonstrates. This essay, included in *Weaving Knowledge Together*, begins with the authors asking "what a reading of our physical place might tell us about who we were or who we thought we were" (Connolly, DeJarlais, Gillam, and Micciche 15). What they discover, via fish lamps and bold posters set up in the writing center by peer tutors, is that their writing center first conceptualizes itself as a "borderland"—a place that stands in opposition to the conformity and ordinariness of the rest of the academic enterprise. What they later learn is that, despite their desire to serve "as the natural location for subversive, counterhegemonic literacy work" (21), their writing center exists via an institutional mandate and budget. When that mandate changes, the writing center changes also. While the authors may abhor having to trade fish lamps for a relatively sterile location and appearance in a typical academic building, that is the reality. While nostalgia for the past and grief over a changing present are valid personal responses, they do not change the realities of academic funding and program design—especially in a world and at a time when philosophical and financial support for education is declining.

Writing centers do change—and must adapt—in response to changes in institutional contexts. While this may be a disappointing fact of life for some, it is also a confirming fact of life for others. The success and commitment of the "Fish Lamps" writing center have prepared the way for a new writing center and staff to take their place in a high-tech location committed to serving the university's composition program. This is not so much a loss as a transition; the loss belongs to those who would prefer a "borderland" writing center, but the loss may not be to the students who will use the new center, the composition program that will benefit, or the literacy education that will occur there in different ways from the original startup idea of the "Fish Lamps" writing center.

Perhaps this movement of the "Fish Lamps" writing center away from the borderlands of the academy toward its center should be seen as emblematic of the direction of educational reform in general. Reviewing Thomas P. Miller's study of the development of English as a college subject, Schilb finds in Miller's work a useful reminder that "changes in educational practices often start at the periphery or from below" (342). Not to see this larger pattern and to react only with nostalgia for the passing of the "borderland" writing center is, in O'Brien's terms, to ignore the institution in which an idea is to be realized. In this context, warnings like those in Terrance Riley's "The Unpromising Future of Writing Centers"—an essay arguing that the growing professionalization of writing center work jeopardizes the ability of writing centers to effect change in academe—appear misguided in the same way. Likewise, for writing center professionals to continue to present themselves as "renegades, outsiders, boundary dwellers, [and] subversives" (Davis 7) can only alienate the administrators who make crucial decisions about the writing center and confirm their tendency to make those decisions without consulting writing center personnel. This is an extremely complicated and dangerous pose in this present era of limited budgets and ofp accountability to administrators, state legislatures, and the public at large, for, as O'Brien states, "When the coffers close, who will decide on the intellectual survivors?" (xvi). As far as writing center and composition professionals are concerned, the issue can be restated in this manner: if the public in general—and legislators in particular—continue to perceive problems in higher education, questions of who owns the text will become irrelevant.

The continuing tendency of writing center literature to focus on the individual student in this way, casting writing center professionals as the revolutionaries or evangelists who will defy the institution in order to lead that student to self-realization represents the more dubious portion of the writing center's inheritance from the process movement. While that movement helped to create, define, and legitimate writing centers as a field of study, it also narrowed the "terminological screen" (Ede 35) through which discussions of writing centers have been formed and debated. In his discussion of terministic screens, Kenneth Burke tells us repeatedly that any way of seeing is inevitably also a way of not seeing (44-62). In the same way, the continuing legacy of the process movement has both illuminated and obscured the truths about writing centers and their roles within the academy.

WORKS CITED

Aristotle. *Nicomachean Ethics*. Trans. Terence Irwin. Indianapolis: Hackett, 1985.
Burke, Kenneth. *Language as Symbolic Action: Life, Literature, and Method*. Berkeley: U of California P, 1966.
Connolly, Colleen, Amy DeJarlais, Alice Gillam, and Laura Micciche. "Erika and the Fish Lamps: Writing and Reading the Local Scene." Haviland, Notarangelo, Whitley-Putz, and Wolf. 15-27.

Davis, Kevin. "Life Outside the Boundary: History and Direction in the Writing Center." *Writing Lab Newsletter* 20.2 (1995): 5-7.

Ede, Lisa. "Reading the Writing Process." *Taking Stock: The Writing Process Movement in the '90s.* Eds. Lad Tobin and Thomas Newkirk. Portsmouth: Boynton/Cook, 1994. 31-44.

Grimm, Nancy Maloney. "Rearticulating the Work of the Writing Center." *College Composition and Communication* 47 (1996): 523-48.

Hairston, Maxine. "Diversity, Ideology, and Teaching Writing." *College Composition and Communication* 43 (1992): 179-93.

———. "The Winds of Change: Thomas Kuhn and the Revolution in the Teaching of Writing." *College Composition and Communication* 33 (1982): 76-88.

Haviland, Carol Peterson, Maria Notarangelo, Lene Whitley-Putz, and Tia Wolf. *Weaving Knowledge Together: Writing Centers and Collaboration.* Emmitsburg: NWCA, 1998.

Kinkead, Joyce, and Jeannette Harris, eds. *Writing Centers in Context: Twelve Case Studies.* Urbana: NCTE, 1993.

North, Stephen M. "The Idea of a Writing Center." *College English* 46 (1984): 433-46.

O'Brien, George Dennis. *All the Essential Half-Truths About Higher Education.* Chicago: U of Chicago P, 1998.

Riley, Terrance. "The Unpromising Future of Writing Centers." *The Writing Center Journal* 15.1 (1994): 20-34.

Schilb, John. "Histories of Pedagogy." Review of *Feminist Accused of Sexual Harassment*, by Jane Gallop, *Pedagogy, Democracy, and Feminism: Rethinking the Public Sphere*, by Adriana Hernandez, *The Formation of College English: Rhetoric and Belles Lettres in the British Cultural Provinces*, by Thomas P. Miller, *Writing in an Alien World: Basic Writing and the Struggle for Equality in Higher Education*, by Deborah Mutnick, and *Pedagogy: Disturbing History, 1819–1929*, ed. Mariolina Rizzi Salvatori. *College English* 61 (1999): 240-46.

Tobin, Lad. "How the Writing Process Was Born—and Other Conversion Narratives." *Taking Stock: The Writing Process Movement in the '90s.* Eds. Lad Tobin and Thomas Newkirk. Portsmouth: Boynton/Cook, 1994. 1-14.

II

RIGHTING THE WRONGS: VOICES FROM THE TRENCHES

7

Readerless Writers: College Composition's Misreading and Misteaching of Entering Students

Ray Wallace and Susan Lewis Wallace

INTRODUCTION

Several decades ago Walter Ong noted in a landmark essay that a writer's audience was always a fiction, and in many ways these words have become more prophetic and, alas, ironic in college composition classes concluding this century. Ong's essay, of course, dealt with audience considerations, and the supposition that writers "invented" an audience for their writing, had to imagine a fictional audience responding to their writing, and had to understand what this fictional audience would and would not comprehend from their writing. What many composition theorists took from this insightful reasoning was that a writer's drafting strategies would gradually clarify a real audience's needs. Implicit in this compelling argument was, of course, an awareness of audience. Unfortunately, today our composition classrooms are full of many shiney, well-scrubbed, expensively clad, functional academic illiterates who have not the first idea of what it is to be considered a reader, let alone think about how a reader (fictional or not) might respond to their attempts at written communication.

We preface this discussion by noting that not all our students fall into this category—many students have already discovered the joy and importance of reading, many read daily newspapers and have subscriptions to several weekly and monthly periodicals, many use the public and high school libraries regularly, and many view a visit to a bookstore as both entertaining and educational.

However, this chapter discusses what for us is an alarming increase in the number of students who are functionally and culturally illiterate and how these students impact both our composition pedagogy and our expectations for their success. The label "illiterate" is a strong one, and we recognize this from the outset; therefore, we do stipulate for this particular discussion that the focus here is the academic illiteracy of many of our students. We deal with a sizable population who after twelve years of education cannot read eighth-grade materials with even the most basic comprehension levels, form sentences correctly, and still have no clear idea about how (and why) to construct an essay (or even a letter). Many of these same students demonstrate an alarming lack of basic factual knowledge about their local, state, regional, national, or international environment. Many of our students have never read a novel, and never read a newspaper or magazine. Many of our students watch five or six hours of television a day, never attend a cultural event (unless forced to for academic credit), and have never been exposed to the joy of learning and had the importance of this learning explained to them. Many of our students have in fact seen those without much formal "book-learning" succeed in employment opportunities. Many of our students have no idea how many states there are in this country, cannot accurately talk about their own culture's history, or cannot find locations on a state, national, or world map.

Every semester we are faced with the task of teaching writing to nonreaders, and unfortunately, composition theory, so clearly developed by scholars so far removed from our classrooms, has not responded to this situation very well. Instead, it seems readily apparent that the students these theorists write about, design overly politicized pedagogical theories and techniques for, and very occasionally teach in their selective admissions doctoral-granting institutions have very little in common with our academically unsuccessful students.

Only when theorists begin to understand the types of students we are actually dealing with in the most common college composition environments, the open admissions environment of two-year community colleges, and public four-year colleges and universities, can they begin to develop more appropriate and realistic curricula for these students. Until then, composition theorists—infamous for not having the time to teach the courses on which they theorize (those who can preach, but not practice)—are simply burying their heads in the pedagogical sands, while those of us in the trenches—those of us who actually teach writing to students who have not yet acquired these skills, semester in and semester out—will be pounding the instructional sand in vain.

TODAY'S ENTERING COLLEGE COMPOSITION STUDENTS: THE STATE WE ARE IN

To preface this discussion, we concede the state we live and teach in has many problems; for many years our state's educational prowess has ranked us at the bottom, or near the bottom, in almost every standard measure of educational achievement and funding. From the outset we recognize that our students are taught by some of the poorest paid teachers in the country, in some of the worst funded schools in the nation, and that many of these students are in fact all that are left, given the fact that many of their former classmates have already dropped out. Frankly, we recognize all too well that many of our students (as many as 50 percent) graduate high school and come to our open-admissions state-funded university to immediately enroll in as many as two years of developmental studies courses; these students have graduated high school but are still judged deficient in writing, reading, and/or math skills, based on standardized test scores and placement tests. We recognize that our state now gives full tuition scholarships to students on the basis of standardized test scores and high school grade-point averages that in other states would consign these same students instantly to developmental studies programs. We recognize that things are bad here! But, frankly, we have also taught in several other states across the nation, and we recognize sadly that many entering college students' writing skills are not much better in other areas of the country either. Why?

A NATION'S LATERAL MOVEMENT: NEEDED INCLUSION

Two major socio-political events took place in the in the middle of the twentieth century that changed the face of higher education in the United States of America, and both events gave rise to and helped propel the open admissions college and university.

First, with the introduction of the GI Bill, the United States took a giant educational lateral step in our educational journey. Before this introduction, this country was like most others in the industrialized world in that university education was a privilege of the rich, the well-heeled, or the religiously affiliated. Until the introduction of the GI Bill, university students were mainly male, white, and of Anglo-Saxon stock. Women, of course, had colleges to attend (and co-ed colleges/universities did prosper before the GI Bill), but again only those women for the most part of a particular social class attempted higher education. This same social class had by and large been educated in a similar fashion, with a reasonably secure cannon of knowledge and religion, and a relatively homogeneous student body and curriculum. A German hybrid of a British education structure was the most common approach, and frankly, the trivium, or a form of it, was the cornerstone of this curriculum. Great books, lots of reading and writing, studies in rhetoric, grammar (supplemented with Latin or Greek instruction) and logic prepared these students for advanced studies at universities. The students who entered these universities had much in common, not least a common-ish high school curriculum. So, university enrollees of a bygone era were homogeneous. They had basically studied the same types of subjects to the same levels, and the admissions procedure assumed this as fact. This is not to say that students' academic weaknesses have not been decried by their academic masters for centuries, but these declarations of woe certainly pale under our contemporary problems—the university before open admissions was a very different institution after open admissions.

The GI Bill helped provide access to higher education for a new class of citizens in American society. The working-to-lower-middle class, traditionally excluded from higher education, came home from World War II eager to enroll and improve their lot in the society they had so valiantly defended. With this rapid increase in enrollment, our nation's campuses also began to burst at the seams. One need only go to an admissions office on any public college or university to explore their yearbooks from the late forties and early fifties to see the measures that had to be taken just to house these many new enrollees. Of course, curricula had to be modified. A young working-class soldier returning after service was not the same academically as the middle- and upper-class highly educated prospective attendee the curriculum has been designed for. However, what these new students lacked in the classics, they certainly made up for in maturity (these veterans were our first nontraditional students), career pragmatism (note the rise in Colleges of Engineering, Science, and Business, and the relative decline in Colleges of Arts, Humanities, and Classics), and work ethic (many of these same veterans had families to support, in cramped living conditions, and with very little extra money) while trying to gain this education. In addition, as universities began to modify curricula to meet these new students' needs, it became clear that more teaching resources would need to be directed toward the earlier college years to bring many of these new arrivals up to the levels of their more traditional classmates. More support courses were needed and offered—tutoring in English composition, in the form of writing labs, began to appear.

Second, a series of social movements and reforms, which helped secure the place of the open admissions university squarely into the landscape of higher education, lead to the inclusion of student populations who had otherwise been excluded from higher education—minorities and women. As a direct result of the civil rights movements in the fifties and sixties and then the women's rights movements of the sixties and seventies, more and more "minorities" fought for and gained access to universities. The inclusion of even more deserving recipients of higher education put even more strain on colleges and universities, and we saw another increase in the size of state colleges and universities, and the building of even more institutions of higher education, most notably more community colleges. Of course, there always remained colleges and universities that excluded students from all these categories (and still do) on the basis of academic standards, but, by and large, most states gradually saw both the moral and financial gains to be made by admitting as many students as they could through these recently federally-mandated open admissions policies.

THE DREAM AND THE NIGHTMARE OF OPEN ADMISSIONS UNIVERSITIES

At face value, this grand experiment to educate all our citizens with as much education as they wanted was intrinsically a novel approach. We had left our European counterparts behind; we were attempting to change higher education from a meritocratic privilege for some to a democratic right for all—and this philosophical change describes how higher education in open admissions state colleges and universities has been administered ever since. Basically, students can enroll in an open admissions college or university as long as they (1) find enough funding for tuition and living expenses through federal and/or state loans/scholarships, work study, athletic scholarships, academic scholarships, private means, and others; and (2) meet minimum academic standards *or* take a series of developmental academic subjects to elevate them to requisite levels of performance. What this actually means for many students is that the high school diploma can be replaced with a GED; high school itself can be replaced with home schooling, standardized tests such as the ACT or SAT can be taken casually, if at all, and a series of institution-specific placement tests can take the place of these standardized tests for admission purposes. Simply stated, students now wishing to gain access to higher education can attend a community college or an open admissions four-year institution with very little academic preparation in their high school careers.

So the noble dream of access to a quality higher education for all who can benefit from it has turned into the nightmare of access to remedial repetition of work these students did not sufficiently acquire in their high-school years. These students are essentially paying for (or the taxpayers are paying for) remedial work to prepare them to take college-level work. This is their right, and open admissions colleges and universities must, by law, provide instruction for these students. Our institutions of higher education are complicit in this national scam—we readily admit students whom we know have little chance of advancing very far in our universities; moreover, we are quick to flaunt our enrollment figures if they are going up, but very quiet about our retention figures or our figures on percentages of students in developmental education courses.

WHO THESE STUDENTS ARE

Each year, immediately after high school graduation, students entering our university discover to their great dismay that their 3.0 (and above) grade point averages, their inclusion in the *Who's Who in American High Schools*, their letter jackets in basketball, their volunteer work at the local hospital, their honors courses, and the fact that they were heavily recruited by all the state colleges and universities can't save them from having to enroll in a battery of developmental reading and writing courses. The one relative measure of their high school career, the one nationally normed test they take, the ACT test, places them, without much fanfare, right in the middle of the developmental range. These developmental courses, in this case courses in reading and writing, usually a year-long sequence of very-basic-to-somewhat-basic courses, are for a sizable number of these students, all they will ever see of college.

Each year, we initially blame their high school teachers—how could these people have been allowed to graduate from high school so deficient in these major skills? But, this finger-pointing soon ceases as the semester begins—there is not enough time for finger-pointing when you have twenty-five to thirty students in each class, four classes per semester, and very few of these students want to be here, or understand why they are there in remedial classes in the first place. After all, they passed English in high school, and they can read already! These students, no matter how much we would like to buy our university's public relations brochures, are not very nontraditional; they are, as we noted earlier, instead generally eighteen-year-olds fresh from their high school graduations. Nevertheless, their standardized scores place them in developmental studies courses and a few regular admissions courses, although it is not clear how anyone really believes that a student placed into Developmental Reading and/or Writing and concurrently enrolled in Survey of American History to 1865 will actually survive (this person generally does not).

Developmental Writing students have yet to master appropriate paragraphing, essay writing, and rudimentary proofreading skills. Many write below the eighth-grade level, and most have not written an entire essay in high school—or at least what their college instructors might call an essay. Developmental Reading students read below the eighth-grade level. This means that they can barely understand an article in *USA Today*, let alone understand the most rudimentary college text. Add to this that most of these students have no study skills habits, no time management skills, and very little realistic chance of success in college—yet they keep coming and coming and coming!

In an open admissions college/university, many students who are judged more proficient than their developmental studies counterparts enter our first-year composition classes with only slightly better skills. These are students, who, by and large, have had average—although with rampant grade inflation their grades are far from average—high school academic experiences. Some have written essays and some have even completed the dreaded book report, a few have written research papers (some even had to type them), and some had to (were forced into) take honors classes of the AP variety but their scores were vaguely reported, if the tests were even attempted. It seems very clear that composition scholars at prestigious doctoral-granting institutions need to be aware that these students are not the same as the mythical ones they think inhabit all composition classrooms all over North America.

Indeed, over the years, through a series of questionnaires, we have collected some observations about these students.

They do not read. Most of our students do not take a daily newspaper, read a weekly magazine, or a monthly periodical. They know people who read, at least they have noted one of their parents or guardians reading in the last six weeks, but a surprising number report that there is no newspaper in their home. At college, they make no use of the general periodicals and newspapers in the library unless forced to for an assignment, and many students could not name a newspaper from a city one hour away. In their dorms, they sometimes glance at teen/fashion magazines and sports magazines, but they don't claim this to be real reading for the most part—they look at the pictures a great deal! The vast majority of our entering first-year composition students have never read a novel!

They watch television. Most of our students claim to watch at least four hours of television a day, but many others consider this a conservative estimate. We, like most colleges and universities today, offer students living in residence halls a wide array of cable television channels, educational television offerings, and now their own twenty-four-hour movie channel system for their extracurricular entertainment. One could only hazard a guess as to whether the library budget has kept pace with the incremental increases in entertainment budgets for our charges!

They are employed. Many of our students come to college with pickup truck and car loans, and they must find or keep jobs to help pay off these vehicles. This is not the same type of student for whom "daddy and mommy" buy a car for graduation—these kids have had cars since they were sixteen and seventeen because in rural northern Louisiana and eastern Texas a car or truck is a necessity. We don't have much in the way of public transport and we don't have cabs at all. Other students must find work immediately because they come from lower income families and, while tuition and room and board might be paid for through loans and scholarships, incidental living expenses and truck/car loans are not! These students work three to five hours a day—often late into the night or early morning to pay for these necessities.

They play sports, hangout, and "party." Many of our student respondents claim to spend at least two hours a day playing sports, three hours just "hanging out" with their friends in the dorms or in apartments, and most claim to have already consumed alcohol to excess since arriving on campus. Much has been written recently about drug and alcohol excesses on college campuses, and the illnesses and lost time students undergo because of this overindulgence is truly staggering. Recently in Louisiana, we have had a number of students seriously hurt with binge drinking, but frankly we will never know how many students we do lose to this excess.

They are not all computer literate. While some of these students do surf the web and make use of e-mail accounts, many more do not have the skills to avail themselves of this technology. True, our open computer labs are generally full, but when we start looking at time spent in these labs it soon becomes clear that many of these students are only sending and reading e-mail a great deal of the time—not actually writing academic papers! Most of these students have limited typing skills, many still exhibit computerphobia, and many still have their mothers type (and presumably edit/proofread) their papers. Many of these students do not have access to a computer in the home, and many still view the computer with distrust. However, others are beginning to use the web for their research purposes more often than they use the traditional library, and this research strategy is one that many college instructors will have to adapt to: we are now seeing more cases of plagiarism from the web than ever before, and perhaps more important, we are now seeing students quote accurately and honestly from web sites that are just plain incorrect! With so many people now having the skills to put text on the web, our students now are even more lost as to what might or might not be factual information than they were with the traditional library resources of yesteryear.

WHAT THESE STUDENTS KNOW

On average half of our first year composition students surveyed don't know how many states there are in the US, while 85 percent could not name all of them in fifty minutes. Ninety percent of the students don't know the dates of either the First World War, the Second World War, the Korean War, or the Viet Nam conflict—many are not even clear in which century these events occurred and which nations were involved. Most students could not name the last five presidents of the United States; many could not name the capitals of Iran and Iraq, countries featured on television for many years. None of our students could accurately place England, Russia, France, Germany, Italy, Japan, and Australia on a map, and a surprising number (60 percent) had difficulty differentiating between Canada, Alaska, Greenland, Hawaii, and Puerto Rico.

Most of our students could not name a living novelist if John Grisham were disallowed. Most could not name a play other than one written by William Shakespeare. Most could not name a living poet, and most could not name a black writer and his/her work. Our students don't know three lines of any poem, cannot recognize book titles of even the biggest literary stars, and most have never been to a play—although many have seen *Cats* two and three times!

Our students have no idea about their own local history. In alarming numbers they don't know when their state became a state, they don't know who the last governor of the state was, they don't know who the last vice president of the United States was, and perhaps most ironic for professors teaching in the Deep South with its deep memories, most of our students cannot accurately (within ten years) tell us about the American Civil War (many believe this event occurred in the early twentieth century). These students know nothing of current politics—unsure who is a Democrat, who is a Republican, unsure in what parts of the world Bosnia or Tibet are located, having seemingly never heard of Yeltsin, Stalin, Marx, or Lenin. They know next to nothing about the Constitution of the United States, and cannot differentiate between Martin Luther and Martin Luther King.

However, these students do know who Oasis is, who Tupac Shakur was, who Seven of Nine is, who Dennis Rodman is; they know what the Taco Bell dog says, and they know all the slang terms for drugs. These students are vitally aware of sports scores and sports trivia, and they know the latest actors' biographies, including their most recent loves and divorces. They can tell the plots of most of the soap operas shown every day, and they know who Letterman's guests were last night.

HOW WE CAME TO THIS SITUATION

Concerns about such surveys of students' current knowledge quickly move to question their validity, but almost as quickly these concerns move to ask whose fault is it? Well, we believe with all our intellectual might that understanding something of Martin Luther King's life and struggle is more important, more culturally relevant, and more academically responsible than being able to name the members of the British pop group Oasis. We believe with all our might that not knowing that we have fifty states in our country is much more reprehensible than knowing that Antonio Banderas is married to Melanie Griffith. We believe with all our might that we have reached an incredibly sad state of affairs when our entering college students don't know which century the Second World War took place in, who the Allied and Axis forces were, and what the results of this war were; moreover, we find it doubly ironic and galling that one of these results was the fact that many of these grandparents were finally able to go to college, move up in social class, and eventually allow their grandchildren the luxury of their own ignorance!

However, the key point here is that these are not the students at whom composition theorists have aimed their theories and designed their overly politicized mission-statements about the purpose of first-year writing. These are not students who can "resist" dominant discourses even if they knew what that meant. These are not students who will explore alternative discourses to subvert the dominant power discourse. These are not students who can take part in a Marxist-inspired curriculum; these students don't know who the Marx brothers were, let alone Karl! These are not the students who will quickly develop women's ways of knowing, feminist perspectives on language, or be able to unpack a Friereian perspective on the oppressed; these are students who are barely holding on linguistically, and have yet to gain much knowledge about the world around them. These students cannot interact meaningfully with this politicization even if they wanted to! The theorists exemplify yet another case of not practicing what they preach—audience awareness. We have little faith that these approaches are even what First-Year Composition is intended to be in any case, and we believe that students trained in these approaches will not be successful in the types and genres of writing that they will face later in their careers.

THE ALARM BELLS ARE SOUNDING

More and more states are requiring departments within colleges and universities to be able to show accountability for what it is that we claim to be imparting to these students, and what they can actually demonstrate competence in. Ironically, English departments are rhetorically suspect in claiming their graduates are prepared adequately in various areas; in reality we know English departments are producing a very flawed, unemployable, yet certified competent, product.

As more and more students leave colleges and universities, having attained very high grades and very impressive-sounding degrees, but, unfortunately, limited applicable knowledge, limited marketable abilities, and limited workforce communication skills, society is beginning to question the extreme difference between the academics' perception of curricular theory and the graduates' demonstration of actual performance.

Another illustration of this practice is when literature professors claim that their students will, through a complete survey of "great books" readings, the acquisition of critical approaches to various genres, and the ability to approach and "unpack" literatures from a variety of critical frameworks (feminist, Marxist, deconstructionist, post-structuralist, and others) be able to transfer those skills in a variety of careers. Employers would beg to differ. Hence, we see a split between a curricular emphasis in theory and in practice.

Even more ironic, perhaps, is that this same split between theory and practice is readily apparent in composition studies, especially in the politicized theories listed above, ironic because at an earlier time we prided ourselves for being in a field that was helping students gain the writing skills to succeed in college and life, and now, if we continue to follow current composition theorists trends, we will be actively trying to get them to "subvert," "resist," and attack the usefulness of the various discourses they will in fact need to show proficiency in to be judged successful! The deeper irony is that if students follow the current politicized mission of composition, then we are in essence setting them up to fail.

THE COMPOSITION CLASS IN THEORY

First-Year Composition is one of very few courses in university curricula across the nation in which all students are required to either take it or test out of it. Across the country, college composition seems, in theory, to be organized centrally around certain key cornerstones.

First, it seems fairly clear that this is a service sequence of courses: usually two, English 1010 and English 1020, but certainly not limited to this structure for the entire university. While situated and generally taught in English departments, and while basically funding all the other courses within these departments, the composition courses and those who teach them have a much broader responsibility to all those in the university.

Second, it seems clear that composition courses are implicitly designed to publicly certify our students' literacy skills to all the university. These courses are seen across the university as places for students to develop the basic writing skills necessary to move forward. This course sequence then is the unofficial certification for all open admissions students—the university community expects the faculty teaching these courses to certify students as literate.

Third, this course sequence is expected to do a myriad of things: teach proper format, teach appropriate language, teach research skills, and teach proper grammar and proofreading skills. For many outside the composition classroom environment, it is seen as a refresher course so that students will all be on "the same page" as they enter their next classes.

It is important to realize that English departments agreed to all these points. English departments, as they saw their undergraduate majors dwindling as more and more new students decided on majors that could actually demonstrate employment opportunities, welcomed their only opportunity to avoid going the way of Classics Departments to virtual extinction. English departments in effect said "yes—send us these students; we are the best trained faculty on campus to deal with them." Of course, the average literature professor was neither trained nor had much inclination in actually teaching these students to write and read to appropriate levels, so the departments went about hiring an "underclass" to do this work for them. This underclass, the compositionists, can now provide a more realistic view of the place of composition.

THE COMPOSITION CLASS IN REALITY

Presently, the composition sequence is still very much embedded in the realm of the English department empire, but the department does not see it as a university core course to prepare students, but instead as a step-child in a new marriage. In sexist terms, the predominately male department does not mind the second marriage to the predominately female composition field because this marriage comes with a healthy financial dowry; but the male does not want to take much responsibility raising his bride's children, born out of wedlock and from an undesirable class.

Hence, college composition is seen as a necessary evil in English departments, as something that most professors are loath to teach and happy to get others to do in their place (as long as they don't ask for too much pay or tenure very often). Therefore, composition instructors are still generally the lowest paid and lowest ranking members of the English department; many are not even members of the department at all, but instead are adjuncts and graduate students who teach an alarmingly high number of these courses.

Second, this course is often not what the rest of the university wants it to be. Many departments have a two-course sequence and much of the writing that takes place here is writing about literature and personal realization writing. Of course this type of writing has its purpose and place, but as a university core course much more should be expected from this class or classes. The literature component plays an interesting role in the composition sequence. Many English departments are not rich enough or sufficiently large enough to be able to hire people to teach this odious sequence, and so literature faculty must from time to time get their hands dirty. Teaching literary works, short stories, poems, and drama in the second half of the composition sequence has become a way for many literature scholars to be seen to be teaching writing, but in fact, they are still teaching literature. What writing skills these prospective scientists, engineers, business leaders, and medical doctors gain from writing about literature has still to be demonstrated, and the call for writing across the curriculum came not from the English department, but from faculty across the curriculum, who still could not see students' writing skills improving sufficiently through this personal essay to literary analysis sequence.

Third, this course is not, no matter what others think it is, a refresher course for skills already learned. Simply stated, for so many of these students these communicative skills have yet to be learned, and the idea of writing as a process toward a product is still alien to most of these students. Many of the instructors and professors teaching these courses lack the training to teach writing, especially from the ground up. This lack of acquired communication skills is the result of a complex cognitive problems, and most, if not all, of the instructional staff are not trained in these areas. Indeed, most of our composition instructors still come to us from literature-based programs, and those who come from composition-based graduate programs (that long ago decided teaching grammar was wrong) still lack the grammatical knowledge and awareness to help students understand and correct their own work.

Fourth, because composition personnel are overworked and undertrained, writing centers and other tutorial centers also have been developed to help individually train these students and to work with more difficult or time-consuming individual writing problems. While in theory these are supplemental workstations for the composition personnel, many writing centers are, in fact, where a great deal of composition instruction actually takes place. For many students entering a writing center, this is the first time they get an individualized conversation about the demands of writing, and, for many, this is the first time they have talked with someone trained in the area, since even their composition instructor may be a literature graduate student just passing through. Unfortunately, the students must return to the writing classroom to an environment generally devoid of tried and tested composition successes.

Fifth, with the introduction of computer labs and electronic classrooms, compressed video labs, and internet-based courses, the composition instructor now has a variety of delivery systems and technologies to become proficient in. However, these technological applications, which promised to make writing easier, composition instruction more cutting edge, and to produce better writers have simply not lived up to their promises. Sure, students seem to like writing on computers more, but we have not seen the hard reliable, replicable results we were promised. In addition, instructors are generally not sufficiently trained in this technology, and at the end of the day the technology is too expensive to implement, too expensive in its upkeep, and too expensive to use given our class sizes.

THE REAL FAILURE OF COMPOSITION THEORISTS: LACK OF REALITY

In the last fifteen years we have seen a gradual change in the demographics of English departments. While certainly most departments are still literature-based, more tenure-track positions are going to those outside the traditional literary fields to meet the ever-rising tide of badly prepared students entering college/university. As we noted earlier, these students must take college composition, and as their numbers have increased, so has the need for better trained writing specialists. Indeed we have seen the rise of undergraduate writing majors, and more masters and doctorate-level degree programs in composition. However, it is the current training of these writing specialists and our own poorly reasoned attempts at gaining professional respectability from colleagues who don't respect our work that have continued to damage the field; those of us who are really in composition know we undercut our own positions of strength in attempts to prove ourselves worthy to join our literature colleagues. Our profession, on the graduate level, quickly moved from what we claimed we were doing, producing writing teachers, to the more lofty, but less realistic, goals of producing rhetoricians and other theorists.

THE POLITICAL DIFFERENCE BETWEEN COMPOSITION AND LITERATURE

After spending years developing some of the best composition programs in the country and helping to produce people committed to making a difference with these new underprepared populations of entering undergraduate students in open admissions universities, composition studies ran off the tracks.

For many of these early years, composition was an honorable field among the minority of graduate students who entered it for the altruistic goals of helping others succeed. Of course, composition was considered a stepchild by our literature colleagues, as a weird subset of English education populated by people who for some odd reason wanted to teach students who should never have been allowed into our universities in the first place. Our first text in the field, Shaughnessy's, was essentially a manual on how to deal with this new population, and our first conferences and journals dealt with the day-to-day instructional needs of our students. We had a room of our own, we had dialogue among ourselves, and essentially we were being left alone to get on with a job no one else wanted to do—to educate people our colleagues wanted no part of.

Then the bottom fell out of the market. Through a combination of more open admissions students entering our colleges and universities, another even more serious decline in liberal arts enrollments, and the subsequent administrative decision to offer more composition classes and fewer literature classes, the market changed. In English departments, literature retirements were now replaced by composition positions, and new positions in English departments went to badly needed compositionists. Developmental Studies departments appeared on many campuses staffed by professionals interested in teaching writing and reading at their most basic levels, and fairly rapidly it became clear that newly minted Ph.D.s in the usual literary specialties were becoming unemployable (the fact that English departments continue to produce more graduates in these areas than there will ever be jobs for is also criminal—yet another, although related, essay).

What happened next was predictable. Composition doctoral programs could not sufficiently produce enough trained professionals fast enough to meet the demand, and the more savvy literature programs began to certify their students as compositionists, while still pushing them to pursue their literature specialties. These people, with perhaps one course in composition theory, a couple of years teaching assistantship duties (teaching a subject, writing, they had next-to-no love for), since their professors would not teach composition, and a literary dissertation with the word "Rhetoric" in the title started to compete and get composition jobs that a few years before would not have been open to them. Indeed, today one need only look at the number of English literature doctoral programs masquerading as Composition programs to see why we in composition have not advanced professionally as we should have. Frankly, taking a course in composition theory, a couple of courses in Classical and Modern Rhetorical Theory, and writing a rhetorical analysis of James Joyce for a dissertation does not a composition expert make.

OUR DISCIPLINE'S LATERAL MOVEMENT

It is perhaps compositionists' own fault that our discipline has become so sidetracked. One need only note just how few composition classes composition experts actually teach. Often these very experts are hired into assistant professorships and immediately take over writing program administration positions. In addition, many neocompositionists have never been entirely content with their role in teaching writing and have looked for more acceptance from their literature colleagues. This need for acceptance has led our field away from work in how to teach writing more effectively and how to more effectively help student writers become more proficient. Instead, because of some compositionists' need for more literary acceptance, we have essentially allowed our profession to lose its way. We were beginning, through empirically, based research, to develop concretely tested, replicable methodologies that helped students acquire certain writing skills; we were beginning to set boundaries for our emerging discipline. However, we fell (or were we pushed?) for the patently absurd notion that a discipline could exist without boundaries, and that anyone who brought the latest theory to our table, linked however thinly to writing, was by definition a compositionist.

Now when we have national searches for the next generation of compositionists, we are faced with applicants resplendent with the heavy respectability of work influenced by critical theory, by Marxist theory, by our supposed liberatory duty to help students resist and subvert the dominant discourse, and by postmodernity, by Habermas, and by Derrida. We saw the beginnings of this nonsense with the call for Students' Right to Their Own Language—a perhaps well-intentioned, although patently maternalistic, call that students never asked for. But now, so-called composition dissertations have been so infiltrated by so much extra-academic, polemic, diatribic influences that it is not clear where we are headed.

What is clear however, it that none of these influences and clever discussions have very much to do with teaching writing. We seem content instead to bring theories from the "outside" and make them applicable to our "inside." Indeed, even the most sacred cow of the profession, the role of rhetoric, needs careful attention. Have we really ever demonstrated that classical rhetoricians have enough to offer the composition classroom, and for that matter have we ever really stopped to reconsider the so-called importance of medieval or contemporary rhetoricians' theories to our students' very current academic lives? The study of rhetoricians (classical to contemporary) may have more to do with looking like a "real field of study" for our literature colleagues than advancing our own!

We must face facts soon! Our students still need—more now than ever—faculty trained and committed to the teaching of writing. We can neither find this practical training in classical rhetoric studies or in the works of Jacques Derrida! Instead, we must recapture the spirit that attracted the early pioneers to our professions—we must return to teaching writing and studying how to do this more effectively for our students. Our greatest paradox to date is that composition theory has been driven lately by too much theory and not enough evidence. As two who have spent a great deal of time in the trenches, what we see as the failure of composition studies is that the people offering the "competing theories" don't spend enough time in the trenches near the same battle as we do. One would think that with the amount of theory being posited that by now we would know more about what actually works—but we don't.

The chilling truth is that we are no closer to knowing how to teach writing than we were at the beginning of the process movement. We have unsystematically bounced from one rhetorical theory to another critical approach to another speculator-du-jour, like sailors in search of wind and bereft of a compass; in this directionless process, we have moved away from many of the key pedagogical areas of writing instruction we needed immediate answers to. We are now instead being swamped by theoretical waves. We have too many competing theories, and not enough people sufficiently trained in research design actually trying to test some of these theories' hypotheses.

QUESTIONS THAT REQUIRE ANSWERS IF COMPOSITION IS TO BECOME A DISCIPLINE

At this point we in composition need to ask ourselves some pretty important questions that are telling about what we value:

1. Why are so many of our newly minted compositionists unable to conduct even the most basic experimental research designs to prove a research hypothesis about a teaching method? We produce people who can theorize until blue in the face and those who can bring in every critical theorist's reading, but they cannot test a basic hypothesis about the field. What happened to empirical studies? Why is it that compositionists don't study educational statistics as part of their doctorates?

2. Why are so many of our newly minted compositionists unable to relate their work to the theory and practice of teaching reading? We produce people who write dissertations on audience considerations, but are unable to talk about the reading process and all the research already conducted on how readers process written texts. How can we miss this obvious connection?

3. Why are there so many of our newly minted compositionists who are unable to draw connections with the wealth of research in text production and text analysis techniques conducted in the study of linguistics? Can we really claim to be interested in all aspects

of language, when we actively steer people away from linguistics?

4. Why are so many of our newly minted compositionists unable to teach and talk about grammatical issues?   At one level, we are a profession that claims to help others produce gramattically correct texts, but why, then, do we have so few people who are able to teach grammar(s), and why do we produce graduates who do not think that grammar instruction and the teaching of writing are interrelated?

5. Why are so many of our newly minted compositionists so unknowledgable about issues related to students' learning styles and matters of cognition? For years, we have spouted the truism that "writing is an individual process" but we have done next to nothing in the training of our next generation of compositionists in how to identify and teach students with different learning styles.

6. Why is it that we all rely so very heavily on so much theory from theorists who do not teach composition regularly? We read and attempt to put into practice (often across the curriculum no less) untested theories proposed by many composition experts who teach at major research schools, where admissions are not open, where the teaching load is ridiculously low, where masses of graduate students and part-timers artificially keep composition classes small, and where the purpose is to publish theory and not practice teaching.

CONCLUSION

With this influx of new student populations, most unprepared to meet the real writing demands of the academy and careers beyond it, we must again begin to provide trained and valued practitioners of composition. We must rebuild our discipline. Only this time we had better do it correctly or we will lose the moral and academic authority to serve this population once and for all. The challenges are great, and we already know many of them.

Our students lack the most basic writing skills. We know they cannot yet process thoughts into relevant, cohesive, coherent academic prose. We know they cannot proofread their written attempts into standard written English. We know they lack the skills to integrate others' work cohesively and correctly into their own writing. We know that they know little about audience concerns, and we know that they are unclear about rhetorical choices available to them. We know they have had limited success in writing; it is an act they detest or, worse, fear.

Our students lack the most basic reading skills. We know that they have trouble reading at age-appropriate levels and lack the requisite comprehension skills to gather information from various sources. We know that their analytical skills are weak, and they have trouble summarizing and paraphrasing. We know they read painfully slowly, and we know that their vocabulary is painfully limited—and that these two deficiencies attribute to poor comprehension and textual misunderstandings. We know they do not view reading as a pleasurable activity; it is an act they detest or, worse, fear.

Our students lack sufficient cultural information to begin to discuss issues they will meet, or are assumed to already know, in many of their university classes. We know they are unaware of the political and social events that have allowed them entrance into our colleges and universities. We know their sense of history and geography is incredibly warped. We know that these students have no real idea what their future holds, and many have only the vaguest ideas of why they are in college or university to begin with.

We hold all these deficiencies to be self-evident, and we need to use what we know about our students to better prepare the people who will teach them. It also seems evident to us that the current method of preparing composition specialists has not really improved our students' lot. We need a radical reformation of our profession and the reform must come from within. We know that jobs in composition are going to be plentiful for some time; more unprepared, than prepared, students are coming to colleges and universities, and open admissions institutions have really not seen the decline in enrollments that our honors colleges and selective admissions schools have. However, this needed reformation is disciplinary in scope; we must be about much more than job acquisition, otherwise we are not a discipline, but an available labor pool instead. We must do a better job of teaching students to write, and so we must do a better job of becoming discipline-specific professionals.

OUR SOLUTION

We see the need for a new academic structure and approach to teaching writing if we are to improve the teaching of writing in American open admissions colleges and universities. Our primary call would be that all developmental reading and writing courses, first-year composition sequences, and advanced writing courses be placed in their own department. We would see this department staffed by compositionists, whose only interests would be the teaching of writing at various levels and conducting applied research into how to teach writing more effectively. We must begin to rebuild our boundaries and in this spirit we posit the following boundary cornerstones:

No One Should Be Forced to Teach Writing Who Does Not Want To

The move from the traditional English department should include only those who have been trained in composition, or those who are willing to join such a department and take part in monthly training workshops. Professionals in literary fields who disdain teaching composition should not teach it. They should remain in the English Department and hope that students will flock to take their courses.

Only Those Trained in the Teaching of Writing and Reading Skills Should Teach Writing

If we are a profession, then let us begin to behave as one. We must exclude those who teach writing simply for job security. We must only employ those who love our profession, not those who simply choose it for employment safety. These people make bad teachers; they are easy to spot, and we all know it.

In addition, the relationship between reading and writing is inseparable. When there is a deficiency in a student's reading comprehension skills, it is quickly evidenced in his/her writing. Compositionists, as academic professionals, should be able to recognize, evaluate, and prescribe solutions for students who struggle with writing because their reading skills are so poor. For too long, students have been encouraged to guess at or parrot the English language, and that is not good enough. We must be able to evaluate our students' reading comprehension skills. No matter what an ACT or SAT score suggests, we must note if a student can comprehend what he/she has learned to "read" through the wonders of whole language. It's time that we ensure that our graduate students, future professionals in the composition field, are securely grounded in the theory and practice of teaching writing *and* reading.

No First-Year Composition Program Should Exist Without a Writing Center

A writing center must play an integral part of any department charged with administering first-year composition. It is an ideal training place for new graduate students, for faculty learning about new techniques, and for outreach programs across the curriculum. This facility should be staffed and directed by professionals in the field.

No One Should Direct a Writing Program Who Is Not a Trained Compositionist

The days of giving the composition program directorship to someone willing to do this "drudge work" or to someone else to keep an eye on it must come to an end. The composition program directorship should never be a "plum job" used to employ another literature specialist.

Composition Directors Should Always Teach Composition Courses

Composition specialists who seek to escape the rigors of first-year composition should be automatically suspect in our profession's eyes, but, at present, they are not. If a Director wants to impose direction, she/he must also be subject to the experience he/she is proposing on his/her teaching staff.

The Use of Masters-Level Trained Compositionists Should Be Encouraged, But Not Abused

These professionals should teach three composition classes per semester, with real salaries and benefits, and no other class loads. The use of personnel trained in real M.A. composition programs, i.e. not those with a glorified M.A. in Literature (with some teaching experience), would greatly cut down on the number of badly prepared students coming out of badly thought out programs.

Graduate Students in Composition Departments Should Always Be Supervised Teachers

In effect teaching assistants should be just that, assistants to the master teacher in the course. They should apprentice with this master teacher before ever getting a class of their own. And even then these apprentice's should be observed and evaluated bi-weekly.

Composition Departments' Primary Focus Should Be on University Service

While the teaching of advanced composition, business communications, technical and professional writing courses, creative writing, applied rhetorical theory, and composition theory and practice, and perhaps even full B.A, and M.A curricula in teaching writing might be added emphases, the composition department members should remember that their primary role must be to train first-year writers to succeed in the university. To do this they must teach composition courses as their first responsibility.

Only Compositionists Should Evaluate Compositionists

In a department designated as the one serving the writing needs of an entire university, compositionists should be reviewed for tenure and promotion by other compositionists who can accurately and fairly evaluate their worth. An obvious point perhaps, but one forgotten in the current academic structure.

Composition Classes Must Be Shown to Work

Compositionists must be able to show empirically that their techniques and approaches actually produce better writers. In order to proceed in this manner, doctoral programs will have to ensure that their graduates can work in this empirical realm, and such research into the effectiveness of approaches must become a natural, ongoing process within this department. This means that compositionists must be more scientific than they have been in the past, and that they must be fully aware of the principles of accountability that are running most universities today.

We are facing uncertain times in composition classrooms. We have to better deal with students who are unprepared for tertiary education, and we must be seen as a community of scholar-teachers who have some concrete answers to some very pressing questions. We must be seen as knowledgeable practitioners of *an art and a science* who can teach students to write and read clearly and effectively. We must be seen as professionals who care about our students as individuals, who understand that not all of them will succeed, and that many of them can be taught to communicate more effectively through methods that have been empirically tested and proven successful.

We must begin to draw boundaries around our discipline; we must build a discipline by recognizing what our mission is, what areas fall "inside" and "outside" these boundaries, and who can and cannot work within these boundaries. We must make promises slowly and carefully to the rest of the academy, and then we must live up to our promises. We must realize that we cannot cure everyones' ills, and that the educational system still will admit people we do not have much hope in reaching. Finally, we must be realistic—we will exist as professionals and be treated as such if we are seen to be providing a service that the students, the university, and industry really need and can profit from.

When we begin to achieve these goals, we will begin to educate future teachers who will in turn begin to send us a better educated, more literate student body. We will end this cycle of miseducation of open admissions students; we can reread our techniques and reteach ourselves in the process, understanding that this process will require our best efforts and challenge us, as well as our students. We must revise ourselves and our philosophies, and from this revision will emerge a revolutionized discipline both worthy of our students' needs and vital to their success.

8

Peer Review and Response: A Failure of the Process Paradigm as Viewed From the Trenches

Lynne Belcher

In 1972 when Donald Murray argued that writing should be taught as a process not a product, he foresaw many implications for teaching the process rather than the product. The first implication Murray lists in his essay "Teach Writing as a Process Not Product" is "The text of the writing course is the student's own writing. Students examine their own evolving writing and that of their classmates, so that they study writing while it is still a matter of choice, word by word" (91). Ten years later, Maxine Hairston argued for a paradigm shift in the teaching of writing in her "The Winds of Change: Thomas Kuhn and the Revolution in the Teaching of Writing." She argued that the new paradigm should focus on the writing process, a process that involves the intervention of readers in students' writing during that process. She also argued that students benefit "far more from small group meetings with each other than from the exhausting one-to-one conferences that the teachers hold" (17).

Clearly, the process method of teaching writing involves reader intervention by students in the writing of their classmates. But how successful has that intervention been in the writing that students produce? Since this part of the paradigm is so important to teaching writing as a process, we need to have some idea as to how well it has worked.

A careful examination of what instructors see happening as student readers intervene in the writing process of their classmates will show how this part of the process paradigm has failed. Students, for the most part, have not, as Murray argued, examined "their own evolving writing and that of their classmates . . . word by word." Nor has small group work been a greater benefit to student writers than the "exhaustive one-to-one conferences" between teacher and student writer, as Hairston argued. What seems to be an essential part of the process paradigm has been a failure in that it has not worked in the way many had hoped.

Much has been written about the work of peer response groups in the past, building on the work of Elbow and Bruffee, but much of that research has focused on what small numbers of students do when they respond to the writing of their classmates. The research generally can be classified into three categories: historical perspectives of peer review and peer response groups, descriptions of what peers do when they respond to the writing of their classmates, and suggestions for improving peer responses. Ann Ruggles Gere's book on peer groups written in 1987 includes both a historical perspective and an exhaustive bibliography. Muriel Harris includes a brief history in her comparison of writing center tutorials with peer response groups. Harris points out that "peer response, having been the subject of numerous studies, has a track record of conflicting results" (377).

Much of the research concluding with claims of the effectiveness or ineffectiveness of peer response begins with descriptions of what peers do when they respond to the writing of their classmates. Thomas Newkirk, Anne Ruggles Gere and Robert D. Abbott, Nancy Grimm, Nina Ziv, and Diana George among others have studied what peer reviewers actually do. Most of them conclude that more research needs to be done. Ronnie Carter concludes that though females outperform males as peer reviewers, "this study points out the lack of demonstrable *short-term* gains in peer evaluation by itself" (13). Carter also concludes that more research needs to be done (15).

Some researchers have tried to help make peer response more effective by looking at what instructors can do to better prepare their students to be good critical readers and responders. Mara Holt suggests a method for helping instructors understand "the kinds of peer criticism that students can fruitfully engage in" (391). Karen Spear in her book *Sharing Writing: Peer Response Groups in English Classes* explains not only what peer writing groups do but also how they can be used more effectively in composition classes. More recently, Candace Spigelman looks at the tension students feel about the ownership of texts in peer writing groups and how that tension can be used productively (250-51).

None of the research really examines what instructors who actually teach multiple sections of writing classes every semester think about the quality of peer responses and whether or not the use of peer response groups actually frees instructors from one-to-one conferencing. To that end, I surveyed writing instructors on two e-mail lists concerned with writing and writing instruction: WCENTER@ttacs6.ttu.edu and ECOMPL@listserv.nodak.edu. The survey reads as follows:

Name:
Semester class load:
Number of writing courses per semester:
Enrollment limits in first year composition:

1. Do you use peer review as part of your instruction in the writing process?
   Yes   No   If you don't, why not?

2. What kind of information do you ask peer reviewers to consider?
   Global revision   Paragraph and sentence level revision   Editing

3. How would you describe the quality of the peer comments?
   Excellent   Good   Fair   Poor

4. Do you grade peer reviewers on their comments?
   Yes   No   If you answered yes, why?   If you answered no, why not?

5. Do you think using peer reviewers makes your job easier or harder?
   Easier   Harder   No difference

6. Do you think using peer reviewers saves you time?
   Yes   No   If yes, how does it save you time?   If not, why not?

7. Which do you think is more effective in helping students revise their work?
   Small groups of peer reviewers working together
   One-to-one conference between teacher and student

8. Would you recommend that a new writing instructor make use of peer review as a part of writing instruction?
   Yes   No   Why or why not?   Other comments?

SURVEY FINDINGS

Kinds of and Locations for Colleges/Universities

Though I did not ask for information about the size and the mission of the schools where the respondents teach, those who answered the survey either included college/university web site addresses or used institutional addresses in their survey responses. I was able to visit the web sites of the schools for all but one respondent who had a commercial e-mail address. Ten of those thirty respondents (33 percent–totals will not always equal 100 percent since those numbers have been rounded off) teach at regional universities where undergraduate education is the primary focus, though most of these schools have some graduate programs. Two (7 percent) of those respondents teach at liberal arts colleges where the focus is on undergraduate education. Four of those respondents (13 percent) teach at liberal arts colleges with religious affiliations and a focus on undergraduate education. One respondent (3 percent) teaches at a larger Catholic university. Six of those respondents (20 percent) teach at community colleges, and five respondents (17 percent) teach at large, land-grant universities, though two of those respondents identified themselves as TA's, two were identified as part-timers, and one was identified as a lecturer. One respondent (3 percent) teaches at a professional/technical university, and one respondent (3 percent) teaches advanced placement writing classes at a high school.

Respondents teach in a variety of places; eighteen states and Australia are represented in the survey. Pennsylvania is most represented with four respondents while Texas and Kansas have three each. New York, Georgia, Wisconsin, and North Carolina are each represented by two respondents. Wyoming, Indiana, North Dakota, Illinois, Nebraska, Massachusetts, Utah, Virginia, Iowa, Connecticut, Georgia, and Colorado are each represented by one respondent.

What I was looking for with the surveys is instructors' attitudes about using peer response work in the classroom. I wanted to see what it is teachers think they are accomplishing when they use peer review. I was also interested in what instructors think of the quality of the comments their students make about other students' writing. I wondered if teachers think using peer review allows students to understand writing word by word and if making use of peer reviewers frees instructors from the demanding work of one-to-one conferences.

Semester Course Loads

Respondents reported that semester course loads range from five classes to one class, though many who teach smaller loads are either running writing centers/labs or are graduate students. In cases where respondents reported two different loads (e.g., three classes for fall, two for spring), the greater number was recorded since those respondents teach the greater number of classes at least one semester of each year. The responses to the question on semester class load are as follows:

5 classes per semester–two	(6 percent)
4 classes per semester–nine	(29 percent)
3 classes per semester–eight	(26 percent)
2 classes per semester–eight	(26 percent)
1 class per semester–four	(13 percent)

Respondents teach an average of 2.9 classes per semester. Eight of the respondents who say they teach either one or two courses a semester explain that they also work in or direct a writing center. Two other respondents identified themselves as graduate students.

Writing Course Load per Semester

Respondents also indicated the number of writing classes they teach each semester:

5 writing courses per semester—two	(6 percent)
4 writing courses per semester—three	(10 percent)
3 writing courses per semester—five	(16 percent)
2 writing courses per semester—sixteen	(52 percent)
1 writing course per semester—four	(13 percent)

Respondents teach an average of 2.35 writing classes per semester.

Enrollment Limits In First Year Writing Courses

Enrollments in first year composition courses range from 16 to 30 students, though five respondents say that the enrollment limits are regularly exceeded. Here are the enrollment limits indicated by respondents:

30 student limit—one ("routinely raised")	(3 percent)
28 student limit—one	(3 percent)
27 student limit—one	(3 percent)
25 student limit—twelve	(39 percent)
24 student limit—one	(3 percent)
23 student limit—one	(3 percent)
22 student limit—five	(16 percent)
20 student limit—seven	(23 percent)
16 student limit—one ("sort of" limit)	(3 percent)

Class size average is 22.5 students for respondents.

Peer Review as Part of Instruction in The Writing Process

All thiry-one respondents said they use or have used peer review as part of their instruction in the writing process. One respondent claimed to be "currently rethinking" using peer review. This respondent said, "I have tried a variety of ways to peer edit. Very few of them [peer reviewer comments] have had positive results; most of the time peer [reviewer] comments are too vague, [peer reviewers] comment on things that are a matter of personal style, or [peer reviewers] are just plain wrong." Another respondent said, "I have used it [peer review] quite a bit in the past. I'm taking a couple of semesters to try teaching without it right now." Though all the respondents have used peer review, not all of them are satisfied with the results.

Kinds of Information Solicited From Peer Reviewers

Most respondents (thirty) said they ask peer reviewers to consider global revision in their responses to their classmates' papers. Almost as many respondents (twenty-one) solicit paragraph and sentence level revision comments. Almost half of the respondents (fourteen) said that they have peer reviewers make editing comments about their classmates' papers. One respondent said that students are required to write "two-page critiques referencing audience, purpose, content, and style." Only one respondent asks students to review "mainly sentence level and editing."

The Quality of Peer Comments

The respondents were asked to comment on the quality of the peer review responses, identifying those comments as excellent, good, fair, or poor. Some respondents said the comments cover a wide range of quality while others said that the quality of the comments improves over the course of the semester. Here is how the respondents categorized the quality of peer reviewers' comments:

Excellent–two
Good–fifteen
Fair–twelve
Poor–seven
(The total is higher than thirty-one because some respondents identified several categories.)

Three respondents said the quality of peer comments improves over the semester. Nine respondents said there is a wide range in the quality of the comments by peer reviewers. One respondent said the quality of peer review comments is "fair to poor, usually. I also think they don't take it too seriously. . . I really wish I could figure out how to induce them to take it more seriously. (One time I tried anonymous peer reviews to see if people would be more candid. Not really–although one usually quiet, diplomatic student wrote a scathing peer review.)"

One respondent voiced the frustrations that many composition instructors must sometimes feel about peer review comments: "I've never been completely satisfied with the way it's gone, and students have consistently indicated on course evaluations that they are frustrated with it. I've tried modeling the process on sample papers. I've tried giving them detailed guidelines for comments. I've tried providing minimal guidance; I've tried putting students in peer revision groups that they stay with all semester. I've tried moving them to new partners every time. The main problem has been lack of thoughtful and useful commentary and/or commentary that directly contradicts my advice to the student. For this reason, students have seen it as a waste of time if not downright counterproductive."

One respondent said that the quality of peer comments is "excellent to poor; some students don't offer any constructive feedback at all; others are excellent at responding–it's too hard to give an overall judgment except to say that I find it valuable enough to continue." For many of the respondents, it seems that in spite of (or because of) the quality of the comments, they will continue to use peer responses to drafts of papers in their classes.

Grading Peer Reviewers on Their Comments

Respondents were asked if they grade the peer reviewers on their comments. Twelve (39 percent) said they do, while eighteen (58 percent) said they do not. Four respondents said they include peer comments as a grade for participation. Seven said they periodically review peer comments. Many respondents commented about the value of grading or not grading peer review comments. One respondent said that the review comments aren't graded, "but I make them sign off on their comments and I review the peer review sheets to identify weaknesses in their process and then focus on those areas more for the next review. A peer review is just as much a learning process for the reader as it is for the writer. This is practice to help them understand how to find mistakes in their work and how to offer critiques of others' work in a manner that is helpful." Other respondents expressed the idea that peer review comments are as much a learning experience for the reader as for the writer.

Several respondents said they do grade the peer review comments as a way to get students to take responding to drafts seriously. One respondent who grades the peer review comments said that "Sad to say, if students know they are accountable, most seem to take the activity more seriously." Another said, "I have found that students spend more time and give better comments when they know they are being held accountable."

Several respondents said they do not grade review comments because of a lack of time: "I think maybe I should [grade the review comments] because that might make students take it seriously," but this respondent also said that the comments are not graded because the respondent is already "too busy." Another respondent replied "no" to the question about grading peer review comments because "I already have too much work with forty-four students." Others said they do not grade the comments but for different reasons: "I am more interested in the social aspect of writing for real readers. Also, I give grades only on midterm and final portfolios, based on writing quality, amount of work (i.e., how much revising, what depth of revising), and participation. Any individual set of peer comments is only a small part of the overall picture. I do ask for peer evaluation of midterm and final portfolios, and I comment on those one- to one-

and-a-half-page evaluations as part of the feedback which the portfolio author receives." Another respondent said that, "I think that would inhibit the comfort level of the groups. I don't want it to be competitive. Also the logistics would be a problem. I can't sit in on all the groups at the same time." Though not all respondents grade the comments of the reviewers, they do seem to spend time looking at the kinds of comments reviewers are making in order to help reviewers become better critical readers.

Peer Reviewers Make Instructor's Job Harder and Easier

Respondents were asked if using peer reviewers makes their job in the classroom easier or harder. Many respondents did not like the choices for answers and so came up with other answers. Ten respondents (32 percent) did say that the use of peer reviewers makes their jobs easier. Five (16 percent) said it makes their jobs harder. Nine (30 percent) said using peer reviewers makes no difference in their workload. Two (6 percent) said it makes their jobs both easier and harder while three (10 percent) said it makes their jobs neither easier nor harder. One respondent (3 percent) said it makes the job more interesting while another (3 percent) said it makes the job different. Many respondents had more to say. One respondent believes using peer reviewers makes the job harder "because I spend a great deal of time trying to teach them the fundamentals of peer review and then I spend time constructing a variety of different peer reviews. It also takes time to evaluate the success of each peer review session." Another respondent said that using peer reviewers makes the job "harder, I think. . . . I'm always tinkering with the process to try to make it work better. I love the idea in theory–and have found it useful in grad courses–but I think it needs to be done differently." Another respondent said that using peer reviewers makes the job harder, "but that's not a bad thing." One respondent who believes using peer reviewers makes the job harder said that, "ideally, it should make it easier. If students are responding as engaged and intelligent readers they should provide backup for my comments and provide insights of their own that I might have missed. However, this has rarely been the case. Instead, I've had to do a lot of extra work preparing guidelines, checking that they did it, etc. That's why I've decided to give it a break for a few semesters. Maybe I'll get some fresh ideas, a new perspective, and try it again."

Respondents who reported that using peer reviewers makes their jobs easier had a variety of reasons for answering as they did. One respondent said, "I'd say that classes involving a lot of workshopping are easier for me–because that's what I know. It has little to do with the time I spend reading papers, however. It has more to do with how class time is spent, and how much I have to allocate in preparing for it. I also sleep better at night knowing that my comments aren't the only comments they are depending on." One respondent said that using peer reviewers makes the job "easier; one less day that I have to lecture, which is often a waste of time anyway." Another said that using peer reviewers makes the job neither easier nor harder: "If I didn't use them I would read every draft, but since I do use them I spend a lot of time modeling and teaching students how to respond to one another's writing." One respondent reflected the views of many in saying, "It helps students to see a variety of opinions (hopefully), but it also gives me more work to do in checking over the responses to grade them."

Peer Reviewers Do Not Save Time For Instructors

Respondents were also asked if using peer reviewers saves time for instructors. While eleven respondents (35 percent) said that using peer reviewers saves them time, seventeen (55 percent) said it does not. Two (6 percent) weren't sure, and one respondent (3 percent) said that saving time isn't a priority. One of those "yes" votes was a probably: "Probably yes, because it teaches critical thinking skills as it has students review their own writing and their knowledge of writing." Another said the time it takes to make use of peer reviewers is "time better spent. . . . Because I don't have to personally respond to every paper, I get better writing from students when I do see it, and I'm teaching them not to be dependent on me for feedback. It doesn't save time compared to a pure lecture, though, because I have to make up peer review sheets and guidelines, facilitate those groups and actively engage students in the process of peer review." One respondent said that "the students quickly begin making comments about problems I used to have to tell them about." Another said that "the peer review substitutes for a conference with me. The papers don't end up as good, but they learn more about working in such groups." Another respondent said, "I don't use it as a substitute for my own work."

Most of those who said that using peer reviewers does not save them time noted that it actually takes more time: "I need to spend a great deal of time setting them up to be good reviewers–that usually takes at least half the semester. Then I work on checklists and comment sheets for each assignment. That takes time. Then I go over the peer comments with my students in conference. . . . Just conducting class and conferences would be less time consuming, but I want my students to learn how to be good writing partners later, so I think the time is worth it." Another echoes that concern: "It is another means to giving feedback on work in progress, and thus can relieve me of some of that load, but students need to learn how to review others' work, and that must be built into class time and practiced." Many of those who said using peer reviewers does not save them time explained that they respond to drafts of papers as well as have peer reviewers respond to them.

Some respondents pointed out that peer review is probably a greater benefit to the reader than to the writer: "The main benefit I see is to the reader, not the writer. The comments they made toward the beginning of the semester were mostly about surface error, even though they had strict instructions to discuss only content issues–I think that is because they didn't really understand what I meant or how to do it. . . . Because I think the helpfulness of their comments is limited until they get some experience, I also read and comment on all their drafts, and meet with them individually. . . . If you start out teaching kids who are more comfortable with writing, then maybe peer editing as a source of information for the writer is more realistic. For me, it is still extremely useful–just more so for the reader." Another respondent expressed a common opinion: "peer review (as you know) doesn't just happen, but like everything has to be taught, modeled, what-have-you." One respondent found that question about saving time "absurd." This respondent said that after many years of teaching, "saving time has not been a priority in my teaching."

Teacher Conferences Are More Effective Than Peer Reviewers

Almost half of the respondents (fourteen–45 percent) believe that one-to-one conferences between teacher and student are a more effective intervention method than peers working together. Three respondents (10 percent) believe peer groups are more effective than student/teacher conferences. Two respondents (6 percent) said a mixture is effective while four (13 percent) said each is equally effective. Four respondents (13 percent) said teacher conferences have a different purpose than peer reviews, and two respondents (6 percent) said each has its strengths and weaknesses. Two respondents (6 percent) said that teacher/student conferences are more effective for the short term but that peer review work has a long-term effect. One respondent said "students learn more from each other than from the teacher and that knowledge is more deeply structured or implanted when students are able to work together to internalize it. Ultimately, students just learn more from collaborative groups than from a teacher trying to impart knowledge." Another respondent supporting the effectiveness of peer review work summed up that opinion by saying, "Students learn more by giving advice than by getting it."

Those who responded that teacher/student conferences are more effective than peer review work seem confident of their opinions about this issue, saying "no question about it" and "definitely one-to-one conferences between teacher and student." One respondent said that "students often ignore peer comments, and many students just can't figure out how to give useful suggestions." Another respondent said, "I am a great fan of one-on-one conferences, and this year have finally managed to bring each in under twenty-five minutes." Another said, "Although peer reviewers are quite useful as a way of giving the student an audience, I think the one-to-one conference between teacher and student is hard to beat. I find I can verbalize suggestions for writing improvement better than the students can." One respondent explained that although a one-to-one conference between teacher and student is a better method, "I can't use it with my teaching load. Too bad."

The fourteen respondents who have mixed opinions about which method of intervention is more effective have a variety of reasons for their mixed opinions. One respondent uses "a mixture of small groups and occasional larger ones. The first for active participation, the second for seeing more how other people comment, and seeing the wide range of things that can be said about student work. One-on-one conferencing can be very effective, but I think only if the students want to–I'm hesitant to assign whole classes to come and see me individually." Another respondent said, "They have different uses. I use small groups to comment on things like coherence and the quality of evidence–that is effective because it lets students develop a 'metalanguage' for analyzing writing. But if student reviewers are less able to say why a text appears disjointed, etc. or how it could be improved, then a teacher-student conference is important." Another respondent said, "Both are effective; for the short-term goal of getting a good grade on the paper at hand, the one-to-one works better, but perhaps for long-term, general growth as a writer, the peer conference is better because writers can see how real people react to confusing, unclear writing, and that makes a strong impression and provides motivation to write more clearly." One respondent who said that both methods are effective added, "But small groups without teacher guidance at the individual level is, I'm afraid, a cop-out. Peers simply do not know what we (presumably) know about the writing process."

New Instructors Should Use Peer Review

Thirty (97 percent) of the thirty-one respondents would recommend that a new writing instructor make use of peer review as part of writing instruction. Some respondents were quite emphatic in their recommendations while others gave more qualified answers. One respondent said, "Beyond the obvious goal of helping each other improve their writing, I think the peer groups have other benefits that are more intangible. Having a real audience fosters the sense of writing as genuine communication as nothing else can. I encourage them to discuss the concepts and learn from each other about all kinds of ideas. They get ideas for their own future writing. They find out that not everyone else is a fabulous writer–that they have similar frustrations with writing. They also are exposed to those students who take the same assignment they had and develop something really insightful and eloquent. Students actually become part of that community of writers we read about." One respondent who has had negative experiences with using peer reviewers said, "Despite my bad experiences with it, I know there are others who've found it very useful. I certainly think new teachers should try it out in a couple of different formats. They may find it very helpful and interesting." One respondent pointed out that "Peers listen to peers–you and I do it, too–but new writing instructors need to learn how to teach peer review–it doesn't just happen." Another respondent believes new instructors should use peer review "Just to begin the practice of de-centering the classroom from the beginning–it's a difficult transition to make." One respondent said that "whether I recommend this or not depends upon the teacher's personality. Peer reading may or may not suit what the teacher wants to do. Although I use peer reading in both comp. classes, many teachers find the second semester of peer reading a waste of time."

CONCLUSION

The original motivation for this survey was my own frustrations with what I saw as the failure of peer review to do what I hoped it would do: free me from the exhausting work of either reading drafts of students' papers or having individual conferences with students, something that is difficult to do while teaching four classes, two of which are writing classes. Since reader intervention is such an integral part of the process paradigm, I have always worried about the problem of giving feedback to all students. Making use of peer responders has not solved this problem for me. Other composition instructors seem to be more optimistic about this practice, though many do not see peer review as a way for writers to learn about writing or as a time-saver for instructors. They see peer review as a way for students to learn how to read critically. The dedication to teaching of the respondents to this survey and their willingness to work long and hard at what they do are impressive. I am amazed at the time and energy this hard-working group of professionals must put into their teaching.

When I was in graduate school in the early 1980s, one of my professors said that teaching writing as a process is much easier than teaching it as a product. I have always wondered how that could be possible given the demands of teaching writing as a process with multiple drafts and constant feedback. I now understand that my professor could say that because most of the people teaching in graduate programs do not teach first-year composition or only teach an occasional honor's section. According to the October 1998 *PMLA*, 96 percent of all writing classes in Ph.D.-granting English departments are taught by graduate students, part-timers, or full-time non-tenure-track faculty members (1157). Also, according to *PMLA*, "between one-half and two-thirds of the total number of professorial-rank appointments are located outside doctorate-granting research institutions" (1166).

Many of us end up teaching three to five classes a semester with half of those classes being writing classes. Not only do we have to teach our students how to write, we have to teach them how to read. What most of us do as composition instructors is complicated, demanding, and time-consuming. Yet in higher education, our work is marginalized at best. Those who teach us may do most of the research and may be among the most recognized in the profession, but they seldom do the work of a composition teacher, and they certainly cannot understand the time that is involved in teaching writing as a process. We do not need another paradigm shift in the teaching of composition; we need a revolution.

WORKS CITED

Bruffee, Kenneth A. *A Short Course in Writing Practical Rhetoric for Teaching Composition through Collaborative Learning*. 3 ed. Boston: Little, Brown, 1985.

Carter, Ronnie. *By Itself Peer Group Revision Has No Power.* ERIC, 1982. ED 226 350.

Elbow, Peter. *Writing without Teachers.* New York: Oxford UP, 1973.

George, Diana. "Working with Peer Groups in the Composition Classroom." *College Composition and Communication* 35.3 (1984): 320-26.

Gere, Anne Ruggles. *Writing Groups: History, Theory, and Implications.* Carbondale: Southern Illinois UP, 1987.

Gere, Anne Ruggles, and Robert D. Abbott. "Talking About Writing: The Language of Writing Groups." *Research in the Teaching of English* 19.4 (1985): 362-85.

Grimm, Nancy. "Improving Students' Responses to their Peers' Essays." *College Composition and Communication* 37.1 (1986): 91-94.

Hairston, Maxine. "The Winds of Change: Thomas Kuhn and the Revolution in the Teaching of Writing." *College Composition and Communication* 33.1 (1982): 76-88. Rpt. in *Rhetoric and Composition: A Sourcebook for Teachers and Writers.* Ed. Richard L. Graves. Upper Montclair: Boynton/Cook Publishers, 1984. 14-26.

Harris, Muriel. "Collaboration Is Not Collaboration Is Not Collaboration: Writing Center Tutorials vs. Peer Response Groups." *College Composition and Communication* 43.3 (1992): 369-83.

Holt, Mara. "The Value of Written Peer Criticism." *College Composition and Communication* 43.3 (1992): 384-92.

Murray, Donald. "Teach Writing as a Process not Product." *The Leaflet.* New England Association of Teachers of English, November 1972, 11-14. Rpt. in *Rhetoric and Composition: A Sourcebook for Teachers and Writers.* Ed. Richard L. Graves. Upper Montclair: Boynton/Cook Publishers, 1984. 89-92.

Newkirk, Thomas. "Direction and Misdirection in Peer Response." *College Composition and Communication* 35.3 (1984): 301-11.

Publications of the Modern Language Association of America. Final Report of the MLA Committee on Professional Employment. New York: *PMLA* 113.5 (October 1998): 1154-77.

Spear, Karen. *Sharing Writing: Peer Response Groups in English Classes.* Portsmouth: Boynton/Cook Publishers, 1988.

Spigelman, Candace. "Habits of the Mind: Historical Configurations of Textual Ownership in Peer Writing Groups." *College Composition and Communication* 49.2 (1998): 234-55.

Ziv, Nina. *Peer Groups in the Composition Classroom: A Case Study.* ERIC, 1983. ED 229 799.

9

The Service Myth: Why Freshman Composition Doesn't Serve "Us" or "Them"

Kerri Morris

My interest in discussing composition and the myth of the "service" course arises from years of frustration with teaching, theorizing about, and determining curricular goals for the freshman composition course. A former director of composition at a university where I once taught confessed that he no longer teaches the first-year course because he has no idea what he's supposed to do in it. I came to sympathize with him more fully than I thought possible after serving at another university on a committee to review the written objectives for our first-year course. We reviewed syllabi of every departmental member because each of us taught the course. The disparity among these documents—in fact the conflict among teaching methods, course descriptions, and course materials—seemed to suggest that we were teaching ten different courses. We were not teaching composition ten different ways, but teaching different disciplines. I doubt anyone—with course name removed from the syllabus—could have grouped all ten into a pile named English 111. Let me hasten to add that my respect for my former colleagues is immense. Each is intelligent; most are kind and dedicated, conscientious, and capable. As a group we were a microcosm of the lived experience of composition in higher education—chaos joined by a course number.

This chaos is systemic. As a discipline, composition has a variegated countenance, seeking to address disparate issues ranging from collaborative learning to the cognitive processes of writers and nature of the composing process, to pedagogical theories and taxonomies governing the universe of discourse. We have long been fascinated by our genealogy and our role in the academy, and have perennial interest in discussing composition's status as a skill or a content course. Recently, discussions of cultural theory, Marxism, and other critical theoretical approaches have filled our journals and syllabi. We write and discuss assessment, portfolio grading, grammar, learning disabilities, writing as therapy, and writing as self-discovery. The sheer variety of the uses of the term "composition," our tacit agreement to avoid defining it, and the lack of any common themes suggest an undisciplined discipline. It is unclear what we are talking about when we speak of the "discipline" of composition.

This chapter concerns the very nature of composition itself, to answer the question, "What is composition?" The answer is frequently that composition is all of these things. I hope to illustrate why that answer is insufficient, and, if true, reduces us to the status of a nondiscipline, to little more than a large gathering of interest groups paying dues to the same professional organization. First, I will explicate the problem, which finds its roots in the political, economic, institutional, and curricular arenas. Second, I will argue that this "diversity" is evidence that we have not become a discipline, lacking the necessary rules that shape such intellectual enterprises. Third, and finally, I will speculate both about ways to begin solving this problem and suggest some rules that might earn us disciplinary status.

THE PROBLEM OF "COMPOSITION" AND SERVICE

While the journals and conferences reveal a more complex story than the one I will tell, the story most frequently told to and by our students, their parents or families, legislators, trustees, and teachers seems to be that first-year composition serves as a foundation upon which our field is built, that it serves students, the society in which they live, and the curriculum as a whole. However, the nearly unavoidable role of composition as a service course is the source of our problems. In this section I will explain briefly why service defines us so completely; then I will discuss the problems that result from service; and finally I will argue that adherence to service limits us to pedagogical discussions, which are not enough to sustain a discipline.

Three aspects of our discipline bind us to a service mentality. Each has been thoroughly and recently discussed in journals and at conferences, and I will repeat them only briefly.[1]

1. Composition is unavoidably linked to freshman composition, responsible for more sections at most institutions than all the other composition-related courses combined.

2. Freshman composition is unavoidably linked to its unique national status as the only specific course required of all college students, and consequently serves to do something for the benefit of the academic community and society at large.

3. Freshman composition is unavoidably linked to a nonspecialist workforce of graduate students, part timers, nontenure-track faculty, and tenure-track faculty with specialization in literature or another field.[2]

Because these three traits so deftly determine the course, many departments have developed an "anything goes" policy of overseeing it. While many institutions have an "optional" syllabus or even a "required" syllabus, and most large institutions have adopted required textbooks, none with which I have been acquainted has imposed order on the course or incorporated substance into the course description. As a practical matter, the sheer number of people teaching the course defies this imposition, and as a personnel matter, respect for individuals—particularly the underpaid nontenure track—encourages acceptance of mushy policies. The familiar chant is: As long as you have a theory and your course is consistent with that theory, then all is well, the "I'm OK, You're OK" method of writing program administration.

We have a broad mission and a heavy mantle as teachers of all students in the university community, that is, if we teach first-year composition. Viewing the course from a service mentality is enabling, but offers only a wobbly foundation for the institutions where we serve and for our discipline. We do a job no one else wants to do when we put freshman composition at the center of our discipline. We have built up a mythology of its importance and worth and either really believe or convince ourselves of its value. And we're probably teaching the course better as a result. But we also wield power by doing the job. If it is in part what "housewives'" power (Grego and Thompson 67) of being needed that "empowers" us, it is also real power. As long as the course remains required for virtually every student in every institution, we ensure ourselves jobs, create ways to fund graduate programs, and become self-perpetuating. While others in the humanities have had to suffer enrollment variability, overflowing first-year courses offer stability in English departments and provide cover for teaching upper division courses. As Sharon Crowley argued at the 1998 CCCC, tenure-track members of the English department depend on this course and upon the adjuncts and students who teach it for the survival of their way of life: "I ask you to remember who it is that puts the bread on our table: the absent multitudes whose labor we exploit, whose labor allows us to enjoy positions as WPAs, researchers, and scholars" (A14). She estimates that 40 percent of lower division instruction is dependent on this workforce, a figure that must soar when focusing on the first-year course (A12).

Like staff at the local diner, however, we serve our customer/students a casserole of expectations from the masters we also serve—our own departments, myriad other departments on campus, curricular goals, and the communities in which these students will eventually work. Even if we wanted to, we couldn't possibly meet these expectations. We must be brave about this and decide why or if every college student needs this course, and we must be accountable for that decision. If we argue the course is necessary and that we are the ones to teach it, then we need to produce results that our various communities can rely on.

These links to a service mentality put us in the unenviable position of having constantly to justify ourselves. We have become an ends-oriented, or teleological, field. In order to maintain integrity, we feel (and should feel) the need to demonstrate the success of our results. Many English departments sponsor computer centers and writing centers, where presumably students can "gas up" with some extra help from the staff. Lately we have become obsessed with assessment, and theories about "what works" have risen to disciplinary status.

I feel certain that assessment is unnecessary and confident in saying that we have failed. Miserably. Most students who pass through our first-year course (or courses in some cases) write no better after the course than they did before, especially if we wait a year or more to test them. Businesses, public schools, accounting and engineering firms all complain loudly about the writing skills of their employees. Law schools and other graduate or professional schools join the chorus. All of which leads us back to our role as servants and to discussions of how to serve better, or to what we professionally call "pedagogy."

The service mentality efficiently and unavoidably links us to pedagogy, with the most common conversation among both untrained and trained practitioners focusing on how we *are* teaching writing, or how we *should be* teaching writing, or how you will be teach writing. Even the professional journals are dominated by pedagogical discussions, the lore of our field turning individual experience into disciplinary truth. There is nothing wrong with pedagogical discussions and quite a bit right about them. But this topic dominates the conversation, turning our attention firmly away from the "what" and toward the "how."

In the midst of the confusion, composition has become a pedagogical "discipline." Denise David et al., for instance, describe the discipline as "adrift" and floundering, but they propose only expressivist theories and teaching methods as solutions (524). This pedagogical turn—common in our field—gives rise to a conviction that we as a group have conflated the matter of *what* we teach with the concern of *how to* teach. This reduction separates us from the rest of the academy. If we look at another discipline, literature, for instance, the problem becomes clearer.

How we teach literature is rarely conflated with what we teach in a literature course. If a colleague asks, "What will you do in the Brit Lit II course?" the immediate response will be a list of literary texts written by British authors after the eighteenth century. Within these boundaries, there is much room for debate and conversation, of course. However, if Norman Mailer's *Naked and the Dead* is on the reading list, our colleague is likely to raise her eyebrows. If Copi's *Introduction to Logic* text is on the list, our colleague is likely to protest, or at least worry.

While there is loud debate about canon, there is little confusion about the boundaries that define or principles that influence a British literature course. In addition, there are many theories about literature that inform the teaching, the reading, and the content of the course, but they exist within the obvious and acknowledged outlines of British literature. Perhaps these clear outlines explain why teachers of British literature, while not always tenured or tenure-track specialists, are usually specifically educated in British literature. Anything clearly does not "go" in the discipline of literature, nor can just anyone teach in the field. Of course, debate punctuates discussions of that discipline. In fact, the debates are more public, more rigorous, more volatile, and more important because the discipline has a clearly understood and accepted self-definition. It also has earned more scholarly, academic clout.

The neglect of the "what" and the edification of the "how" have defined composition for ourselves and for the academic community within which we work, much to our professional detriment. We are considered just slightly more erudite than our education colleagues down the hall who are rumored to teach courses in constructing bulletin boards and writing on the chalkboard. Worse still, because of curricular chaos, conversations about what freshman composition is or should be doing have ceased altogether at the institutions with which I have acquaintance. It is difficult even to know how to get the conversation going or to know what we will discuss. We have been rendered inarticulate because we are no longer confident what it is that we are talking about.

In some cases, members of other departments have entered the conversation for us, making up committees to assess the course, determining the content of the course, and stating its objectives for us. Without a clear disciplinary sense of what constitutes "composition," questions about first-year composition will drive the discipline further into a corner. Our conversations will remain stuck in a defensive mode as a response to "comp-bashing," as John Schilb describes it at the beginning of a recent review of books about pedagogy (340-41). Meanwhile our own disciplinary discourse will continue to be of the tail-chasing variety, rehearsing the same debates, which are typically grounded in the "evidence" of experience.

THE RULES OF DISCIPLINE

The philosopher John Rawls clarifies the nature of the problem in his 1955 essay, "Two Concepts of Rules." Rawls proposes two types of rules: summary rules and rules of practice. In the Summary Conception, rules follow action and are "rules of thumb," maxims, general guidelines. Each person in this view "is always entitled to reconsider the correctness of a rule and to question whether or not it is proper to follow it in a particular case" (285). In the Practice Conception, rules are prior to practice, offering a system or pattern of rules that define the practice. People come under the authority of the rules in the Practice Conception:

It is the mark of a practice that being taught how to engage in it involves being instructed in the rules which define it, and that appeal is made to those rules to correct the behavior of those engaged in it . . . . Thus it is essential to the notion of a practice that the rules are publicly known and understood as definitive, and it is essential also that the rule of practice can be taught and can be acted upon to yield a coherent practice. (286)

It seems to me that we are operating within a Summary Conception of Rules when we reduce our discipline to a pedagogical one. "How we teach," what Stephen M. North has called practitioner lore (21-55), is a process by which we determine rules after the experience of walking into a classroom, deciding what method will "work" best. Because each person may develop her own "rules of thumb," determining the correctness of past rules for current situations, she may determine her own actions subjectively—for instance, that the study of grammatical principles followed by drills has helped her composition students write better.

The teleological force of being defined by summary rules—where ends justify means—undermines our disciplinary status and transforms us into what "they" have wanted us to be from the beginning: utilitarian and itinerant teachers of skills. As such, we are left floundering, attempting to "prove" that the portfolio method improves student writing or that Marxist cultural theories improve critical thinking and writing. We are forced to demonstrate what few others in the humanities are asked to. While philosophers probably hope that teaching ethics will strengthen their students' ethical behaviors, no one argues for the course on those grounds. Instead, ethics is seen as important for the curriculum on disciplinary grounds. Meanwhile we have become what Richard Marius calls "practical" because of the "death of rhetoric as a discipline" (466, 471).

A further trouble with summary rules in composition is that the "success" or perceived success of a method and the method itself is left up to the teacher and not governed by or even necessarily informed by prior rules. Rules have no force. In fact, each time a person questions a rule or changes a rule, she also challenges the nature of the discipline itself. Every question becomes metadisciplinary. For "disciplines" operating under a Summary Conception, it's a new world every morning.

In contrast, when we operate under a Practice Conception of Rules, we legitimize ourselves through public self-definition of a practice whose rules have force and whose nature is acknowledged by all participants. To be a participant in this kind of practice is, in fact, to be knowledgeable of and proficient in its rules. The rules of practice proceed our walking into the classroom. The Practice Conception of rules offers many advantages: its participants must be specifically educated about the practice; the authority of the rules themselves determine actions, causing consistency and predictability; the rules are public and definitive, allowing competing theories within the practice to enrich rather than threaten it.

Instead of recreating a discipline each time we confront conflict, the Practice Conception demands that our questions and concerns fall clearly within the practice. The question, "Should I teach grammatical principles, followed by drills in my Brit Lit II course?" would not only lack sense in the discipline of literature, it would never be asked by an educated participant. More likely, an educated participant might ask, "Should I teach mostly women authors in my Brit Lit II course?" This question is not only sensible, but debate over it has enlarged and improved the discipline.

For our own discipline, the question has been more troubling. "Should I teach grammar with drills in my freshman composition course?" is usually followed by the answer, "No, we've found that it interferes with improving students' writing." Or, among the adjuncts with whom I teach, more likely the answer will be, "How can you not teach grammar? They don't know what they're doing. It certainly helps my students." However, the question is much more sensibly debated over disciplinary rules or definitions. "Is grammar an intrinsic part of what we do in composition? If so, should it be introduced in the first year or later?" Surely no one doubts the importance and worth of grammar as a field of study. What many of us do doubt, however, is whether it needs to be formally taught to nonmajors, and especially to first-year composition students. The answer to that question simply must move beyond the subjective and utilitarian world that composition has become.

If rules must be established prior to practice in order to have a legitimate discipline, and if those rules must be publicly known and understood as definitive, then composition is not a discipline. Instead we have a group open to anyone who teaches writing or has an interest in teaching writing, regardless of preparation or knowledge. We have no more or less disciplinary weight than Culinary Arts or Creative Writing—all I might add that have a value and lofty character of their own. Note, however, that if we are in the same category as these groups, which are also defined by the Summary Conception of Rules, then our hiring practices should change dramatically. Instead of scholars or specialists, we should hire successful writers, just as flute teachers must be accomplished in their art and instructors of chefs must be chefs themselves. We will become practitioners of an art rather than practitioners of a discipline.

However, if we want to be a discipline—and I urge that we follow this path—then we must set about establishing a Practice Conception of Rules, with the authority and coherence that they afford.

NEEDED REFORM AND RULES OF PRACTICE

My recommendations for reform are not new and have been suggested by many others, but if put into practice would cause huge upheaval to English Departments, particularly at the graduate level, to textbook publishers, and to the academy in general:

1. The teaching of writing needs to be termed a skill for which every faculty member shares the responsibility of teaching. As the Boyer Commission suggested in 1998, all of us teaching in higher education should make writing "a central component" of

our courses and writing "should be linked to course work" (V, 1).

2. Abolish the first-year writing course and any courses at the sophomore level that are really freshman composition delayed. If teaching writing is everyone's responsibility, then we must drive that point home by eliminating this course that suggests writing can be learned in one or two courses taught by English teachers.

3. Move composition and rhetoric out of English departments. By doing this, we will eliminate with one stroke the second-class-citizen status we have come to endure and will be forced to obtain disciplinary status on our own terms.

4. Establish a discipline-based first-year course that is a part of the general education requirement, but not a course that every student is required to take. The course should be an introduction to rhetoric and composition.

5. Continue to associate the discipline of rhetoric and composition with serious attention to pedagogy. However, make clear that the discipline's basis is no more about how to teach than is any other discipline in the humanities.

6. Encourage every colleague within the academic community to pay closer attention to pedagogy, sharing with them the treasure trove of riches that we have compiled over the past several decades, including collaborative learning, one-to-one conferencing, peer editing, process-based teaching, and portfolio grading.

7. Eliminate the nomenclature of "writing teacher" as a description of someone whose discipline is rhetoric and composition.

The economic effect of making such changes is enough for most people to ignore them at first glance. But the time has come for us to suffer these consequences. We can no longer base graduate programs and their funding on unfair labor practices, which most part-time and untenured persons suffer under. We can no longer churn out graduates who will never get academic jobs and for whom teaching an ill-conceived course at less than minimum wage without benefits is not enough like the Peace Corps to satisfy, despite what a former MLA chair has suggested. We can no longer tolerate a textbook industry that profits from an ill-conceived course taught to many students in no economic position to support the industry. We can no longer claim that freshman English is accomplishing something when it neither represents our disciplinary interests nor accomplishes what it claims to do. Instead, we need to regroup and begin anew to clarify ourselves as a discipline.

More difficult, however, is the process of determining our Rules of Practice, though not impossible. By rules, I do not mean the handbook type of rules, with which we are all too familiar. Instead, I mean the rules that define us, in fact that preceded us, as a discipline. I suggest the following as a beginning:

1. Rhetoric and composition are concerned with the contextual nature of discourse.

2. Rhetoric and composition are concerned with the ways in which language shapes the culture and culture, in turn, shapes the language.

3. Rhetoric and composition are concerned with the production and reception of discourse.

4. Rhetoric and composition pay attention to effects on audiences of discourse.

5. Rhetoric and composition are concerned with the ways through which producers of discourse represent themselves.

6. Rhetoric and composition are concerned with the way discourse makes its appeal to audiences.

7. Rhetoric and composition both are interdisciplinary by nature, inquiry-driven like philosophy and text-focused like literature.

These rules are only suggestions, a place to begin the process of establishing a disciplinary charter. While my suggested reforms are perhaps extreme, my intent is not. Rather, I want to reclaim our ethic of inquiry, analysis, and interpretation to serve our students with an intrinsic disciplinary merit rather than to serve them with false claims and expectations that will consistently fail them.

NOTES

1. See Sharon Crowley's "A Personal Essay on Freshman Composition" for a particularly helpful discussion of some of these points.

2. Clearly, first-year composition is taught by specialists as well, both in adjunct and tenure-track status, but the strong link to nonspecialists is also evident, most of whom are underpaid and under supported by their departments and their institutions. For a helpful discussion of the adjunct work force, see Trainor and Godley's "After Wyoming."

WORKS CITED

The Boyer Commission on Educating Undergraduates in the Research University. *Reinventing Undergraduate Education: A Blueprint for America's Research Universities.* http://notes.cc.sunysb.edu/Pres/boyer.nsf April 24, 1998.

Crowley, Sharon. "Excerpt from 'Early Concerns of CCCC.'" *College, Composition and Communication* 50 (September 1998): A12-4.

———. "A Personal Essay on Freshman Composition." *Pre/Text* 12:3-4 (1991): 156-76.

David, Denise, et al. "Seeking Common Ground." *College Composition and Communication* 46 (December 1995): 522-32.

Dobrin, Sid. "The Politics of Theory-Building and Anti-Intellectualism in Composition." *Composition Forum* 6 (Summer 1995): 90-99.

Fleming, David. "Rhetoric as a Course of Study." *College English* 61 (November 1998): 169-91.

Grego, Rhonda and Nancy Thompson. "Repositioning Remediation: Renegotiating Composition's Work in the Academy." *College Composition and Communication* 47 (February 1996): 62-84.

Lazere, Donald. "Teaching the Political Conflicts: A Rhetorical Schema." *College Composition and Communication* 43 (May 1992): 194-213.

Marius, Richard. "Composition Studies." *Redrawing the Boundaries*. New York: MLA, 1992. 466-81.

North, Stephen M. *The Making of Knowledge in Composition: Portrait of an Emerging Field*. Upper Montclair, NJ: Boynton/Cook Publishers, Inc., 1987.

Rawls, John. "Two Concepts of Rules." *20th Century Ethical Theory*. Eds. Steven M. Cahn and Joram G. Haber. Englewood Cliffs, NJ: Prentice-Hall, 1995. 273-90.

Schilb, John. "Histories of Pedagogy." Rev. of *Feminist Accused of Sexual Harassment*, by Jane Gallop, *Pedagogy, Democracy, and Feminism: Rethinking the Public Sphere*, by Adriana Hernandez, *The Formation of College English: Rhetoric and Belles Lettres in the British Cultural Provinces*, by Thomas P. Miller, *Writing in an Alien World: Basic Writing and the Struggle for Equality in Higher Education*, by Deborah Mutnick, and *Pedagogy: Disturbing History, 1819-1929*, ed. Mariolina Rizzi Salvatori. *College English* 61 (January 1999): 340-46.

Trainor, Jennifer Seibel and Amanda Godley. "After Wyoming: Labor Practices in Two University Writing Programs." *College Composition and Communication* 50.2 (December 1998): 153-81.

Preparing Composition Students for Writing in Their Careers

Donald Samson

As a composition student a long time ago, my climactic assignment was to tell the story of Orwell's "Shooting an Elephant" in the style Lawrence used in *Twilight in Italy* and in the style Hemingway used in *In Our Time*. A little over a year later, I left college and worked as a technical writer for a manufacturer of outdoor lighting equipment and traffic signals. I described how various parts were cast, machined, and assembled into finished products. To determine a product's cost, I described very specifically on an operation sheet the raw materials or components in the product and the steps necessary to create it. I had to be concise, because each letter or number I wrote had to be hand keypunched for loading into a computer. Imitating the styles of Lawrence and Hemingway, and my other composition assignments, had done little to prepare me for writing outside academe. Over the last thirty-five years, some say, the situation hasn't improved much.

The gulf between academic and nonacademic writing has widened. Heather MacDonald says that current writing instruction is "not just an irrelevance, it is positively detrimental to a student's development . . . an indigestible stew of 1960s liberationist zeal, 1970s deconstructivist nihilism, and 1980s multicultural proselytizing" (3). In a widely circulated article that appeared in *U. S. News and World Report*, "The Answer Is 45 Cents," John Leo surveys reports of graduates' writing skills, citing an article in *English Leadership Quarterly* "urging teachers to encourage intentional errors in English as 'the only way to end its oppression of linguistic minorities and learning writers'" (14). Leo quotes James Sledd's opinion in *College English* that Standard English is "'essentially an instrument of domination'" (14). For Sledd, the villain is the "military-industrial-educational complex," which aims "to maintain and extend corporate control of schooling and–more generally–corporate control of the accumulation, storage, and dissemination of knowledge" (168).

Writing program staff have moved beyond confrontational attacks on "the executives of the transnational corporations and their flunkies" (Sledd 173) to see the importance of gaining support from business and determining how to prepare students for the writing they will do in their work as college graduates. *Programs That Work* describes several such programs, including that at the University of Chicago, where faculty recognize that their graduates will not only write in their work but will go on to become "the managers who will have to pass on the writing of those they supervise" (Williams and Colomb 87).

Clearly, most of our students will work outside academia after they graduate, and our function as writing instructors should be in part to prepare them to succeed in the writing they will have to do–and have them as allies of our programs because we helped them prepare to succeed.

Not only in Writing Across the Curriculum and Writing in the Disciplines programs has increasing attention been paid to preparing students for writing in their work. The rapid growth of undergraduate and graduate programs in technical writing attests to increased attention to preparing students for nonacademic writing. However, despite more opportunities for students to prepare for writing in their work, many students receive no formal instruction in writing after first-year composition. Many, if not most, college and university students will not take a writing course after composition. All the writing instruction they will get to prepare themselves for writing in their careers is what they get in composition. If we want to empower our students for success, we should teach them how to write for nonacademic audiences.

To determine how composition might prepare students better for writing in their careers as well as in their studies, we should consider some generalizations about composition students and composition instruction, and some specific approaches for composition courses. The generalizations here have many exceptions, but they can help us consider how to prepare students for writing in their work.

SOME GENERALIZATIONS ABOUT COMPOSITION

Most composition students are straight out of high school and have limited work experience. Some have served in the military or have held full-time jobs, and there are increasing numbers of these "nontraditional" students with work experience and "life experience." Such students usually raise the level of discussion in composition classes, but, for most of us, a composition class means twenty to twenty-five (or more, unfortunately) teenagers in transition. Most composition students have limited familiarity with career-type work and therefore do not recognize the importance of developing writing skills for their work.

Most composition students aren't going to be English majors, much less English teachers. Most composition instructors no longer assign analyses of literature, but some still do. Others have students writing poetry in expository writing classes, and personal narrative and expressive writing are common approaches. Clearly, such assignments can help students develop writing skills, but they are far removed from the types of writing our graduates will do in their work. Practice presenting information and argument to an audience other than the instructor would be more relevant.

Many composition students don't know what they want to do in their work after college; those who do usually find themselves working in another field, often doing something they never imagined themselves doing. When they understand the realities of the job market (and Career Services staff can help them through class presentations), students become more receptive to the idea of preparing for a range of possible vocations.

Many composition students didn't like English in high school. Often, they had to write essays on literary works they didn't understand. Many didn't read well or never really learned to do more than tell the words. Many couldn't spell and wrote papers that received failing grades for spelling errors. Nothing frustrates students more than failing when they are trying, and many writing students failed in high school (and fail in college) not because they can't write but because they can't read, or can't edit or proofread. When we fail to determine why an individual student has trouble writing, we can't do much to help. All we can do is drop back to the mass-production approach that administrators seem to promote. And when the student is a first-year student who feels awkward about approaching an instructor for help, it becomes all the more difficult to get to the bottom of a writing problem.

Most composition students can write better than they (and we) think they can, when we help them understand the writing process and invite them to write about what they care about. However, we need to help them recognize that in their work they will write about what they know, not what they care about, and they will write to communicate information and/or persuade, not to explore their thoughts and feelings or to develop as thinkers and writers.

Most composition students have little familiarity with the types of documents created in business and government agencies: proposals, reports (progress, final, monthly, interim, case, feasibility, recommendation, evaluation, incident, trip, planning, annual, etc), letters, memos, instructions (including hardware and software documentation), resumes, briefing materials, speeches, financial statements, budgets, articles, monographs, books, and so on. Just skimming the indexes of three or four good texts in technical or business writing will reveal the range of types of documents that composition students will go on to write or contribute to in their work. Most composition students are not familiar with such documents; neither are many composition instructors.

Most composition instructors are more comfortable when they have students write the types of documents that the instructors themselves are familiar with:

personal narratives, argumentative essays, and research papers (which very few composition students will go on to write in their work). Unfamiliar with what their students will have to write when they graduate, many instructors rely on academic assignments–research papers, even analyses of literature. This approach prepares students to do academic writing, especially if they major in the liberal arts. But how many students write research papers these days outside of composition courses?

Although training in academic writing serves a valuable purpose, it can only do so much to prepare students for writing in nonacademic settings, where writers have a different audience and purpose. Students write over and over for an expert audience: an instructor. Their reader knows more about the subject than they do, or knows better how to write that kind of assignment. Professionals in business and government usually write for readers who know less than they do about what they are writing about. Students write in school to show how much they know about a subject; the primary use for writing in schools is for testing, of course. Professionals, though, write to communicate information to readers who know less than they do about the subject. It is essential for students (and professionals) to recognize these differences in audience and purpose to be successful in nonacademic writing.

Much student writing is writer-centered. Good nonacademic writing, however, is reader-centered. Although writing writer-centered prose can help a writer get started, as Linda Flower noted (1979), writers in professional settings need to write reader-centered prose. Students write to show how much they know; nonacademic writers (successful ones, at least) write not to show how much they know but to inform their audience. At least some of the assignments in a composition course should help students learn how to convert writer-centered prose to reader-centered prose.

Many composition courses don't teach students how to write good sentences, much less how to analyze and improve writing at the sentence level. Students are warned about comma splices and fragments and run-on sentences, but in most composition courses students don't study syntax and style enough that they understand the different ways to state a sentence, much less enjoy capturing the nuance that understanding syntax permits.

Many composition courses are taught by the English faculty least prepared to teach writing–graduate students one or two years removed from the academic writing they did as English majors (and still doing academic writing in their course work or on a thesis or dissertation), junior faculty not long removed from work on a dissertation, and experienced faculty who would rather be teaching something else. Many of us have actually heard an administrator say, "Anyone can teach composition." That's true. But then, anyone can do brain surgery. The trick is to do it well. Composition is hard to teach well, for reasons reviewed in these generalizations, but sometimes it is taught by those least prepared or inclined to teach it.

Many composition instructors have little experience doing nonacademic writing, the matter-of-fact, unadorned, straightforward prose that is at the heart of good written communication in business and government. So it is difficult for them to prepare their students to write successfully in those environments. To compound the problem, many composition teachers, especially part-timers and nonprofessorial level staff, are overworked (as well as underpaid).

SOME APPROACHES FOR COMPOSITION

In composition courses, we might do some things differently to prepare students better for the writing they will do in their careers.

Have Students Write Reader-Centered Prose

The tendency to ask students to write about personal experience may stem in part from instructors' fear that students don't know much except what's current, and that when most students write about current issues, even less controversial ones, they quickly get in over their heads. So students are asked to write about personal experience, in the hope that introspection and reflection will produce something of substance, and it often does. However, in their careers no supervisor will ask them to analyze their personal experience and write about it as part of their work. Instead, our graduates will be proposing and reporting on projects, disseminating information to clients or the general public, writing letters, and so on. Writing about personal experience in composition doesn't prepare them to do that. It can motivate writers and make them feel good about themselves and about us (we're interested in and care about their experience), but it misleads them into thinking that their experience is what is important. To be successful when they write in professional settings, they must remember that they write not for themselves but for their readers and the organization they represent.

Have Students Present Information to Different Audiences

When students write to other students who know less than they do about what they are talking about, they must consider how to approach an audience other than the expert (the teacher). This "lay" audience more closely resembles the audiences they will write for in their careers. Writing for less-informed readers, students learn that they need to provide background information, avoid or define unfamiliar terms, motivate the reader to read the piece, slow the pace, simplify the style, and use other techniques. Toby Fulwiler has stressed the importance of students' awareness of other audiences, including "an external, outside-the-classroom audience" (24).

Some of the information and argument we invite students to present should come from their own discipline. Suggesting Writing-to-Learn strategies here may seem adverse to what is being argued, as Writing-to-Learn focuses on the writer, not the reader. However, the aim of such programs–to allow students to explore and inform themselves about their subject–is consistent with an emphasis on writing to inform readers. Students should be encouraged to present information from their specialty (or a course) to less-knowledgeable readers, as they will usually do when they write in their careers.

We should teach students how to write for readers who do not know much about their subject. A common assignment in the second semester is a set of instructions explaining how to do something they know how to do but the reader doesn't. To avoid students' choosing to explain how to tie a shoe or make a pizza, the instructor might specify that the procedure come from their field or one of their courses, or from work in their field.

Another assignment often used to introduce the concept of a different audience and to prepare students for work is the resume. The resume assignment doesn't work well, however, for composition students (but high school and even middle school students in Virginia write one as an assignment). Most composition students have so little education and experience relevant to an entry-level position in their field that they must focus on personal information. The exercise usually does not prepare students to write a professional resume, because they're just not ready to have a resume. Similarly, many composition students aren't ready for collaborative writing projects, but composition should involve some collaborative work, as it is the norm in nonacademic writing. Peer review is a good introduction to collaborative writing, though, and after peer review is working well collaborative projects might be assigned.

Several writers have examined how instructors invite students to address nonacademic audiences in writing assignments. In their analysis of writing assignments in an anthropology course, Anne Herrington and Deborah Cadman discuss the instructor's emphasis on writing for nonacademic audiences. Of the four assignments, one article reported research to other specialists, and the next reworked that information into an article designed for a general audience such as the readers of *Smithsonian* or *Natural History* (193-96). Lester Faigley and Kristine Hansen suggest that "differences in the expectations and beliefs that readers bring to a text tend to be ignored in freshman English courses . . . [but] teachers of courses on writing in the disciplines . . . collide head on with these differences, which handbook notions of correctness and narrowly construed ideas of process cannot accommodate" (148). Anne Herrington's discussion of reports in two chemical engineering courses, Lab and Design, examines students' and instructors' perceptions of the audiences, who differed in their knowledge of the subject, and reinforces the need to define audiences carefully (109-13). Douglas Eagles reports using peer review "to make the students aware that they were writing for the audience that would judge their work for the rest of their careers: their peers" (20). How instructors might vary the audiences of related documents is exemplified in William Mullin's discussion of assignments in physics in *Programs That Work* (212-14). Anne Herrington's discussion of lab reports illustrates how the purposes of related documents might differ for different audiences (114-16).

Teach Students How to Use Illustrations

Except in engineering, technical communication, and scattered courses in business and science, students are not taught how to use graphics to present information. However, anyone who reads a business or government agency report, or an article in a newspaper or a magazine, recognizes how much writers rely on illustrations. They present information that is difficult to present in text, break up the text, invite readers into the discussion, emphasize important information, and so on. Many composition texts have no more illustrations than an occasional cartoon, although discussion of graphics for papers and reports will soon become common in composition texts. Composition courses should stress communication through illustrations, as classes in the sciences do with lab reports, because it is only in some academic writing that the words do it all.

Teach Students How to Use Peer Review Productively

Peer review of drafts and final documents is standard in professional settings, and students should be taught how to review peers' drafts. Gail Hearn's discussion of peer review of assignments in ecology (*Programs That Work* 148-54), which provides an excellent model, establishes the connection between the peer review and collaboration that students do and their work as professionals.

Peer review of a draft should address content, organization, format, and appropriateness for the audience. However, composition students often mistake peer review of a draft for proofreading, so the instructor must clarify these steps in the writing process. Students will still tend to look for spelling mistakes and awkward phrasing, just as some less useful reviewers do in business and government. We should encourage students to avoid addressing such issues, possibly by asking that all comments be made on a review sheet, with no notes on the draft.

Peer review will be difficult when surface errors distract the reviewer, so we should stress that each draft be well edited and proofread. Unfortunately, many writing teachers still use the term "rough draft" to refer to a draft prepared for peer review. No one but the writer should see a rough draft. For review, writers should prepare a first draft that is as good as they can make it on their own. When students bring to class for review a draft that has been well written, edited, and proofread, reviewers will not be distracted by sentence-level problems. Then, with training and practice, they will be able to make more useful suggestions about content, organization, format, and appropriateness for the audience. We need to help students learn how to use peer review effectively and be able to rely on themselves and their peers, rather than a supervisor, for critical comment on a first draft.

Have Students Research Writing in Their Field

Having students find out about the writing that professionals in their field do can be very useful. A common assignment in professional writing classes is a report on what professionals in the student's field write–the types of documents and their audience, purpose, frequency, length, and so on. For this assignment, students often interview professionals in their field (academics as well as nonacademics) to gather information. This introduces students to the way professionals in business and government gather information–not by going to the library or getting on the Internet.

Such an assignment can be difficult for those composition students who have no idea what they want to do in their careers, but they might be encouraged to choose a field for the purpose of this assignment, and doing so can help them see whether they might be interested in that field. When students have a sense of what they will need to be able to write in their careers, and when they have heard from professionals other than English instructors how important writing is, they often work harder in writing courses.

Encourage, but Limit, Revision

We all encourage revision, but we should discourage more than one revision after we have commented on a paper. Some instructors allow a student to revise over and over until the student is satisfied with the grade the latest revision has earned. At first this policy seems good, as students should be encouraged to revise and polish their work through drafts, but it may create a dangerous sense that a writer doesn't have to get it right the first or second or third time. No employer wants an employee drafting a document repeatedly, although in some ill-managed situations that does happen, as Susan Kleimann has shown (1991), especially in government agencies.

We need to encourage students to make their first draft as good as they can make it on their own. The second draft should be as good as they can make it with reviewers' comments and subsequent revising, editing, and proofreading. And the final draft must be as good as they can make it using the instructor's (supervisor's) comments. In an efficient business or agency, writers don't work a document over and over, and we should not lead students to think that they will be able to revise a document continuously until they get it right.

Insist on Correctness

Mistakes in spelling, grammar, and usage damage professional documents, and we should help students understand the need for correctness. Too often, instructors dismiss spelling errors as "typos," suggesting that they are not that significant. However, some instructors and programs have had a "three spelling mistakes and it's automatically an F" policy. Clearly, there's disagreement among instructors about how significant spelling and other such errors are. In business and government, however, there's no disagreement. For Gail Hearn, in the report on scientific research "there can be absolutely no error in spelling, grammar, or English usage," because "skillfully written, well-illustrated, and error-free manuscripts come to represent to the stranger reading the report the quality of scientific research" (149). Julia Harding stresses that in business, "the writing must be perfect . . . business writers jeopardize their credibility if they commit errors in spelling, word choice, format, and sentence structure" (209). In professional documents, errors in spelling, grammar, or usage suggest sloppiness or ignorance, and some readers question the accuracy of the information in a document with errors in presentation. So it is important that we help students understand that correctness does matter.

As Toby Fulwiler and Art Young rightly note, "teaching grammar and usage is not teaching writing" (292), but we must teach grammar and usage as we address editing. In writing in business and government, correctness is essential to create the sense that the organization pays attention to detail. We should also encourage students to pay attention to "little things" such as formatting, spacing, justification, and margins. We should require proper margins, spacing, type font and size, and page numbering, and the reference format that is standard in the writer's field, not necessarily MLA. Students should be encouraged to identify and learn the proper reference format(s) in their field–and if they don't have a major, they should learn APA format, as it is so widely used.

We should teach sentence structure and punctuation to all students, and teach grammar individually as needed. Students need only a few punctuation guidelines to cover most of the internal punctuation needed in papers and reports, and it is easy enough to teach students how to punctuate if the instructor can talk about parts of speech, phrases, and especially main clauses. Recent approaches to teaching punctuation, such as John Dawkins' (1995), simplify concepts and emphasize the role of grammar and punctuation in clarifying meaning. Similarly, five or six guidelines about sentence structure can help students control their writing. Richard Lanham's "Who's Kicking Who?" is a good way into discussing word order and emphasis, and it allows the instructor to move into guidelines for effective sentences (1-6).

Web sites such as Jack Lynch's provide instruction in grammar and usage; a listing of other such sites can be found at Linda DeVore's site and in library databases. Articles such as those in *Newsweek* by Charles Larson (1995) and Patricia O'Conner (1996), and by Frank Grazian in *Public Relations Quarterly* (1997), address grammar issues with humor and are entertaining, as are William Safire's columns in *The New York Times Magazine* and whatever Steve Martin writes about writing in *The New York Times Magazine* or *The New Yorker*. Such materials, which are easily accessed, can encourage students to think about grammar, punctuation, and usage and keep instruction in these areas from being the parsing and dull memorization that bored so many of them (and us).

Avoid Using Letter Grades

Very few people outside academia use letter grades to evaluate a document, and to prepare students for writing in their careers we should evaluate their work the way it will be evaluated by a supervisor or client, with evaluative comments or a point system. Most composition students receive far more thorough feedback on their writing than they will get in their careers, but the letter grade an assignment receives may be all that the student really pays attention to. We need to encourage students to solicit and consider readers' responses to their writing rather than risk discouraging such behavior by assigning a letter grade, even to an excellent paper.

Make Sure Students Are Computer-Literate

We should encourage students to become skilled with a word-processing program and familiar with at least one operating system. More and more students enter composition courses competent in word processing, but many still do not. Because most will be doing their own typing until they are well into their careers, they need to be proficient with this writing tool, and unless the school offers tutorials, composition becomes the place for students to learn how to process words. Instructors need to be familiar with common programs such as Word and WordPerfect to help some students learn the basics and to help all students become more proficient. Instructors need to be able to explain the limitations of writing aids such as spelling and grammar checkers.

Encourage Students to Identify Their Subject, Audience, and Purpose

Most students focus their writing better when they identify clearly in their introduction the paper's subject, audience, and purpose (unless the audience and purpose are understood from the assignment, as in many traditional composition and academic writing assignments). Some instructors argue that we should discourage students from "mapping the particular (concrete) language of the assignment into the opening paragraph of the paper" (Williams and Colomb 102), but a clear indication of the subject, audience, and purpose of a document in its introduction is standard in business and government writing.

Teach Students How to Read

We ask students to read, assuming they can. However, too many composition students read poorly. Rightly or not, most people assume that English class is the place for them to learn how to read better. Few composition instructors, however, have been trained to teach reading. The ability to read and the ability to write are inextricably linked, and we cannot assume that we can help students develop one ability when most of us are not qualified to help them develop the other. Instruction in teaching reading should be a significant component in any program in teaching writing.

Drop the Research Paper from Composition

Outside of English and a few other programs in the Humanities, fewer and fewer instructors are requiring a traditional research paper. When instructors outside of English assign research papers, they often complain about the quality of the papers they get and fault composition instructors generally. They complain that the students haven't been taught how to do research (and write up research) in that field–and of course, they're right. So unless we teach discipline-specific research papers and the methodology they involve, perhaps we shouldn't try to teach first-year students how to write a research paper. As Lester Faigley and Kristine Hansen point out, however, teaching students how to write such a paper requires that teachers learn about the discipline, not just the characteristic parts of a report on research in that discipline (149).

Most English instructors are understandably reluctant to teach students how to do research in biology or finance. As WAC programs have shown, it makes sense for the biology or finance instructor to teach the students how to do research and then teach them how to write it up. Students writing the review of literature for a research article in a field in which they have done research will be more motivated than students in second-semester composition, because they see its applicability. "Writing development is, in part, context-dependent," found Lucille McCarthy, based on a study of a student writer's work in different courses, and "skills mastered in one situation . . . did not automatically transfer to new contexts with differing problems and language and differing amounts of knowledge that [the writer] controlled" (152). When we teach students from many majors about research, we can only generalize, but in writing in their majors, especially in the sciences and business, they need specifics about research.

Reconsider Requiring Composition

To prepare students better for nonacademic and academic writing, we should design and teach courses that students will elect rather than have to take. If composition were no longer a requirement, students who do not need it–and there are many who did not–would have two (semester) or three (quarter) courses for other interests. Many who needed it would elect it and approach it with more enthusiasm. Many who needed it but avoided it would write poorly in courses in their major, and their major professors would have to address the problem rather than just blame writing teachers. Absolved of responsibility for poor student writing, English department and writing faculty could go back to what they were trained to do–to teaching the English language and literature in English, and teaching writing to students who want to learn to write better.

True, English departments and writing programs might have to reduce their staff, but the part-timers and temporaries who are exploited by departments on a term-to-term basis would be encouraged to find full-time or less seasonal/migratory work. And if some tenured faculty had to be let go due to financial exigency, surely each English department has a few tenured faculty (often senior and well paid) who no longer contribute but have not yet retired. Getting rid of the requirement for composition could have other benefits too–Kristine Hansen has recently explored them (1998). Perhaps the best reason to do away with the composition requirement is to refuse to accept the idea that our students don't know what's good for them but we faculty do–not the best approach to ensure a positive attitude toward composition.

CONCLUSION

Composition is perhaps the most difficult writing course to teach well, so we should be staffing sections with experienced staff. Composition should no longer be a probation where students earning MAs or Ph.D.s in literature or cultural studies or critical theory do hard time to learn how to teach. (Has anyone ever demonstrated that teaching composition makes such specialists better teachers of their specialty?) If we want students to improve their writing skills and enjoy writing, and to take more courses in writing, language, and literature, and to succeed in their writing in their work, we need to give them our best teachers. If we cannot staff all sections with experienced writing teachers who know about nonacademic writing, such teachers should help new composition instructors decide what to teach in composition and learn how to teach it. And we should prepare our students for nonacademic as well as academic writing. Writing skills will be too important in our students' careers for us not to.

WORKS CITED

Dawkins, John. "Teaching Punctuation as a Rhetorical Tool." *College Composition and Communication* 46 (1995): 533-48.

DeVore, Linda. Grammar NOW! URL: www.grammarnow.com.

Eagles, Douglas. "Writing in Environmental Zoology." In Fulwiler, Toby, and Young, Art, eds., *Programs That Work*, 20-21.

Faigley, Lester, and Kristine Hansen. "Learning to Write in the Social Sciences." *College Composition and Communication* 36 (1985): 184-99.

Flower, Linda. "Writer-Based Prose: A Cognitive Basis for Problems in Writing." *College English* 41 (1979): 19-37.

Fulwiler, Toby. "Writing Is Everybody's Business." *Phi Kappa Phi Journal* Fall 1985: 21-4.

Grazian, Frank. "Who Really Cares about Grammar and Usage?" *Public Relations Quarterly* 42.3 (1997): 5-6.

Hansen, Kristine. "Serving Up Writing in a New Form." *College Composition and Communication* 49 (1998): 260-64.

Harding, Julia. "Writing in Business." In *Programs That Work*, 209-11.

Hearn, Gail. "Writing in Ecology and the Ecology of Writing." In *Programs That Work*, 148-54.

Herrington, Anne. "Writing in Academic Settings: A Study of the Contexts for Writing in Two College Chemical Engineering Courses." In Bazerman, Charles, and David Russell, eds., *Landmark Essays on Writing Across the Curriculum*. Davis, CA: Hermagoras Press, 1994. 97-124.

———, and Deborah Cadman. "Peer Review and revising in an Anthropology Course: Lessons for Learning." *College Composition and Communication* 42 (1991): 184-99.

Kleimann, Susan. "The Complexity of Workplace Review." *Technical Communication* 38 (1991): 520-26

Lanham, Richard. *Revising Prose*. New York: Scribner's, 1979.

Larson, Charles. "Its Academic, or Is It? Soon, no one will care about correct grammar, and the apostrophe will disappear into infinity." *Newsweek* 126.19 (1995): 31.

Leo, John. "The Answer Is 45 Cents." *U. S. News and World Report* 122.15 (1997): 14.

Lynch, Jack. Grammar and Style Notes. URL: www.english.upenn.edu/~jlynch/grammar.html.

MacDonald, Heather. "Why Johnny Can't Write." *The Public Interest Summer* 1995: 3-13.

McCarthy, Lucille. "A Stranger in Strange Lands: A College Student Writing Across the Curriculum." In Bazerman, Charles, and David Russell, eds., *Landmark Essays on Writing Across the Curriculum*. Davis, CA: Hermagoras Press, 1994. 125-55.

Mullin, William. "Writing in Physics." In *Programs That Work*, 211-14.

O'Conner, Patricia. "Like I said, don't worry; as an 'expert,' I find that people love words but grammar gives them the willies." *Newsweek* 128.24 (1996): 12.

Sledd, James. "Product in Process: From Ambiguities of Standard English to Issues That Divide Us." *College English* 50 (1988): 168-76.

Williams, Joseph, and Gregory Colomb. "The University of Chicago." In Fulwiler and Young, eds., *Programs That Work: Models and Methods for Writing Across the Curriculum*. Portsmouth, NH: Boynton/Cook P, 1990. 83-113.

Young, Art, and Toby Fulwiler. "The Enemies of Writing Across the Curriculum." In *Programs That Work*, 287-94.

Coming to Terms with the Freshman Term Paper

James C. McDonald

There is a long tradition of complaint about the required research paper in the freshman composition course that dates back almost as far as the assignment itself, as Robert W. Frederick's 1929 survey of educators indicates. Articles questioning the value of the freshman research paper, such as Paul F. Fletcher's "Should Term Papers Be Abolished?" John W. Stevenson's "The Illusion of Research," Thomas E. Taylor's "Let's Get Rid of Research Papers," and Richard Larson's "The 'Research Paper' in the Writing Course: A Non-Form of Writing," go back as far as Roy C. Woods's "The Term Paper: Its Values and Dangers" in 1933. A few choice words of condemnation or ridicule are almost expected in any article or book that discusses the freshman research paper. Describing students that he observed working on research papers in the library, Michael Kleine laments, "Not only were they not writing, but they were not reading: I detected no searching, analyzing, evaluating, synthesizing, selecting, rejecting, etc. No time for such reading in the heated bursts of copying that interrupted the conversations" (151). The research paper "trivializes the process of knowledge acquisition," Sharon Crowley writes, "Any subject whatsoever can be read up on and mastered for the occasion" (*Methodical* 163-64). To Ken Macrorie, student research papers are "inane productions" (xi), "bad jokes" (161), "the most unoriginal writings the world has ever seen" (54), and "an exercise in badly done bibliography, often an introduction to the art of plagiarism, and a triumph of meaninglessness—for both writer and reader" (xi).

Yet the research paper remains the 400-pound gorilla of the first-year composition course, probably the most institutionalized undergraduate writing assignment in higher education. James E. Ford and Dennis R. Perry, in their 1982 survey of first-year writing programs, found that 78.11 percent required the research paper (827), only slightly fewer than the 81 percent Ambrose Manning reported in 1961. Some freshman programs, as well as a number of high schools, devote an entire course to research paper instruction. Anecdotal evidence suggests that the percentage may have decreased since 1982, particularly after that year's publication of Larson's "The 'Research Paper' in the Writing Course: A Non-Form of Writing," but it's difficult to find evidence of a major change in composition textbooks, which continue to devote more space to this assignment than to any other. Teachers spend far more classtime on this one assignment than on any other (over one-third of the average course, according to Ford and Perry [828]), and the time they spend responding to and grading bibliographies, notes, outlines, drafts, and revisions, as well as dealing with suspected plagiarism, is a legendary burden for teachers. This assignment also burdens others on campus. Writing program directors probably deal with more plagiarism cases involving this one assignment than with all other assignments combined. And Ford and Perry documented the amount of work librarians put into supporting the freshman research paper: 87 percent of college libraries in 1982 organized tours of the library specifically for students learning to write the research paper, 66 percent arranged for librarians to meet with freshman composition classes to lecture them about research methods and materials, and over 50 percent of the schools gave faculty and/or librarians special training on how to instruct and support undergraduates writing a research paper (829).

And despite a myriad of articles on reforming research paper instruction (see Ford, Rees, and Ward's "Research Paper Instruction: Comprehensive Bibliography of Periodical Sources, 1923-1980," as well as Ford's 1995 *Teaching the Research Paper*), students are usually taught to follow a composing process not much different from the one James M. Chalfant recommended in 1930, in the first article that *English Journal* published on the research paper: choose a subject and narrow it, compile a bibliography, take notes, write an outline, and finally compose the theme paying close attention to the conventions for documenting quotations and paraphrases to avoid plagiarism. Later textbooks added the step of revising the draft, and now most textbooks discuss keeping a research journal as an alternative to note cards, but the process for composing a research paper as it has appeared in composition textbooks has changed remarkably little in seventy years, especially given the long-standing, widespread dissatisfaction with the assignment.

This mechanical process of writing a research paper is a legacy of current-traditional textbooks, which dominated composition instruction as the research paper became a requirement in the freshman English course. From a current-traditional standpoint, neither reading nonliterary texts nor writing about them should be a problem because the language in these texts is merely a conduit for transferring thoughts from speaker to hearer. Writing is a simple matter of translating thoughts into words and reading a matter of translating the words back into thoughts. If the writer has written clearly, transmission to a reader should be automatic. Reading instruction for the research paper, therefore, has been confined to some instruction in extensive reading practices required in much research, how to skim and scan many texts for information, but has ignored the need for intensive reading strategies to analyze and evaluate sources. In the first edition of the *Harbrace College Handbook* John Hodges gave students this advice for reading and using sources:

Seldom will a whole book, or even a whole article, be of use as subject matter for any given research paper. To find what the student needs for his particular paper he must turn to many books and articles, rejecting most of them altogether and using from others a section here and there. He cannot take time to read each book carefully. He must use the table of contents and the index, and he must learn to scan the pages rapidly until he finds the passages he needs. (370)

Hodges assumed that reading is merely a matter of recognizing words and the ideas they represent and that knowledge is a commodity that one possesses; careful reading unnecessarily slows and distracts the student trying to complete a research paper in a few weeks. The assumption that knowledge is a commodity, of course, explains the current-traditional obsession with plagiarism and acknowledging proper ownership of ideas. If one can possess knowledge, one can steal it (or kidnap it, as the Latin origin of the word "plagiarism" suggest). With proper documentation, however, the writer merely "borrows" another's knowledge. Books and articles here are merely containers of bits of knowledge and data that can be labeled, located by indexes, and recorded on four-by-six-inch note cards—only one item per card, please. At best, language is a see-through cellophane wrapper that allows readers to view knowledge inside the containers. Hodges's advice suggested that students use indexes much as shoppers use signs and directions in a giant mall to guide their searches to the right stores and aisles for items they are searching for. The long history of complaints about the assignment from both teachers and students and the success of a black market of student research papers, however, testify to the difficult of learning research writing and the inadequacy of research paper instruction.

The remarkable endurance of the freshman research paper despite the long history of complaints about the assignment may suggest that the problems with the assignment cannot be separated from problems of the required first-year composition course, which has survived even longer despite its own lengthy history of discontent. The problems and debates generally reflect conflicts between the research and teaching missions of the university that go to the heart of the service function of the course and a failure to define clearly the content and purposes of the first-year course, especially regarding research writing.

The undergraduate research paper developed out of the shifting priorities of the modern research university, as the research mission of the university came to influence the education faculty desired for their students. Nineteenth-century American colleges were small colleges whose main function was to instruct an elite student body in the traditional liberal arts preparing for leadership roles in society in a small assortment of professions, medicine, law, and religious ministry. Faculty took it as their responsibility to conserve the wisdom of the ages and transmit it to the next generation. After the Civil War, the modern university began to develop into large knowledge-producing institutions with an important role in the economy of the information age, and faculty took on the new responsibility of teaching and credentialing an ever-growing and ever more diverse student population for an increasing number of professional careers. In contrast to the nineteenth-century college library, which was typically smaller than the local public library, the modern research university library underwent a vast expansion and fostered the development and publication of a growing number of readers' guides, indexes, and bibliographies.

Students needed instruction in navigating these large and complicated libraries, and because freshman English was the only universally required course in the curriculum, it likely seemed the natural place for this instruction. By 1920 composition textbooks were including a chapter on the library, and universities such as the University of Chicago began to require a research paper in the freshman English course shortly after World War I. The requirement was an established part of the freshman English course by World War II. By the time the general education movement led universities to develop other universally required courses that could have covered library instruction, that instruction had been established as the responsibility of the freshman English course, and the research paper assignment had become the core of this instruction.

Whether or not this instruction should be the responsibility of the first-year English course, it would be difficult to argue against teaching student writers how to conduct library research. But whether college freshmen (and high school students) should be taught to write the academic article is much more debatable. Writers need to conduct research for many situations, but few students write academic articles after they graduate—not that there are no benefits to undergraduates who learn to write an academic article. I have yet to find evidence, however, that composition faculty considered alternatives for incorporating library research into freshman English when the research paper became a standard requirement in the course. The main reason that the research paper became the dominant genre of research writing in the first-year course is the service nature of freshman English.

In his history of writing across the curriculum, David R. Russell discusses an unresolved tension in the university's research ideal between its "elitist tendency . . . to promote disciplinary excellence" and its "egalitarian strain . . . that insisted that all students should have some experience in individual research on an important and interesting subject" (86). As it became the dominant production center of knowledge in society, the research university abandoned the oral declamation, a public oration on a political or moral issue important to the general public, and replaced it with the research paper as the dominant genre of extended student discourse, "a comprehensive display of learning on a narrow topic" that addressed experts on "questions of interest to a discipline rather than to the general public" (Russell 79, 81). "Student writing increasingly became research writing," Russell writes, "an imitation of the writing that the institution valued most: the documented or 'research' paper and, to a lesser extent, the laboratory or experimental report" (72; see also Berlin 70). This change involved a shift "from student-as-public-performer to student-as-disciple or apprentice, conducting individual research under the guidance of a professor and producing critical, 'original' interpretations of documents and data using the methods, conventions, and assumptions of a specialized discipline—not the 'common knowledge' of a particular social class" (80). Rather than future citizens and leaders of a community, colleges perceived students primarily as apprentices in a discipline, and the value of a course "lay in its relation to the discipline, not to general culture or public discourse" (Russell 85). Robert Scholes argues that the graduate course became the model for the entire undergraduate English curriculum, including the general education courses, with English faculty treating all students as apprentice English professors.

Russell writes that while the university's research ideal "narrowed the focus of instruction to the content and issues addressed by research and thus narrowed the range of genres acceptable in academia," it also "distanced the faculty from lower-level instruction" (72). As university faculties gave more time to their research and their discourse became more specialized and removed from the discourse of the student and the public, Russell writes, educators simply "developed ways of living with [this tension], ways that marginalized writing instruction" (86-87), including research writing in the disciplines. At first students learned research writing in the courses in their major under the tutelage of professors in their major discipline, but research faculty abandoned much of this time-consuming work, assigning research papers but more and more expecting the freshman composition course to teach students how to compose them.

Composition faculty also had reasons for wanting to teach the research paper in the first-year course. Some may have been eager to take on research paper instruction at first as a way to enhance the prestige of the freshman English course, to move it beyond a course to correct students' literacy deficiencies by providing instruction in the dominant genre of the research university. Robert J. Connors, however, holds that composition faculty embraced the research paper to help them move the course beyond personal writing and introduce students to academic writing and to help them manage how students used library sources when they wrote. Personal writing had become the emphasis of the first-year course partly because access to the modern research library had made it too easy for students to crib a paper together from secondary sources. In addition, the concept of intellectual property had become so critical to the research university that composition faculty believed it was important to teach freshmen to avoid plagiarism. The research paper was a way to assign academic topics, to begin to teach freshmen an academic research attitude and methodology, and to ingrain in freshmen a respect for intellectual property laws (Connors 321-23). It was a movement away from teaching writing to explore personal subjects or issues of public import.

The assumption that students can learn to conduct research, evaluate sources, and write research articles as part of an introductory writing course, only to hone their research writing skills in later courses, is problematic, to say the least. The freshman research paper clearly has not satisfied the desires of the disciplines for students to learn to do academic research. As Richard Larson has argued, instruction in a generic research article cannot take into account that each discipline has developed its own research methodologies and discourse conventions even if each composition instructor could learn enough about other disciplines' research practices to instruct students in them (16-17). But the problem that Larson describes is not a problem of the research paper alone but endemic to the first-year composition course. As Sharon Crowley discusses in *Composition in the University*, for decades the first-year English course has "taught 'the academic essay' as though it modeled all possible genres of academic discourse" (28). The service of function of the freshman English course, to teach students academic prose for all departments in the university, necessitated the fiction of the generic academic essay, and the freshman research paper developed as a logical extension of that fiction.

Shifting the main responsibility for research instruction from the research faculty to the teaching faculty of the freshman composition course undermined the apprenticeship approach to teaching research. Rather than learning research writing under the watchful eye of a practicing, experienced academic researcher, the first-year student normally learns to conduct research from a graduate assistant, an apprentice scholar herself, or from a non-tenured faculty member who usually is given little time or incentive to conduct research and who may have little inclination for traditional academic research. The fact that these composition faculty frequently teach too many students and too many classes further erodes any apprentice approach to research instruction. The decision of research faculty to consign research writing instruction to the teaching faculty of a single discipline has also discouraged active discussions of the function and place of research instruction throughout the undergraduate curriculum.

To deal with the problems of the assignment, composition instructors devised an oversimplified and vastly distorted version of academic research procedures and a mechanistic and formalist approach to writing the research paper that freshmen could learn in a few weeks and that faculty could grade for adherence to format fairly easily. Just as the freshman composition course treated the long heritage of rhetorical theory and practices in a radically reductive way, it also represented the discourses and methodologies of the disciplines of the modern research university in a vastly oversimplified way. The process for writing a research paper that has dominated freshman composition instruction since the introduction of the research paper—select and narrow a topic, compile a bibliography, take notes, compose an outline and then a draft, and revise and edit the draft—and the common practice of students grabbing any sources that they can find off library shelves until they have enough to meet the assignment's minimum requirement for works cited parody the research methods of scholars and provide little help to a student asked to write something original. Textbooks have typically represented research as little more than using catalogs and bibliographies to find texts about a subject and then taking notes. And instruction on research writing in English 101 has seldom been followed systematically by more sophisticated instruction in sophomore, junior, and senior courses.

Perhaps the greatest problem of research paper instruction has been a failure to treat this assignment as a reading-to-write assignment that requires instruction in critical reading strategies of sources. Although most textbooks tell students to distinguish between "biased" and "unbiased" sources, instruction on how to do this is slight. "Instructions on detecting bias often amount to not much more than whether an argument sounds good," Kathleen McCormick concludes after examining several recently published research paper textbooks (217). According to McCormick, textbooks usually credit students "with having an intrinsic ability to distinguish—without training or even explicit instruction—biased from objective sources" (216). That has begun to change. Chapters on critical reading strategies have become popular in recent composition textbooks, and composition scholars such as McCormick, Doug Brent, and Margaret J. Kantz have developed research paper pedagogies that apply reading theories and research. But a serious attempt to address the importance of critical reading in research and in writing in general is difficult to implement in one already crowded course, again raising questions about the content and functions of the course. Just as important, serious implementation of reading instruction into the course would have to involve significant changes in how graduate students are educated to teach writing. On most campuses the composition movement has succeeded only in establishing one practicum course in teaching writing usually coupled with some observation, mentoring, and/or interning of teaching assistants as the standard education for writing instructors, hardly an adequate amount of instruction considering the complexities of writing instruction. To add adequate instruction on theories and approaches to teaching reading of nonliterary texts would probably need to involve an expansion of this instruction and changes in the graduate curriculums in composition studies to include reading research, not to mention adjustments in college English departments' assumptions that reading instruction is the job of high schools and remedial programs.

The situation suggests that universities' desire to teach most undergraduates how to conduct academic research may not be a strong one. If it were, universities should have abandoned their present approach to research instruction long ago. Graduate school enrollments and the oversupply of Ph.D.s in many fields suggest that the current system prepares more than enough students for graduate school to supply colleges and universities with the faculty and research assistants that they are willing to hire. One reason this haphazard approach to teaching research has continued may be that it encourages future professionals to become consumers of the knowledge that the research university produces. Despite recent definitions of reading and writing as "meaning-making activities" and students as "makers of knowledge," textbook representations of the composing process of research papers have been dominated by a reverence for expert knowledge and opinion that encourages students to be uncritical consumers of the knowledge and claims of university scholars. A common assumption of textbook instruction, as Crowley writes, is that "opinion could be accepted as fact when the person who expressed it was an authority" (*Methodical* 110).

Such a position makes it unnecessary to use critical reading strategies when conducting research. Most textbooks have instructed students to evaluate a source before reading it, to trust in the credentials of the author. Hodges instructed students to evaluate a source much as one should evaluate merchandise, checking for signs about whether the information inside the source was good: "One important consideration always is the reliability of the source. Does the author seem to know his subject? Do others speak of him as an authority? Is he prejudiced? Is the work recent enough to give the information needed?" (370). Some knowledge goes bad after a while. Once a text is certified, the information should be good. Kathleen McCormick's examination of recent research paper textbooks suggests that textbook advice on evaluating sources has changed little since Hodges. Textbooks often signal that sources that support the dominant view of a subject are not biased, recommending that students only check the credentials of the author and publication and rely on their "common sense," which, McCormick writes, "is surely the most unreflective means of passive acquiescence to the dominant that exists—and something that research should help to problematize rather than justify" (217). Textbooks privilege "objective" and "authoritative" sources as political and moral authorities, describing them with terms such as "reliable," "authentic," and "trustworthy" (McCormick 213-14). "Sources that are outside the mainstream, in contrast," McCormick writes, "are 'worthless, silly, and misleading,' 'controversial,' and of course 'biased'" (214).

The research mission of the modern university, the service nature of the first-year English course, the gulf between the research faculty who establish many of the demands of the first-year course and the graduate students and the nontenured teaching faculty responsible for carrying out these demands, and the current-traditional rhetoric that dominated composition instruction during the development of research paper pedagogy have worked together to create a required writing assignment that does not prepare students for the audiences, purposes, situations, and genres that most will face in their writing projects after college; to foster an unreflective acceptance of expert opinion; and to develop a pedagogy that teaches a mechanical and inadequate approach to writing, research, and reading. There are, however, movements to reform the research paper. Ken Macrorie's I-search paper, which tells the story of the writer's research on a matter of personal importance, has become a popular alternative or supplement to the academic research paper and an argument that research writing does not have to be academic discourse. The concept of student research has been expanded to include more than library research, to include interviews, field research, and the Internet. Composition scholars like Doug Brent, Margaret J. Kantz, and Kathleen McCormick have developed reading-to-write pedagogies to teach students to read their sources critically and assess what they have to say. Computer developments likely will lead to adjustments in teaching the research paper. Concerns about the quality and reliability of sources on the World Wide Web have made evaluation and critical reading of sources a more important concern—current-traditional instruction tacitly depended on editors, publishers, and librarians to steer students away from sources that were not authoritative. And the availability of simple and inexpensive bibliography programs should make it unnecessary for teachers to spend much classroom time lecturing on MLA format.

But tinkering with the assignment probably is not enough. University faculty as a whole, research faculty and teaching faculty, need to discuss the purposes for teaching research to undergraduates, what research methodologies undergraduates should learn, how research instruction should work together with writing instruction, and how undergraduate curriculums should try to accomplish these pedagogical goals. These discussions should consider not only disciplinary interests in teaching research methodologies but also the uses students will likely make of research in their lives and careers. While writing based on research certainly has a place in the first-year composition course, it is not at all clear that there is a compelling need to teach freshmen to write a generic academic article. If it is important for students to learn to compose academic articles, it is also important that they learn to use research to write other genres for other purposes and audiences.

I doubt that we can come to terms with the freshman term paper without first coming to terms with the purpose and content of the required first-year composition course. The history of complaint about the assignment has been too long and ineffectual and the problems with the research paper are too closely connected to unsettled questions about who the first-year course should serve and what writing it should teach to expect easy reform or abandonment of research paper instruction. It may be, as Crowley has argued, that the first-year requirement is holding us back, that the universal requirement makes the first-year course too much a matter of contention among different factions in the university, that the requirement discourages other university departments from taking their share of the responsibility for teaching students writing and research, and that the first-year course is saddled with impossible demands. Clearly it is important now to discuss what the content and function of this course should be, what genres and research methods students need to learn in the first-year course, and what writing instruction students will receive after freshman English.

WORKS CITED

Berlin, James A. *Rhetoric and Reality: Writing Instruction in American Colleges, 1900-1985*. Carbondale: Southern Illinois UP, 1987.

Brent, Doug. *Reading as Rhetorical Invention: Knowledge, Persuasion, and the Teaching of Research-Based Writing*. Urbana, IL: NCTE, 1992.

Chalfant, James M. "The Investigative Theme—A Project for Freshman Composition." *English Journal* College ed. 19 (1930): 41-46.

Connors, Robert J. *Composition-Rhetoric: Backgrounds, Theory, and Pedagogy*. Pittsburgh: U of Pittsburgh P, 1997.

Crowley, Sharon.. *Composition in the University: Historical and Polemical Essays*. Pittsburgh: U of Pittsburgh P, 1998.

————. *The Methodical Memory: Invention in Current-Traditional Rhetoric*. Carbondale: Southern Illinois UP, 1990.

Fletcher, Paul F. "Should Term Papers Be Abolished?" *Clearing House* 38 (Sept. 1963): 32.

Ford, James E., ed. *Teaching the Research Paper: From Theory to Practice, From Research to Writing*. Metuchen, NJ: Scarecrow, 1995.

Ford, James E., and Dennis R. Perry. "Research Paper Instruction in the Undergraduate Writing Program." *College English* 44 (1982): 825-31.

Ford, James E., Sharla Rees, and David L. Ward. "Research Paper Instruction: Comprehensive Bibliography of Periodical Sources, 1923-1980." *Bulletin of Bibliography* 39 (June 1982): 84-98.

Frederick, Robert W. "The Term Paper as a College Teaching Device." *School and Society* 29 (23 Feb. 1929): 256-57.

Hodges, John C. *Harbrace College Handbook*. New York: Harcourt, Brace, 1946.

Kantz, Margaret J. "Helping Students Use Textual Sources Persuasively." *College English* 52 (Jan. 1990): 74-91.

Kleine, Michael. "What is it we do when we write articles like this one—and how can we get students to join us?" *Writing Instructor* 6 (Spring/Summer 1987): 151-61.

Larson, Richard L. "The 'Research Paper' in the Writing Course: A Non-form of Writing." *College English* 44 (Dec. 1982): 811-16.

Macrorie, Ken. *The I-Search Paper*. Rev. ed. of *Searching Writing*. Portsmouth, NH: Boynton/Cook, 1988.

Manning, Ambrose. "The Present Status of the Research Paper in Freshman English: A National Survey." *College Composition and Communication* 12 (May 1961): 73-78.

McCormick, Kathleen. *The Culture of Reading and the Teaching of English*. New York: Manchester UP, 1994.

Russell, David R. *Writing in the Academic Disciplines, 1870-1990: A Curricular History*. Carbondale: Southern Illinois UP, 1991.

Scholes, Robert. "An End to Hypocriticism." *South Central Review* 8 (Spring 1991): 1-13.

Stevenson, John W. "The Illusion of Research." *English Journal* 61 (Oct. 1972): 102-32.

Taylor, Thomas E. "Let's Get Rid of Research Papers." *English Journal* 54 (Feb. 1965): 126-27.

Woods, Roy C. "The Term Paper: Its Values and Dangers." *Peabody Journal of Education* 11 (Sept. 1933): 87-89.

The Bytes Are On, But Nobody's Home: Composition's Wrong Turns into the Computer Age

J. Rocky Colavito

We haven't asked enough about the basics [of communication in the information age].If information is doubling every three or five or seven or ten years, where has all that information gone? Is the world really awash in information? And if it is, is that the end to all the world's problems? We are counting articles and pointing to large numbers, but not looking closely enough at the information being generated. . . . we are arrogant about out own abilities to handle information despite endless examples of our frailties.

—William Wresch,
*Disconnected: Haves and Have-nots
in the Information Age* (5)

Are the new technologies a magic bullet aimed straight at success and power? Or are we simply grasping at a technocentric "quick fix" for a multitude of problems we have failed to address?

—Jane M. Healy,
*Failure to Connect: How Computers Affect Our
Children's Minds—for Better and Worse* (18)

"ESSAYING" THE TERRITORY

In a flashback to the 1980s, I'm reminded of a popular Talking Heads song with memorable lyrics about being "on a road to nowhere," and as I muse over the now taken-for-granted place of technology in the teaching of writing, I sometimes find those lyrics apropos to the current state of affairs. The road composition is currently on is one way toward technology, and rest stops are few and far between. The "enthusiasm . . . and . . . optimism" are augmented by the "increasing professional influence of computers and composition specialists who. . . entered the field in the early 1980s" (Hawisher, et al. 267). This "enthusiasm" and "optimism" also renders the road downhill, thus precipitating a headlong, inexorable rush to incorporate more and more technology into our classrooms. The pace is sometimes too fast to pick up those "disconnected" folks to whom Wresch refers. The rapid pace also makes us forget some of those "other" educational issues (e.g. classroom practice, teacher training, institutional awareness, and public accountability) that Healy suggests we haven't addressed. Consequently, we at times seem to have made a series of "wrong turns" onto this particular road. This chapter, then, assesses and critiques of some of these literal and figurative "wrong turns" that composition theory and practice has taken into the Information/ Computer/Technological age. The experience starts, for me, about twelve years ago.

And So the Story Starts

> *Our profession is not preparing teachers to deal with technology in its current forms, and we are certainly not preparing them to deal with technology as it changes in the future. . . . attention is focused on specific hardware configurations; demonstrations of existing software packages, programming languages; or computer-assisted instruction and computer-managed education (cf. Lathrop and Goodson; Lucking and Stallard; and Standiford, Jaycox, and Auten). Almost no time, unfortunately, is spent in teaching educators to think critically about how and when virtual environments can support the educational objectives of teachers in English classrooms.*
>
> —Cynthia L. Selfe,
> "Preparing English Teachers for the Virtual Age: The Case for Technology Critics," in *Re-Imagining Computers and Composition: Teaching and Research in the Virtual Age* (24)

> *Computers complicate the teaching of literacy. . . . Technology, along with the issues that surround its use in reading- and writing-intensive classrooms, both physically and intellectually disrupts the ways in which we make meaning–the ways in which we communicate. Computers change the ways in which we read, construct, and interpret texts.*
>
> —Cynthia L. Selfe and Susan Hilligoss
> "Introduction," in *Literacy and Computers: The Complications of Teaching and Learning with Technology* (1)

My first experience teaching composition with a technological component was in the fall of 1986. The preceding spring, I was called to the office of the Director of Composition and told, as only he could, that I was being granted the opportunity to "test-pilot" a section of English 102 (part of our first-year sequence focusing on writing about literature) in our brand spanking new "computer lab." Said lab had six x-shaped tables, with space for four computers upon each. One "work station" was reserved for faculty use exclusively, so there were twenty computers available for student use. The computers were equipped with a now deceased (I think) word-processing program known as Edix-Wordix, whose chief claim to prominence was its ability to split the screen into quarters and allow for viewing four different files at once. There was no network, no Internet, not even modem access (that came a year and a half later). There was also no budget to purchase educational software, and there was no training for me other than a two-hour "how-to" session on running the software.

Preparing the class without guidance was, as you might expect, quite challenging, what with writing new assignments, reconfiguring everyday tasks to incorporate computer use, retooling the syllabus to accommodate training the students in using the software. The class itself went a lot smoother than I could've hoped; I had three students who were very computer literate who gladly served as "teaching assistants," and most folks managed to pick up the word-processing component after a fashion. Still, the problems of access (I had to come in on Saturdays and Sundays to accommodate several students), lost assignments (one poor student never quite managed to get the hang of saving), swapping disks in order to "network" freewriting and other materials, and computer crashes got in the way. I regret to say that my report at the end of the semester about the experience wasn't all that positive, and the Director of Composition subsequently wrote the whole thing off as an experiment that failed.

In retrospect, I believe my initial lack of formal training in using technology, coupled with the institution's desire to move ahead without adequate considerations of what "costs" the technology would incur, created a negative view of the whole experiment. What I needed was a viable framework for bringing technology into the class as a supplement for writing instead of approaching using the computer as course content in and of itself. I needed, as Eric Schroeder and John Boe suggest, a more "minimalist approach"(29) to matters of computing. Trouble was, all my forays into reading the existing research turned up precious little in the form of "how-tos."

Same Stuff, Different Decade

> *The digital computer provides a richly textured writing space. Computer writing can be as abstract as alphabetic writing. It can be as fast and effortless (as apparently untechnological) as mental writing. Computer writing is primarily visual, rather than oral, and can be as silent as the picture writing of preliterate peoples . . . . The computer rewrites the history of writing by sending us*

back to reconsider nearly every aspect of the earlier technologies. In particular, the electronic medium gives a renewed prominence to the long discredited art of writing with pictures.

—Jay David Bolter,
*Writing Space: The Computer, Hypertext,
and the History of Writing* (45-46)

The computer indeed facilitates the production and revision of text . . . but the ease of word processing tempts novice writers to verboseness and blurs for them crucial distinctions between proofreading and revising. Students are tempted . . . toward premature closure. Deceived by polished output, they come to equate good formatting with good text . . . . A coherent pedagogy for computer writing ing has been slow in emerging.

–Kathleen Skubikowski and John Elder
"Computers and the Social Contexts of Writing," in
*Computers and Community: Teaching Composition in the Twenty-
First Century*, ed. Carolyn Handa (90)

For a lot of compositionists, this story sounds hauntingly familiar. Trouble is, we have much more to deal with today than I did thirteen years ago. There has to be some level of success to some of those early experiments, because now we have whole writing courses whose raison d'etre is using the latest technological gizmo or add-on. Some of these successes are qualified ones, but enough positives have occurred to firmly entrench the computer within the space of the composition classroom. Trouble is, there are still some shortcomings as teaching writing with technology lurches toward the year 2000.

These shortcomings include the following:

1. A pressing lack of training for faculty in using technology as a teaching supplement.

2. Reliance upon questionable or insubstantial research findings that raise too many questions.

3. Research geared toward the study of atomistic minutiae when the real need is for holistic assessment and unity of the findings.

4. Little or no concern for questions of student access to computers.

5. Almost no consideration for the "have-nots" in the Information Age.

6. A failure to reconcile tensions between faculty and students over disproportionate amounts of knowledge about computing.

7. Most important, a seeming failure to accept the burden of proof regarding the postive

influences of technology in education as a whole, and writing instruction in particlar.

I could go on, but the point of this chapter is to be both critical and conciliatory. Instead, let's group these shortcomings into the age-old categories of theoretical and practical concerns. Seems almost like an even split, particularly in terms of problematic research findings that fail to contribute to directing or informing practice. There's lots of positive apocryphal lore surrounding computers and composition, and some of it, on the surface, can sound pretty convincing. The scholarship is careful to list numerous studies where positive effects arose. The positive findings of the studies on the whole, however, can be reduced to the following:

1. Students write more.

2. Students complete more surface revision.

3. Growth in quality of writing is often linked to experience as a computer user and experience as a writer.

Students writing more, for example, sounds good on the surface until a close look at some studies (e.g., Burley 1998) reveals that students are writing *lengthier* texts rather than writing *more numerous* texts. And the longer texts, according to Burley's findings, "were unwieldy and rambling, lacking focus and adequate coherence" (90). Students revise more, sounds great, too, but how many of us have returned less-than-satisfactory essays and heard students claim that "But I spell/grammar checked it!" The amount, and overall quality, of revision fostered by writing with a computer is still open to question. Give a good writer a tool that can influence amount of text produced and streamline the whole process of revising, bravo, we've verified that a good writer can used new tools to improve. Where is the treatment of the less-experienced writer? What good did technology do them?

Jane Healy's comment about the lot of research in this area becomes all the more viable:

The few studies showing positive results for educational technology have been largely funded by computer corporations or conducted by educators who are (or would like to become) consultants for the technology business. Even glowing anecdotal reports from classrooms turn out to have been written by "teacher-techies." (22)

What's missing in all this research? In a word, lots. Where, for example, are multiple studies of writing apprehension and cyberphobia as stumbling blocks in the composition classroom? Aren't both of these issues important to informing how we might teach such students? Where can we find measurements of sustained changes in *writing* quality in light of access to in-class discussion groups or Internet resources? Much of the work here has been focused on class-room networking as a means of fostering dialogue. Or, where has there been investigation into the influence of writing on-line in chat groups upon diction, tone, style, or rhetorical a/eptitude? Most significantly, where are the connec-tions between what existing studies reveal and how we can use these results to better inform classroom practice, particularly at the college level? All too often the practical research for college-level teachers is not easily accessible (i.e., the texts don't get publicized) and is still looked down upon as a vehicle for pro-motion and tenure. Much of what we can find concerning classroom practice is geared primarily to K-12 teachers, thus suggesting (wrongheadedly) that the pro-cedures are out of place within the college curriculum. A lack of training that models application and extension of such practices described in the research is "short circuiting" many writing classes that attempt to use technology.

PREACHING, BUT NO PRACTICE

> *A new, more mature research agenda will aid us in understanding how com-puter technologies, literacy, thinking, and culture are connected. Such research is crucial for informing the design of curricula for teaching writing and can guide the wise use of technology in writing. But an even more critical (and, to our minds, heretofore unacknowledged) justification for such research is that it can help authorize our voices not just in the proper* use *of computer tech-nologies for literacy but in the very* shape *such technologies should take. A crit-ical reason for conducting research, then, is to help us give shape to the tech-nologies that, in turn, shape our literacy acts–to "write" the technology that "writes" us.*

—Christina Haas and Christine M. Neuwirth
"Writing the Technology That Writes Us:
Research on Literacy and the Shape of
Technology," in Selfe and Hilligoss (320)

> *Conventional texts have certain limitations. Print's truest products, as Alvin Kernan recently insisted, are "ordered, controlled, teleological, referential, and autonomously meaningful" (Death of Literature 141). When literacy serves the interests of individual authority, monological discourse, and linear argument, these qualities may be essential; but they come to have less value as we come to define literacy in terms of communities–positing dynamic, collaborative, and associative forms of writing*

—Stuart Moulthrop and Nancy Kaplan
"They Became What They Beheld: The Futility of
Resistance in the Space of Electronic Writing,"
in Selfe and Hilligoss (221)

The most damning wrong turn of writing instruction's foray into the computer age is the shocking absence of any sustained body of scholarship geared toward discussing the practical side of teaching with technology. When we do find such information, it's either embedded in descriptions of testing procedures disguised as classroom activities found in research studies or relegated to state English journals. I suspect part of the absence is due to the still-existing tension between theory and practice as types of research, but the lack of resolution in this area is compromising this segment of the field of composition. I concede to the argument about some faculty being resistant to change, but I can also suggest that part of the reason for this resistance is the absence of a coherent and sustained system of retraining all faculty in computer literacy and application. Doris Lee suggests several key needs of trainees in this area:

1. Make the training content interesting and relevant to their experience

2. Practice in a risk-free, competition free environment

3. [Focus] on tasks that are germane to their work, interests, or area of specialty.

4. [Ensure] they should be able to gain confidence in the training tasks they perform. (140)

The hands-on portion of the training is crucial, as is accounting for varying paces in knowledge acquisition. But there's still a pressing need for concrete lesson plans, activities, and mechanisms teachers can use in the classroom. More in this area will give faculty greater confidence about using the computer as a teaching tool, particularly when confronted by students who are more expert computer users. More significant, however, is a seemingly universal failure by educational institutions on down to individual faculty to acknowledge how many students lack the necessary tools to succeed in computer-supported classes. Requiring word processing of papers, for example, begs the question of both student access to computer resources and student ability to complete essays on disk. Again, training in word processing isn't normally part of the course content of a writing class, and I suspect most purists would argue that the course is still First-Year Writing, not First-Year Word Processing. But look at what goes begging here, the assumption is that students will come in (to grade level/college) proficient in word processing. This simply isn't the case, and we err by catering writing classes to the "haves" in the Information Age. Believe it or not, some students come to college with no keyboarding skills, and that includes typing.

There is a like amount of assuming that goes on with regard to having access to computers. Schools feel that having open labs, computers in the library, and mandatory "field trips" to the lab as part of course curricula is sufficient time to access technology. Many schools also assume that students can have access to computers at home. Cynthia Selfe, in a recent *CCC* illuminates the disproportionality in computer possession/access, noting that whites have greater tendency to possess and have easier access to computers, and that whites are more likely than African Americans to access the World Wide Web (Donna Hoffman and Thomas Novak 390, quoted in Selfe 421). Throwing vast amounts of money into technology in the schools still doesn't seem to be improving access, and the only way to assure access to all students is to require possession of a computer for attendance at an institution, or to literally have a computer on the desk of every student. This whole question of access is just as damning as a lack of faculty training because both compromise the integrity of the classroom by calling into question our even-handedness. On the classroom level, students who lack resources or time to get access are at a disadvantage, particularly if word processing, on-line discussion, or Internet research are course/assignment requirements. On an institutional level, if we continue to surreptitiously, rather than forthrightly, "require" access to technology we send the message that those who lack access are second-class students. Better that we take our lumps financially by either providing more computers than is necessary in order to ensure access, and/or by requiring purchase or leasing of computers as an entrance requirement.

RE-ORIENTING OURSELVES

> *Although computer technology has altered reading- and writing-intensive classrooms in some dramatic ways and at many levels . . . it has not brought the deep, systemic changes in education for which many computer-using English teachers hope. Some theorists have suggested that far from bringing change, computer technology may have a complex and over-determined tendency to inhibit change.*
>
> —Gail E. Hawisher, Paul LeBlanc,
> Charles Moran, and Cynthia L. Selfe
> *Computers and the Teaching of Writing in American
> Higher Education, 1979-1994: A History* (8)

> *Despite our best efforts, the computer, in the early stages of learning, steals center stage from the writing (Flinn and Madigan). It's like bringing an iguana into a fourth-grade classroom. Some kids play, others panic, but nobody is thinking about long division!*
>
> —Jane Zeni
> "Literacy, Technology, and Teacher Education,"
> in Selfe and Hilligoss, eds., *Literacy and Computers: The
> Complications of Teaching and Learning with Technology* (79)

I don't pretend to have all the answers for all the issues raised here, but I do think it's time for the field of composition studies to re-evaluate where technology has brought us and what it has wrought upon our theories and classroom practices. Most pressing is our need to devote significant amounts of attention to articulating standards and practices to students, faculty, and the public at large. We call it the Information Age, but there's sadly been too little information disseminated in these areas and to these constituencies. Unfortunately, the flow of information has to be on multiple fronts:

1. Colleges need to decide how much influence technology is going to have upon the classroom, and then provide faculty with suitable training and students with sufficient resources. If that means buying everyone computers, then so be it. At the very least, students need to be told about any and all new "requirements."

2. The educational system as a whole, K-Advanced Higher Education, needs to develop and disseminate a concrete set of standards for computer skills gained in each level. This must happen in tandem with increased access, so that content and skill mastery along each level are preserved. Colleges, in particular, need to adjust curricula to allow for training of students in word processing and general Internet research exclusive of content areas.

3. Faculty need to be trained on the institution's time and dime. The pace needs to be slow enough to allow all faculty to be brought up to speed. The content needs to be extensive enough to allow faculty to efficiently incorporate technology with their own methods and course content, yet not so voluminous that faculty get overwhelmed. The key question to ask is how much knowledge is needed to function effectively in a technologically supported classroom? Give the teachers what they need to thrive rather than simply exist.

4. Theoretical research needs to address heretofore underexamined areas, with an eye toward discovering and illuminating concrete influences of the computer upon writing *practices* rather than outcomes. Such studies can better serve educators because of the focus upon the *process* rather than the product.

5. The profession as a whole needs to develop more venues for giving practical scholarship a voice. Technology in the classroom raises far too many questions about things that we take for granted as teachers (e.g., being able to see the students's faces; how to arrange a room, et al.), and sometimes it's difficult to get answers to these basic questions. Scholarship is available in this area, but its presence is not high profile. As noted, theoretical scholarship can assist in this area by paying more attention to the practical tasks given to students. But giving practical scholarship more visibility and louder voice is necessary, too.

6. Teachers need to admit their fallibility as experts in this area, and not let this quality get in the way of maintaining an authoritative stance in the classroom. Need I point out that the teacher is still the expert when it comes to matters that are associated with becoming a better writer, which is still the aim of a writing class?

7. Above all, I think we need to see technology for what it is—the latest in a long line of supplemental teaching aids. It mustn't become the raison d'etre for any class (except those in computer engineering or Information systems). It is just a tool! It's a "machine that can help . . . students solve their writing problems . . . it will not magically

transform them" (Strickland 1).

Do we need to be afraid of technology? No, too many of us have learned enough about it by being dragged or thrust kicking and screaming into using it. It's time to share with those less up to speed. Make no mistake, the information underclass is fast becoming the newest misconstrued "minority" in education today. The have-nots still outnumber the haves, and that alone is enough to necessitate reorientation. So let's take out those road maps, see where we got off the Information Superhighway, and locate the next, though not necessarily the nearest, on-ramp.

WORKS CITED

Bolter, Jay David. *Writing Space: The Computer, Hypertext, and the History of Writing.* Hillsdale, NJ: Lawrence Erlbaum, 1991.

Burley, Hansel. "Does the Medium Make the Magic? The Effects of Cooperative Learning and Conferencing Software." *Computers and Composition* 15 (1998): 83-95.

Haas, Christina, and Christine M. Neuwirth. "Writing the Technology that Writes Us: Research on Literacy and the hape of Technology." *Literacy and Computers: The Complications of Teaching and Learning with Technology.* Eds. Cynthia L. Selfe and Susan Hilligoss. New York: MLA 1994. 319-36.

Handa, Carolyn, ed. *Computers and Community: Teaching Composition in the Twenty-First Century.* Portsmouth, NH: Heinemann-Boynton/Cook, 1990.

Hawisher, Gail E., et al. *Computers and the Teaching of Writing in American Higher Education, 1974-94: A History.* Norwood, NJ: Ablex, 1996.

Healy, Jane M. *Failure to Connect: How Computers Affect Our Children's Minds—for Better and Worse.* New York: Simon and Schuster, 1998.

Hoffman, Donna L., and Thomas P. Novak. "Bridging the Racial Divide on the Internet." *Science* 17 April 1998: 390-91.

Lee, Doris. "Factors influencing the success of computer skills learning among in-service teachers." *The British Journal of Educational Technology* 28.8 (1997): 139-41.

Moulthrop, Stuart, and Nancy Kaplan. "They Became What they Beheld: The Futility of Resistance in the Space of Electronic Writing." *Literacy and Computers: The Complications of Teaching and Learning with Technology.* Eds. Cynthia L. Selfe and Susan Hilligoss. New York: MLA 1994. 220-38.

Schroeder, Eric James, and John Boe. "Minimalism, Populism, and Attitude Transformation: Approaches to Teaching Writing in Computer Classrooms." *Computers and Community: Teaching Composition in the Twenty-First Century.* Ed. Carolyn Handa. Portsmouth, NH: Heinemann-Boynton/Cook, 1990. 28-47.

Selfe, Cynthia L. "Preparing English Teachers for the Virtual Age: The Case for Technology Critics." *Re-Imagining Computers and Composition: Teaching and Research in the Virtual Age.* Eds. Gail E. Hawisher and Paul LeBlanc. Portsmouth, NH: Heinemann-Boynton/Cook, 1992. 24-43.

————. "Technology and Literacy: A Story about the Perils of Not Paying Attention." *CCC* 50.3 (February 1998): 411-36.

Selfe, Cynthia L. and Susan Hilligoss. "Introduction." *Literacy and Computers: The Complications of Teaching and Learning with Technology.* Eds. Cynthia L. Selfe and Susan Hilligoss. New York: MLA 1994. 1-11.

Selfe, Cynthia L. and Susan Hilligoss, eds. *Literacy and Computers: The Complications of Teaching and Learning with Technology.* New York: MLA 1994. 1-11.

Skubikowski, Kathleen, and John Elder. "Computers and the Social Contexts of Writing." *Computers and Community: Teaching Composition in the Twenty-First Century.* Ed. Carolyn Handa. Portsmouth, NH: Heinemann-Boynton/Cook, 1990. 89-106.

Strickland, James. *From Disk to Hard Copy: Teaching Writing with Computers.* Portsmouth, NH: Heinemann-Boynton/Cook, 1997.

Wresch, William. *Disconnected: Haves and Have-nots in the Information Age.* New Brunswick, NJ: Rutgers UP, 1996.

Zeni, Jane. "Literacy, Technology, and Teacher Education." *Literacy and Computers: The Complications of Teaching and Learning with Technology.* Eds. Cynthia L. Selfe and Susan Hilligoss. New York: MLA 1994. 76-89.

13

Technology, Distance, and Collaboration: Where are These Pedagogies Taking Composition?

Linda Myers-Breslin

Over the last five years, computer-assisted composition instruction (CAI) has grown and changed considerably due to a shift toward network use. Initially, technology allowed pedagogies to focus on revision and editing. Then, pedagogical movement toward collaboration was furthered by local-area-network (LAN) discussion software like Daedalus Interchange and stand-alone hypertext programs such as Story-space and Hypercard. More currently, wide-area-network (WAN) Internet technologies such as e-mail, MOOs and MUDs, Usenet news, inter-relay chat (IRC), and the World Wide Web allow for larger, more public collaborative ventures. When embarking upon such ventures, we need to recognize not just the important differences between the LAN-based and WAN-based discussions, but also the differences between contribution, conversation, community, and collaboration. This chapter describes a three-year study that explored the effects of technology on freshman student collaboration. The information reviews the motivation, methodology, and theoretical underpinnings of the study. The chapter then moves into a discussion of findings and their pedagogical implications, as well as areas for future research.

To those of us looking for new ways to invigorate our CAI pedagogy and to those new to computers-assisted writing instruction, the Internet appears as a big public writing space, a larger version of our LAN-based writing spaces. As we move students from private to public audiences, it makes sense to place students into the Net. There we can ask them to write in a space where anyone and everyone can read their words, and students can exchange ideas in a more real world setting, with people situated in the real-world. Through World Wide Web pages, newsgroup threads, chat rooms, MOOs and MUDs, students and nonacademics alike have a space in which to place their words. Naturally, as teachers implementing collaborative pedagogies, we would like students placed into an electronic space to mean that they form an instant writing community. We would like to assume that the interaction mimics that of the collaborative conversations we see in our classrooms and on our LANs. We hope that students read what others have to say and convey their own ideas, forming a community of writers who write carefully and critique thoughtfully. But is this what is really happening? I think not.

Students intermingling ideas in the same writing space does not necessarily equal students collaborating in that space. As technology permeates composition classrooms and collaborative pedagogies, students spend more time in shared writing spaces. This can be a good use of time. Unfortunately, this preliminary study shows that students spend more time avoiding work, hiding from teachers and groupmates, and planning social events than they do understanding each other and the task, sharing on-task ideas, and completing the assignment. Thus, as teachers using computer-assisted writing instruction, we must ask ourselves key questions: Is the collaborative use of electronic writing spaces helping our students write well as well as continually improving their composition skills or is the technology distracting students from writing well and hindering improvement of their composition skills? How can we best use technology to engage and teach our students writing, the subject at hand?

Networked writing does not constitute community, collaboration, or even conversation. Writing out thoughts and placing these ideas into a space (private or public) is brainstorming. Brainstorming helps create potential paper topics and development. Conversing is more than this. To converse, students must read what others write and respond directly, not just place ideas into a space. Conversation helps students further develop and clarify these ideas for a paper. Collaboration furthers conversation. To collaborate means more than reading what another person writes and placing one's own thoughts into the same space. Collaboration is a concerted pedagogical effort toward the creation of an end product. The terms community, collaboration, and conversation, when applied to the Internet, need more thorough consideration than most of us have given up to this point.

We must remember that the LAN-based software is created by programmers in conjunction with teachers. Thus, pedagogy is integrated into the structure of these writing environments. The intent of these programs is clear to the student as well as the teacher: collaboration toward creating an effective final document. The Internet is not created with any pedagogical emphasis. We might easily envision the Internet as a large LAN for academic writing with connections to students from other schools and countries. Or we can envision connections with nonacademic users, placing our students in more authentic, real-world rhetorical situations. Do these connections and the ensuing discourse benefit our students as we envision? Perhaps there is benefit; however, there are several aspects of our beneficial intent that must be considered. Three aspects are particularly problematic: (1) the teacher's concept of collaboration might be quite different from the students' concepts, (2) collaboration is not a natural by-product of conversation, and (3) collaboration requires deliberate and concerted pedagogical efforts.

STUDY MOTIVATION

Almost two decades ago, computers changed the face of composition. Computer-assisted composition instruction became an important subdiscipline within Composition and Rhetoric. Most articles proclaimed a miraculous increase in student interest and participation (Hawisher, Selfe, Spitzer, etc.). I saw these wondrous examples in few of my classes. Thus, I began my own studies, examining how students use technology to collaborate on assigned tasks and papers. Do they use technology as we suggest, or do they use technology as they desire? Do students collaborate on ideas and writing or do they cooperate by writing separate sections and later combining the sections into a whole paper? With answers to these questions, I hoped to better devise a pedagogy that would increase student participation toward the assigned tasks. The primary study described here displays low student involvement in CAI tasks. The study results presented may help us examine practices that we should avoid and stop, and may show us practices that we should use and improve.

To increase student task involvement in CAI tasks, we must consider how students prioritize their behaviors. We must discover what *their* process is: not the process that we make for them, but the process they actually use when working together via technology. We must know the rationale behind the decisions they make and all that influences their attitudes toward their groupmates, the task assignments, and the work/products. Once we have this information, we can create informed pedagogical strategies that will affect student interaction. We can stop laying our templates on top of their existing interaction or assuming that they behave as instructed. Student collaboration is about students finding the niche that allows them to get what they want.

Because the student collaborative process is more complex than previous composition literature reveals, we need new strategies for studying this process. This preliminary study provides a model strategy. This model for analysis of student collaboration includes cross-disciplinary protocol analysis. Surveys and interviews over time reveal the complexities of student collaboration (and our false assumptions about this collaboration) that might allow us to create better informed collaborative assignments that increase student involvement and interaction.

STUDY METHODOLOGY

Informed by cross-disciplinary research, this study examines ways in which information technologies alter the social and organizational dimensions of student interaction. In order to explore the effect of electronic communication on small-group, collaborative interaction, ideas from communication studies, behavioral science, and social science are employed in this ongoing research project. In order to examine classes as a whole and case study small groups, data was gathered from a variety of sources.

The students, all seventeen to nineteen years of age, were enrolled in first-year writing courses. They were grouped randomly. Case study groups were selected at random. There were two class types taught each semester; one served as a study group and the other as a control group. The study group was given information regarding group dynamics. This included a basic outline of how groups function, the usual group life span and its phases, inherent conflicts and how best to deal with them, the usual group pitfalls, and ways to achieve optimum productivity within the group. The other class was the control group: students followed the same syllabus as described above, but they did not have information about group dynamics. The basic objective was to see if instruction in group dynamics would help groups function more efficiently. The case study group members agreed to meet with me and to be interviewed four times during the semester.

The initial survey and the initial case study interview were created to determine the students' experience and comfort in three specific areas: writing, group work, and computer use. I met with case study students before they met with their groups in order to get an idea of "who they were" before finding out "who they were in their group." Surveys were given to all students after each paper was completed in order to determine each group's process and effectiveness.

Whole Classes

1. *Surveys*—colleagues in social psychology helped construct Likert-scale surveys that were administered at the beginning and end of the courses. These surveys measured student comfort with technology, group work, and writing. After each paper, students were given an open-ended questionnaire, also developed with the assistance of social psychologists. The questionnaires probed student feeling about the writing process, about each group member's participation in the process, and about the final product itself.

2. *Synchronous interaction*—a MOO was constructed for the class. The MOO contained recorders and the transcripts were coded according to Bales.

3. Asynchronous interaction—a conference board was created for the class. Conference interactions as well as e-mail interactions were coded according to Bales.

4. Assignments—all classes followed the same syllabus, used the same texts, received the same assignment descriptions, completed the same process tasks, and answered the same questions.

Case Study Small Groups

1. Interviews—the case study group members were interviewed after each group project to discover their attitudes toward group work. Transcriptions were typed out and used as a basis for many of the results noted below. Student contributions were rated according to Bales

2. Ethnography—an anthropologist observed small-group discussions. She rated group member contribution according to whether students were on task or not on task, in order to determine if group members shifted from task more often during face-to-face interaction or electronic interaction.

In order to begin to address student apathy, I decided to inform groups about group dynamics. My thoughts concerning the dynamics described were that if students knew ways to work together effectively, they could consolidate their efforts, collaborate and cooperate efficiently, and therefore achieve a better process and product with less effort and time than when working alone. They could focus on the task, use each other's thoughts, skills, and experiences, and proficiently complete the assignments.

THEORETICAL UNDERPINNINGS

The theoretical underpinnings of this study, of the pedagogy employed, and of most networked writing software (such as Daedalus and Connections) stem from Kenneth Bruffee's collaborative learning approach to composition pedagogy. Bruffee argues that knowledge is not an accumulation of facts gathered, memorized, and regurgitated over the years, nor is knowledge information passed directly from tutor to student; instead, knowledge is communally acquired experiences, discussed by many, and agreed upon en masse. In other words, knowledge is socially constructed through the consensus of those participating in a given community. The challenge that Bruffee's ideas pose to writing teachers is one of transition. We must help students transition from their extracurricular, real-world communities to their academic or professional communities. Bruffee suggests that the best way to accomplish this transition is by placing students into learning groups and asking them to work collaboratively, socially constructing their knowledge base.

Each of Bruffee's assignments contains a two-stage process. The first stage asks students to pull from their own experiences and knowledge groups; the second stage asks students to contribute this knowledge to their current knowledge community. For example, a teacher provides a piece of writing and asks students to analyze it through a feminist perspective. Students work together, analyzing and discussing the piece in order to decide if the author achieves his or her goal(s). Bruffee's first stage is to place students in small groups, allowing students to talk with each other in their own terms, free from the teacher's ears and judgments. This stage encourages students to express themselves and explore their ideas freely without fear of "sounding stupid" in front of the teacher.

In the second stage, once the groups have completed their analysis, the teacher asks the groups to report their analysis and opinions to the class. This stage asks students to elevate their language in order for all to understand. Through reports and discussions, the teacher helps the students reach consensus. The teacher may read, distribute, or describe some professional, published critiques written about the piece, and by doing so, help students compare their analysis to those of scholars. In the second stage, students often delight in the similarities and learn from the differences between their words and the words of the critics. They begin to see, hear, and sense their transition into the academic (in this case feminist) knowledge community. Because students are in academia, they most often desire entrance into the academic community. The above example allows them to attempt entrance as a group and then to validate themselves through comparison with those already in the academic community.

Classroom networking software (such as Daedalus), or MOOs and MUDs on the Internet, manifest Bruffee's notions of collaborative learning by providing virtual writing spaces in which students can converse by simultaneously contributing their ideas, reading others' ideas, and giving and receiving feedback. Within these spaces, the teacher can create discussion spaces and threads for student groups or for the class as a whole. Students can also group by threads that help students interested in the same idea find each other for further topic discussion. Students enter these spaces readily and willingly; however, collaboration will not occur unless the teacher arranges and presents clearly defined tasks. The goal of transition between extracurricular and academic/professional discourse can only be achieved when the teacher successfully helps the groups reconcile their responses with the decided scholarly discourse community. In other words, the technology does not cause collaborative learning; instead, collaborative learning results from successful application of the technology within a particular social setting, a classroom of college students struggling through their course curriculum. The setting and the curriculum pre-establishes boundaries for conversations and creates a transitional community of students who hold a shared interest in gaining membership into the knowledge community presented by their teacher. Thus, the challenges for the teacher are also pre-established.

STUDY FINDINGS

The Initial Challenge for Teachers Is to Form a Clear Pedagogy and to Focus Pedagogical Efforts

These actions are challenging because the administration as well as our human nature want us to use the technology with as many bells and whistles as we can cram into each lesson. This is a mistake. Teachers need to bring themselves and their students into the electronic environment slowly, always thinking about what will best enable students to succeed at the given task. Most imperative is the teacher's preplanned pedagogy. Teachers must be aware of their course goals and use technology to realize those goals. Far too often the technology drives our pedagogy. We must stop this trend. Our pedagogy must drive our technology. Only then can technology be used in productive (instead of merely intriguing) ways. It is all well and good for the technology to add motivation to students' learning, but what are students learning? On this last point/question we must be clear.

For those of us utilizing collaborative pedagogies, we must remember that placing or intermingling words in the same writing space does not mean that students are conversing, much less collaborating. Students most often believe that collaboration means that they share ideas, then separate and write their papers for submission. In other words, they have a conversation on a particular topic, then write on that topic, edit, and submit the paper. Perhaps they will be asked to read a classmate's paper and edit it, but we should have students more involved in one another's process throughout, not just initially or at the end. In order for students to be invested in the collaboration, they must be involved with one another's papers from invention, through development and revision, to editing and evaluation. We need to make our expectations clear to students. We cannot assume that they know what we mean when we say "collaboration." Even in our classrooms, group work is rarely collaborative. The students do the work and then compare answers; collaboration comes next, when (off-task) they discuss, plan, and organize the evening festivities. We need to channel this later energy into the work at hand. Networked technology is not enough to focus students and spur collaboration. Clear, focused pedagogical efforts are required.

Another Challenge Is the Fact that Creating and Maintaining a Structured Setting Conducive to Collaboration and Transition is Deceptively Difficult

Effective pedagogy requires more than constructing a networked learning environment, such as building a MOO, installing software, or locating an Internet space. Regardless of where your class is located, instituting policies and procedures for the space is crucial to running a productive class on the Internet. For example, the teacher must set a task, including goals and evaluation criteria, and a time limit in which to complete the task. If these parameters are missing, students will chat about themselves and their activities, not getting to the task until the end of the class period, when they realize the activity is due. The teacher must also decide what activities are pedagogically valuable. For example, a teacher might interpret student interaction with nonstudent users as productive collaboration. This may be true, but again, the only way to keep communication valuable is to set goals and criteria, checks and balances. Otherwise, students may become fluent in the discourse of a particular chat room, but this discourse might not be the discourse of the academic knowledge community. Thus, the students learn to chat in a particular way, but such chat does not give them access into the desired academic/professional knowledge community intended for the course.

The instructor must locate or create nonstudent users who will help students transition into the desired knowledge community, not resist the discourse of that community. Such transition can be achieved by contacting outside users and establishing an agreement with them, or by limiting the users of the group. Establishing agreement can take time, but it is not difficult. For example, if students are writing a travel journal, they might want firsthand information. The teachers should locate some travel chat rooms, go in, and ask if users are willing to converse with students (in an appropriate manner). If some or most agree, then that is a productive place to send students. Or the teacher may create a MOO room for the course and invite outside users, who agree to use the desired discourse, into this space. Both arrangements lead to another challenge: maintaining focus on the collaborative goal.

A MOO space is a superb environment for individual users to explore and express themselves and to read what others have to say; however, unless the task is an integral part of the MOO environment, such discovery activity is inherently thwarted. Students wish to talk, but usually about topics they create. The teacher must define and explain collaboration, clarify the assignment, and set a time limit. Because actions within the MOO such as movement, posting, whispering, paging, and so on, can distract rather than help accomplish the task, the teacher may choose not to explain these functions.

Because Play-Tasks Are as Important as Project-Tasks, Teachers Must Create and Assign Both Task Types

To avoid difficulties with collaboration, trust is essential. In order to build trust, there is a need for two task types when combining students into a collaborative venture: (1) community-building tasks and (2) project-building tasks. Community-building adds the element of play, of getting to know each other in an informal sense, to the act of collaboration. A sense of community and trust won't develop through project-tasks. This sense builds with what goes on around the project-tasks. Play is the best way to allow students to get to know each other and to develop a level of trust vital to accomplishing a group goal.

We can bring students into the unfamiliar academic arena with some playful, not-so-academic exercises like the following:

1. Assign the following letter: Your folks/significant other just hollered at you last night about your huge phone bill. They told you to start saving. Now the bill just came in for those concert tickets you ordered. You have to pay this bill now. Write a letter to your folks or significant other, asking for money. After the letters are written, exchange and comment of their effectiveness. These letters let students get to know about one another's domestic lives, relationships, and writing styles.

2. Request the following information: Write three to five facts about yourself, one of which is a lie. The partners on the other end have to guess which fact is a lie.

3. Set up an information gathering scavenger hunt. Ask the others to list three foods they hate, their least favorite nickname that people have given to them, their favorite place as a kid, their favorite place now, questions about family, pets, schools, favorite classes, teachers, books, artists, and so on.

4. Encourage students to get the most esoteric information that they can from their partners. Once the student community is formed, collaborative, project-building tasks are more easily accomplished.

At the Beginning of the Course, Limited and Fully-Detailed Assignments Are Most Effective

We must remember that students are not always used to working in a virtual environment. Thus, just as we need to define our terms, we also need to define our assignments. When we place students into small groups within the classroom, they often know what we expect. This understanding does not transfer into the Internet. Therefore, for the first two or three weeks of the semesters, the more detailed we are and the more swapping of information we do, the better. This practice will come to be the norm for students and they will know what to do, but this understanding is not a given at the start of the course. For example, students working on a travel journal might receive the following assignments to get them started:

Write five assumptions you hold about your group's country of choice. Saving a copy for yourself, send these assumptions to your groupmates. Select the assumptions that overlap with yours, elaborate on why you held that assumption. Saving a copy for yourself, send your elaboration to your groupmates. Look at the list you have received. After each elaboration, write any evidence you have that supports the assumption. Saving a copy for yourself, send this information to your groupmates. Now you are ready to create a draft. Select the assumptions for which you have evidence or decide from where you might gather evidence. Revise your groupmates' information, reconciling it with your own. Decide if your thesis will claim that the stereotypes about the country are true or false. Form this information into a draft. Saving a copy for yourself, send this draft to your groupmates. Discuss and decide which claim your group will take, and revise the draft that the group like best. Then decide who will do what in order to gather supporting information.

The students decide whether they wish to do these tasks together or separately and which technology will best accomplish a particular task. Although we might know computers and CAI, our students benefit from specific, deliberate work. "Baby steps" are the way to go for students when they are just starting out. Students learn what is expected of them, as well as what they can expect from groupmates.

Basic Instruction About Group Dynamics is Helpful Toward Project-Building Tasks

Members of the informed groups' avoided pitfalls such as groupthink (in which students grab onto the first idea mentioned and run with it, although it might not be worthwhile or the most appropriate choice). These students left themselves open to a range of ideas, voiced dissenting opinions, and made sure that all members were heard in order to arrive at a well-considered topic. Out of urgency for consensus, the uninformed groups seemed to accept the first topic mentioned or the topic stressed most adamantly by a member. This urgency caused them to select topics that were not as challenging and interesting as the informed groups' selections.

Initially, the group dynamics instruction was problematic for the informed groups. Instead of seeing the group as a means to an end product, the informed group saw the group as a task in itself. Each group member was too focused on his or her role in the group. For example, a basic of group dynamics is group member roles. Four has been the number of member found to work most effectively within a group. There are four roles they can take to aid group effectiveness: leader—keeps the group focused and moving toward goal; recorder—notes discussion ideas and conclusions; encourager—provides ideas to keep discussion going; and reporter—reports group findings to the whole class or organization.

Preoccupation with roles hindered some "recorders" from contributing ideas because they were so concerned with getting down everything said that they could not think of ideas. Similarly, group "reporters" were so concerned with how to report the information that they did not contribute much. The "encouragers" felt that they did not have to give ideas but had to get others to talk, and the "leaders" were stressed that the others were not contributing and the group was not progressing with the assignment. Once the problem was realized and addressed by the teacher, the roles were helpful. The teacher must make it clear to the group that all students must contribute; then all can help the recorder note the highlights of the group interaction, and help the reporter plan what he or she is to say.

By contrast the uninformed groups were not informed about group roles, and therefore they were not overly concerned about their performance within the group. These groups used the group as a means to an end—a well written paper. However, these groups also had more complaints regarding group members who did not "pull their weight." Thus, a bit of instruction regarding the basics of small group dynamics and about the major pitfalls that groups encounter proved quite helpful. Teachers must be wary, however, that they do not overly emphasize these issues to the point that students feel their grade depends on how well they perform within their group. This point relates to the first challenge regarding a focused pedagogy: we might ask, are we evaluating the students' writing or their group work?

Teaching Students Only the Basics of the Available Technology and Encouraging Them to Use It At Will is More Effective than Assigning Use and Explaining Every Step

Again, less information worked best for students. Both sections were taught how to use the available technologies: the MOO, conference board, e-mail, and nickname file. Members of the informed groups received information regarding which technologies could prove helpful at various stages of the writing process. It was suggested, for example, that the MOO could support brainstorming, the conference boards could support peer review, and e-mail could support revision and editing. Unfortunately, as with group roles, the informed students felt that they had to use the technologies as suggested. This seemed to stifle rather than enhance students process. This difficulty had to be realized and rectified.

Members of the uninformed groups, on the other hand, who had no suggestion regarding when to incorporate specific technologies, immediately began to decide which technologies to use and when. Most of these students used the technologies as described above. But the fact that they created their own group system of operations removed the stifled feeling and allowed students to focus on their writing rather then the technology.

All Spaces Need Auxiliary Features to Support Student Collaborative Work

Teachers should include the following features in their learning spaces: a particular place for the teacher's assignment, separate sessions for the various student interactions and assigned tasks, an accessible database of class documents including student papers, and an archive of previous discussions with easy retrieval for student research. Such ancillaries help the teacher situate the assignment within the larger classroom context, thereby fostering the transitional discourse and desired knowledge community.

The World Wide Web is another area that needs auxiliary features in order to help students collaborate. Although websites provide much information for students to explore, the opportunity to consider the information in a collaborative way does not readily exist. While users can easily surf through the Web's many hypertextual threads, users cannot synchronously interact with others seeking the information. Browsing and research on the Web does not help students make discursive connections with a new knowledge community. If the Web is going to support student collaboration, it will need sharable virtual spaces that allow students to navigate the Web together and converse about what they see. Only through such spaces can students collaboratively research information via the World Wide Web.

Course Information Should be Made Available in Electronic and Paper Copy

Placing all course expectations, assignments, and assignment expectations on the computer is a good idea, especially if this information is placed on the Web, which is always available. Placing course and assignment information onto the Internet eliminates excuses such as "I forgot we had to read that," "I did not know that was due today," and "It had to be five pages?" With the information constantly available, the students have no reason to claim that they did not know, or could not find their assignment sheet.

Equally important, however, is providing this information to students in hard copy. Many teachers have begun to utilize the concept of a "paperless classroom," which means that assignments are given and received on computer without the use of paper. This technique causes many difficulties, especially for those of us new to the computer classroom or particular technologies. Should the server go down, the teacher's Web page not save, or some other catastrophe occur, at least the students have the information. Should a student not have access to the technology at home or dorm or elsewhere outside of the classroom, he or she still has the information in order to complete the assignment. Plus, students can easily make personal notes as the teacher verbally explains the assignment, if they have the assignment in front of them.

Finally, dual notation of the course policies, procedures, and assignments is just a good idea. All students can locate the information and none can claim that the information was unavailable.

Short, Three-Week, Five-to-Ten Page Writing Projects Help the Writing Groups Establish a Group Process and Effective Strategies for Technology Use

Initially, the course change suggested most often by students was to reduce the number of papers. Students find it difficult to complete a group paper in the time usually allotted to complete a single authored paper. Although theoretically it seems that with technology and a group, students should be able to complete a paper, group or single authored, within two weeks, but this is often not the case. When the number of papers is reduced to four for the semester and when the students are given three weeks to complete a paper, not only are the teachers happier with the grades, but so are the students. Most students comment that they have time to complete what they consider the full writing process. They also stop using the excuse that they "do not have long enough to write a good paper." Once the time is extended, students have to claim responsibility for the product. Thus, students are not "getting away with something" because, with the extended time, the teacher can expect a bit more in quality.

An Emphasis on Technology Throughout the School Has an Effect on Groupware Use

Once the freshmen students realize the extent of technology use at our university, they are more eager to learn the technology, particularly the MOO and e-mail systems. Through our school's e-mail system, students have access not only to each other and students at other schools, but to course listings and all that the World Wide Web has to offer: postings of social events, bulletin boards for selling and buying, or boards dedicated to Star Trek, soap operas, parasailing, religious affiliations, Chaucer literature, psychology, and computer groups. Most any interests that students might have is listed, and students can join a conversation with others who have the same interests.

Most groupware, such as Daedalus Interchange and MOO programming, allows students to locate discussion threads. Threads are contributions that discuss (or mention) a particular topic. Students follow the thread, see who is contributing, contact these people, and begin an in-depth discussion of the topic. In a MOO, students can tell the contributors to meet in a specific room in order to isolate and focus discussion. Or students can form their own conference topic on a conference board and contribute asynchronously.

Teachers should emphasize the prevalence of technology throughout their schools in all disciplines. Use of technology in other disciplines is a valuable discussion to have near the beginning of the course. Discussion regarding group work and collaboration in other disciplines and in the work-world is also quite helpful toward motivating student interaction.

Teachers Cannot Assume That Students Will Use the Technology as Suggested, or Even as Assigned

One of the challenges of CAI is the assumption that students will use the technology the way that the teacher suggests. For example, the teacher usually introduces ways in which various communication technologies can be used at each point in the writing process: MOO or Interchange for brainstorming, e-mail and conference boards for exchanging drafts, peer reviewing, and revising, and the conference boards for peer editing sessions. Students most often do not use these technologies as described. For students, Interchange does not always encourage brainstorming opportunity. Instead Interchange and MOOs allow opportunity for getting to know each other, a safe forum in which to tease, joke, and play. When surveyed, a few students referred to the synchronous conferencing system as "a toy."

Similarly, instructions regarding e-mail might provide a way for students to plan group meetings, share writing, and exchange criticism. For students, however, it can provide a subversive way of avoiding work for the assigned project. A few case-study students, for example, did not check their e-mail, even after repeated reminders from the teachers in classes and from their group members out of classes. Thus, these "avoiders" forced other group members into using low-level communication technologies (the phone), and when the avoiders did not respond to calls, the group had to move on without them. These avoiders used the technology to hide from work.

Another assumption held by educators in computer-assisted instruction is that students will be so mesmerized and seduced by the technology that all of them will want to use it. We do not consider that some students might simply choose not to use the technology for whatever reason. For some, it is simply unfamiliar. For others, personal interaction is easier and more rewarding. This case is exemplified by students' complaints that they preferred to talk in person, rather than over the Internet, (which they described as a "toy"), when in the same room. Students resented the technology and found it frustrating when all those conversing were in the same room. Students must be allowed time to speak orally. Yes, we are teaching students to write, but many of them also like to talk.

Students process information in very different ways; some need to verbalize their ideas, to hear them aloud. Students seem most content when there is time allotted for both writing and for speaking in class. We should ask them to write for a while and then MOO, or the other way around. We just have to be sure that we have different topics for the verbal and written discussions, unless the students MOO as a small group and then verbally report back to the class.

Students Need Technology Modeled for Them in Order to Realize Teacher Expectations

Students model their technology use after the teachers technology use. Thus, the we should demonstrate the types of communication we desire over the MOO and over the conference boards. Initially in the study, for example, I placed assignments on the MOO and the conference boards, and I sent e-mail messages when I forgot to tell students something in classes. Unfortunately, students closely followed my model. They tried technological short cuts or avoided the technology. Because I never engaged in discussion with the students on the computer, neither did most of the students. I found that students were just sending each other short, instructional e-mail messages, such as "Let's meet in the library at the big table at 8 tonight," or "Call him again." They did not post papers for review or send messages discussing the paper or ideas for it. They missed out on an efficient and productive way to convey their ideas. In later classes, when I engaged students in the types of electronic discourse that I wanted them to pursue, they did so. Thus, we cannot assume that telling students to communicate on the computer means they will do so without any example or participation from us.

The Grade Is the Ultimate Student Motivation

Student motivation is an area also under examination in this study. Are students prompted to use technology or to participate in the group due to personalities (theirs and others'), by popularity, by technological expertise, by adeptness of writing skills? In light of the findings, instructors must consider the following questions: What then can we do to effectively encourage student participation? And does motivation simply result from the paper grade or course grade? Apparently the answer to the second question is more important to a significant number of students. This study indicates that "the grade," in fact, is the primary motivator for subjects' performance.

By the third project/paper, students (whether working together or individually) forgot about the group and focused on achieving a high grade. Students cared that the product was acceptable to the teacher; they showed limited concern for their group members' opinions.

The Collaborative Writing Experience is Valuable for Students

On the final survey (distributed to all students) is an open-ended question:

Should I teach a classes using the collaborative techniques again? If not, why not? If so, why so?

Of the 242 students, only eighteen stated that they did not benefit from the group writing experience. I was surprised and pleased that the students appreciated being forced to write in a group and felt they had benefited from the experience. Of course, I wanted them to have gained awareness of their writing style and confidence in expressing themselves through writing. A few students mentioned ideas corresponding with my wishes; most, however, noted learning about personal process.

QUESTIONS FOR FUTURE RESEARCH

Software Learning

Although most groups in this study used the available technologies, some did not; thus, leaving many questions unanswered by the work reported here. Of the groups that opted to use electronic communication as suggested, how did they learn the technology? How do students best learn software packages? In our classes, the technology was taught; then its implementation left up to the students. Would students learn better and be more motivated to use the technology if it were peer taught by tutors, by fellow group members, or by reading printed or on-line documentation? Is the simple trial-and-error method the best teacher? Is a combination of these methods most effective? Is the combination different for different groups—suiting the learning style of the group members? Can we discover a group learning style? Can we motivate hesitant students to learn and use technology? If so, how?

Voice

If a collaborative writing group uses electronic communication, how does their computer voice differ from their verbal voice? Does their personal etiquette differ from their electronic etiquette? If not specifically asked to create rules, does the group create rules? Are rules necessary? If a group is required to create rules, what types of rules are created?

Gender

Gender bias was intentionally omitted as part of this study. Many studies show that gender clearly influences interpersonal collaboration. Does it cause similar effects in electronic communication? What about in a mixture of electronic and personal communication? Do same-gender groups or mixed-gender groups work best together, develop the better process? Which group type creates the better product?

Task Type

Consider the task type and technology and collaborative uses. How does technology use differ between collaborative and cooperative writing tasks? Are all types of technology employed? At what stages, if any, in the writing process are students more apt to turn to each other for face-to-face meetings? How satisfied are students with multiauthored rather than single-authored texts?

CONCLUSION

Although this study answered many of my questions about instructing student collaborative writing groups in an electronic environment, obviously there is much left to research. As schools continue to acquire computer technology, I hope that more departments join efforts in developing new teaching and learning strategies for collaborative writing efforts as well as composing interdisciplinary research teams to pose and answer questions.

WORKS CITED

Baron, Naomi. "Writing in the Age of E-mail: The Impact of Ideology versus Technology," *Visible Language: Journal of Typographic Research*, 32, (1998): 35-47.

Bruffee, Kenneth. "Collaborative Learning and the 'Conversation of Mankind.'" *College English*, 46 (Nov. 1984): 635-52.

Forsyth, Donald. *Group Dynamics*. Pacific Grove, CA: Brooks/Cole Publishing Co., 1990.

Hackman, J. R. "The Design of Work Teams." In J. W. Lorsch, ed. *Handbook of Organizational Behavior*. Englewood Cliffs, NJ: Prentice-Hall, 1987. 315-42.

Holdstein, Deborah H. "A Politics of Composition and Technology: Instructions and the Hazards of Making New." *Writing Program Administration*, 20, Fall, 1996: 19.

Lively, K. "New to MOO? What Is This Internet Environment with the Funny-Sounding Acronym?" *Link-Up*, 14 (1997): 21-25.

Olson, Gary. "Writing Literacy and Technology: Toward a Cyborg Writing." *Journal of Advanced Composition*, Winter 1996: 1-16.

Spitzer, M. "Computer Conferencing: And Emerging Technology." In G. Hawisher and C. Selfe, eds., *Critical Perspectives on Computers and Composition*. New York: Teacher's College Press, 1989. 187-200.

Tabbi, Joseph and Joseph Shade. "Postmodern Sublime: Technology an American Writing from Mailer to Cyberpunk." *Technology and Culture*, 38 (1997): 957.

Trimbur, John. "Consensus and Difference in Collaborative Learning." *College English*, 51 (1989): 258-71.

Linguistics and Composition

Sara Kimball

It's very rare that you ever get a free ride from some other field.
—Noam Chomsky (Olson and Faigley 34)

Linguistics has long informed teaching and research in composition. During the 1950s, insights into the systematic nature of language from American Structuralism, the dominant linguistic theory in American universities, helped bring about a significant reorientation in the perspective of composition teachers, allowing them to see themselves not as linguistic police enforcing prescriptive etiquette but as observers of student language. Later, the influence of sociolinguistics encouraged composition specialists to regard themselves as observers of the social and interpersonal contexts in which students write. These changes in orientation not only made composition pedagogy more humane, but without such fundamental shifts in attitude, composition research would not have been possible (Nystrand et al. 273).

Since the 1960s, scholarship in second language acquisition and sociolinguistics has aided composition researchers trying to devise approaches that would meet the needs of speakers of nonstandard English and English as a second language. For example, the concepts of error analysis, first-language interference, and interlanguage, a learner's approximation of a target language that is systematic and a sign of learning rather than a random collection of errors, has informed the work of Mina Shaughnessy, David Bartholomae, and other researchers and teachers of basic writing (Bartholomae 68-70, 76-79,

Montgomery (99-104). Sociolinguistic notions of dialect variation have contributed to an increased awareness that the students in our classes are not linguistically deficient but are competent users of varieties of language with systematic structures and histories of their own. As Lester Faigley notes, the *NCTE Statement on Student's Right To Their Own Language* of the 1970s is the product of an intellectual climate heavily influenced by sociolinguistics (81). Later research within sociolinguistics has helped researchers in composition to understand that difficulties experienced by nontraditional students are not simply linguistic but also have to be understood as rhetorical, cultural, and political (Montgomery 104-8). Work from the anthropological and ethnography of the speaking side of sociolinguistics, for example, Shirley Brice Heath's *Ways with Words*, published in 1983, has influenced both research methodology in composition and fundamental ways of thinking about literacy. By the 1970s and 1980s, scholarship influenced by pragmatics, discourse analysis, and functionalist linguistics appeared with some frequency in composition journals and monographs (Nystrand et al. 285-88, Faigley 80, 89-91, Larson 219-23).

AN UNWARRANTED PESSIMISM

By the late 1980s and early 1990s, however, linguistics had apparently become a less salient influence within mainstream composition scholarship. Lester Faigley, for example, notes that Stephen North ignores linguistics in his book *The Making of Knowledge in Composition* (80). In her survey of the impact of linguistics on composition between 1950 and 1980, Sharon Crowley concludes that while linguistic theory was attractive to teachers of composition in the 1950s because of the intellectual poverty of composition teaching at that time and the long association of composition with grammar (481), its influence on the whole has been disappointing and that linguistics "cannot provide teachers with the wider focus on composing that is necessary to develop a comprehensive theory of composition" because it offers "an extremely narrow, noncontextual view of what it means to be a user of language" (499). Even Frank Parker and Kim Sydow Campbell, who criticize Crowley's limited presentation of linguistics, are fairly circumspect in their claims about the possible benefits, restricting their illustration of the relation between theory, application, and practice to speech acts and pragmatics and dismissing Sledd's observation that the study of language structure, history, and the social functions of dialects provides useful intellectual grounding for writing teachers as special pleading from an expert in these fields (311 n. 5). To cite a more recent example, neither North in an assessment of possibilities for research in composition published in 1997, nor any other contributors to the volume in which his essay appears, mention linguistics as an influence on research.

At first glance, the pessimism seems justified. Institutional changes such as the formation of linguistics departments separate from language departments, a process that started in the late 1940s but accelerated in the 1960s and 1970s, in part because of the prestige of transformational-generative grammar in the academy, tended to isolate linguists from composition (Faigley 85). The increasingly abstract nature of theoretical linguistics has perhaps made it seem irrelevant too. The ethos of linguistics as a field that presents itself as scientific and empirical (and in the case of generative grammar, mathematical) has long proved uncongenial to the more humanistically oriented elements in English departments,[1] but since the early 1980s the emphasis within Chomskyan linguistics has been on finding universal properties of language rather than on the constructions and rules of individual languages, a set of goals that seems to have little to offer either the researcher in composition or the teacher (Faigley 83).

But the picture of linguists isolated within linguistics departments pursuing syntactic esoterica is not entirely accurate, and much of the pessimism is unwarranted because it is based on limited and inaccurate views of linguistics. Linguists have always been part of English departments, and especially in the many universities that do not have separate departments of linguistics, English and other language departments often provide linguists with institutional homes. Many English department graduate and undergraduate programs require at least some coursework in English linguistics or the history of the language, and it seems a safe bet that most students and faculty in English departments and composition programs have had at least some exposure to linguists and their ideas.

Although transformational-generative grammar is the branch of linguistics most readily identifiable to outsiders, and Noam Chomsky is perhaps the only linguist well known to the educated public, not all linguists work within the Chomskyan tradition. It is perhaps safe to say that any linguist trained within the past thirty years is a Chomskyan in the sense that the gospel according to MIT provided part of our training and has helped shape our outlook, but many of us, including those in phonetics, some types of phonology and morphology, anthropological linguistics, sociolinguistics, educational linguistics, psycholinguistics, second language acquisition, discourse analysis, pragmatics, and historical linguistics have stuck to chugging along on Faigley's "slow, data-gathering local" (84) and have prospered in our own ways. Chomsky's idealization of language as the theoretical competence of an idealized speaker-hearer using an invariant idiolect was a productive abstraction on the theoretical level, but it has not gone unchallenged,[2] and challenges to concepts from Chomskyan linguistics have provided productive avenues for research in empirically oriented fields within linguistics such as psycholinguistics and second language acquisition (Newmeyer and Weinberger "Otogenesis," Cahill).

In some ways, theoretical linguistics and sociolinguistics have been such intimate parts of the formation of composition as an academic field that ideas from these fields are no longer easily recognizable as foreign. If we strip away some of the misappropriations and misunderstandings of the past forty years—for example, the confusion of "generation" or "derivation" with invention implicit in some of the early enthusiasm about generative rhetoric, the confusion of the syntactic notion of "transformation" with the writer's notion of stylistic option implicit in early work on sentence combining, and the use of "recursive," a term describing the mathematical properties of rules in early generative grammar as a synonym for "nonlinear" in process research—there is a solid core of intellectual influence that is so fundamental to modern composition thinking that its origins are no longer salient.[3] It seems unlikely, for example, that any scholar in composition would seriously question the notions that power relations are enacted through language or that speakers and writers signal various aspects of their social identity through their use of language, ideas that have been developed and examined in sociolinguistic research. Many ideas from sociolinguistics in particular are most familiar as sociolinguistics in the literature on basic writing, but the fact that so much of literary theory has been deeply influenced by linguistics, especially the European version of Structuralism (Nystrand et al. 282-84; Faigley 88) also contributes to the sense that concepts originally from linguistics (e.g., discourse community as an extension of speech community) are simply part of the intellectual landscape in composition.

Although some of the reluctance to acknowledge the influence of linguistics may stem from widespread attitudes toward scientific, empirical, or mathematical approaches to knowledge, some of the inability to recognize the influence of sociolinguistics in particular may come from a tendency within composition to regard knowledge as dialectic rather than cumulative, an attitude that is sometimes too ready to discount old knowledge in favor of novelty. The discouragement about linguistics is analogous to the fate of process within composition scholarship: the idea of writing as process was embraced as a virtual panacea, commodified by the textbook industry, and then widely rejected as a topic of research, both in reaction to initial excesses and because of its more or less accidental historical ties with expressivism (Tobin 7-9).

The embrace of novelty is no doubt in part a reflection of fickle academic fashion, but it is also a function of the fact that, as a field, composition is driven by a pedagogical imperative. A large part of our job, which is made more difficult by unrealistic demands from administrators and the general public, is to find effective ways of intervening in writing. Unlike linguists, we do not have the luxury of description without action. But the danger is that we can be moved by the pedagogical imperative into ill-informed action. We sometimes look for quick fixes—Chomsky's free ride from some other field—without necessarily thinking through the relation between theory and practice, forgetting that our job in its largest sense is to articulate theories appropriate to our own concerns, both as the backing for effective pedagogy, and as knowledge for its own sake.

And this is precisely where things have gone awry historically in the relation between linguistics and composition—when linguistic theory has been applied directly to practice, for example, in teaching transformational-generative grammar as stylistics or invention. After forty years of research, it should be clear that teaching students linguistics, or any form of formal grammar, will not improve their writing.[4] Expecting students to master style through the study of grammar, whether traditional or according to a particular linguistic theory, makes about as much sense intellectually as expecting pitchers to study physics in order to improve their pitching, even though a pitch can be described in the equations of physics.

LINGUISTICS AS INTELLECTUAL GROUNDING

Crowley is right to criticize the quick-fix mentality in attitudes toward linguistics (498), but the solution is not rejecting linguistics as a field that can inform composition theory and practice. As Faigley notes, "a categorical dismissal of linguistics from rhetoric and composition may be premature" (83). The pitcher may not have to learn physics, but the people responsible for the conditions under which the game is played can contribute to better pitching by knowing enough about the physics of pitching to design better balls and practice activities that do not wreck pitcher's arms. Similarly, acquiring a background in the structure and history of the English language is one of the intellectual responsibilities of composition professionals in their roles as researchers and teachers because such a background can help teachers fashion classroom environments that allow writing to flourish, and it can provide productive directions for research into the nature of writing.

In the remainder of this chapter I would like to illustrate how linguistics can provide perspectives on writers and their work by looking at two areas in which the concerns of linguists and those of compositionists intersect. The first—in some ways easier because it is less obvious—is how definitions of language from formal linguistics can contribute to an understanding of writing. The second is perspectives from linguistics on the relationship between spoken and written language.

DEFINITIONS OF LANGUAGE

Writing involves using technology to make thought manifest in visible symbols with a relationship to language.[5] To intervene effectively in the work of writers, we need to separate out and understand the parts of writing that belong to language, thought, and technology. Linguistic definitions of language help separate the linguistic aspects of writing from the cognitive and technological.

All natural languages exhibit dual articulation: they consist of sounds and meanings linked by a system of rules called a grammar. A central tenet of linguistics since de Saussure is that, whatever the shape of the rules, the link between sound and meaning is arbitrary. No sequence of sounds uniquely, or ideally, conveys a particular meaning.

This is a formal description of language as an observable phenomenon. The generative tradition in its various manifestations has always had as its goal going beyond formal description to explain language as a biological faculty and to explain how it is acquired (Olson and Faigley 10-13). Current theories try to isolate Universal Grammar, those aspects of language that are hard-wired in the human brain at birth and that constitute a common human inheritance (Chomsky and Lasnik 14). The working hypothesis is philosophically nativist; its premise is that human beings are born with a set of principles common to all languages already present in brain structure and with knowledge of how these principles may vary along a limited set of parameters. Language is acquired as the result of exposure to particular languages during the first years of life, and acquisition involves learning the values appropriate to each parameter—in other words, learning how the principles are embodied in the language the child hears. For example, a principle that seems to be universal is that syntactic rules are structure-dependent: they rely on structural relationships for their conditioning not on the linear order of words (Cook 2). The ordering of elements within constituents, however, differs from language to language. A child is born knowing in some sense both that rules depend on structure and knowing possible structures; exposure to language teaches her to select particular structures. Exposure to English, for example, teaches her to generalize (apparently quite rapidly) that the head of a noun phrase or verb phrase (e.g., the noun in cat in the hat or the verb in caught the mouse) comes to the left of the phrase. A child hearing Japanese, by contrast, learns that heads come to the right (roughly the equivalent of cat hat in and mouse caught). This process of acquisition is natural, unconscious, and biologically determined. Chomsky has repeatedly likened human linguistic capacity to a bodily organ, viewing acquisition as the natural growth and development of this organ (*Rules* 134-35).

At first glance, none of this seems directly relevant to teaching writing. But it is very directly relevant to one's sense of what one is doing in the classroom. First, it provides the warrant for regarding all of our students—no matter what their level of preparation or social background—as competent users of language. Universal Grammar and dual articulation provide intellectually sound arguments for viewing all languages, and all dialects of a language, as linguistically equal. If the relation between sound and meaning is arbitrary, then judgments about the superiority or inferiority of a language or dialect are social; they have no linguistic basis. If all human languages are at some fundamental level the same, and we are all born with the capacity to learn any human language, then all human languages are, in linguistic terms, equal. The equality of linguistic codes cannot be dismissed as a sentimental trope of the political left or a fond hope of optimistic but naive teachers; it is a consequence of human biology.

A biological theory of language also implies a theory of translatability. It is possible to express any thought capable of being held by a human being in any language. Labov, for example, in a paper that has been highly influential in composition and language education, demonstrates that it is possible to construct a syllogism in the most colloquial variety of Afro-American Vernacular English (12-15). A theory of translatability implies that whatever the relation between language and thought, it is not direct. Chomsky, for example, has long described language and thought as interrelated but fundamentally separate cognitive systems. Although there are challenges to this view from within cognitive science and linguistics (Kempson), and it is possible that features of grammatical systems, such as marking of tense, aspect, and plurality may mediate thought, shaping and constraining speakers' worldviews (Lakoff), a number of considerations should suggest that, ultimately, language is not thought. People without language (aphasics, deaf people who acquired neither spoken language nor sign language in infancy, and infants) are capable of various cognitive activities, for example, computation (Pinker 67-69). Anecdotal accounts of thought without language, (e.g., thinking in images) receive some empirical support from experiments (Pinker 70-73), and any writer who has ever struggled to find the proper words to express her thoughts is deeply familiar with the idea that thought is possible—if not necessarily satisfying—in the absence of language. But more important, no human language is an adequate medium for the mental computation that underlies thought, because, as Stephen Pinker explains, language does not in and of itself offer the means for resolving coreference, deixis, or lexical ambiguity, and natural languages lack the logical explicitness necessary for mental computation (78-82). It takes more than linguistic knowledge to understand or produce a sentence like *Norma cut a piece of pie, put it on the plate she'd taken down from the shelf, and gave it to her sister.*

If language is biological and organized along universal lines, writing is artificial because it is always mediated by technology, and unlike spoken language, it is explicitly taught and learned. The distinction is a crucial one and in part what linguists mean when they speak of the primacy of speech. One of the benefits of recent research in computers and writing is that it foregrounds the technological aspects of writing, but it should not be forgotten that the simple writing tools we often take for granted—pencils, pens, and paper—are also technology. Because writing inevitably involves the use of tools, it ineluctably intertwines language and thought as cognitive systems with cognitive systems involved in the manipulation of tools.

Some of the difficulties writers face may be primarily technological rather than linguistic or cognitive, or they may reflect the complexities inherent in trying to integrate three different systems. This should not be an idea foreign to our experience as teachers and writers. Teachers of basic writing, for example, have long known that some of their students' problems stem from unfamiliarity with the tools used for writing (Shaughnessy 14-16). If successful writing depends upon the fluent integration of thought, language, and tools, someone unaccustomed to manipulating a pencil or pen may in part be hobbled by the tool-using aspects of the task and unable to deploy language and thought with spontaneous fluency, a phenomenon that should not be alien to anyone who has struggled to learn a new word-processing program. But difficulties integrating technological, cognitive, and linguistic aspects of writing are probably not unique to basic writers and novice computer users. One cause of some types of writer's block may be interference among competing systems under conditions that force the writer to focus on one aspect at the expense of others.

One of our goals as teachers should be to arrange conditions to allow students opportunities to practice integrating thought, language, and tool-use. We can also reformulate some basic research questions by defining their domains more clearly. For example, one source of disillusionment with sentence combining is that no one has provided a satisfactory account of how it works (Strong 337; Crowley 490-91). It is possible, however, that under the right circumstances sentence combining can increase syntactic flexibility not by tapping directly into linguistic competence, but by providing an opportunity for practice. As Larson, for example, notes, sentence combining seems to work best as a technique for revision that engages students in reshaping their own prose (218). Perhaps it succeeds when writers are actively engaged in the linguistic manipulation of intellectual content that they have created because it allows them to practice integrating the linguistic and tool using aspects of writing without undue interference from the cognitive aspects. In other words, it functions as exercises do in sports or music, as a way of isolating, practicing, and making automatic a small part of a larger, more complex whole in a context free of the stresses of real-world performance (Strong; Elbow 238).

LINGUISTIC PERSPECTIVES ON SPOKEN AND WRITTEN LANGUAGE

The idea that some of the features viewed with disfavor in student writing have their source in spoken language is not new to composition. It figures prominently, for example, in work on the influence of nonstandard dialects on the writing of so-called basic writers. The ideas of Walter Ong, who claims that differences in the syntax of written and spoken language reflect cognitive differences between "literate" and "oral" thinking have also been influential, if not uncontroversial, in composition, and the increasing use of real-time and delayed conferencing systems in networked composition classrooms has recently stimulated thinking on spoken and written linguistic strategies.

How might a perspective from linguistics inform thinking within composition on the relation between speech and writing? Over the past twenty years linguists have published a number of studies of spoken and written language based on corpora of various sizes that have the virtue of providing empirical evidence to confirm or challenge common-sense assumptions. For example, the vocabulary deployed by writers in a variety of genres tends, on the whole, to be more extensive than that available to speakers (Chafe and Danielewicz 87-89). There are also differences in the stock of vocabulary items typically used in writing and speaking, especially at the extremes of formal, highly informational writing on the one hand and casual conversation on the other. Writing, especially when it is highly informational in focus, tends to favor nominalizations (Chafe and Danielewicz 99; Biber 104), and it typically shows greater lexical density, or a higher proportion of content words to function words (e.g., prepositions and articles) than speech (Halliday 59-62).

The differing relations of speakers and writers to their audience are also marked linguistically. Chafe and Danielewicz, for example, find that their written samples show a higher degree of referential explicitness than their spoken samples (90). They see spoken language as showing indications of speakers' involvement both with their audiences and with themselves, which they define as a concern for concrete aspects of linguistic interaction and concrete reality marked in linguistic features such as use of first and second person pronouns and in the use of spatial and temporal adverbials (105-7). The written language in their sample, by contrast, shows markers of detachment, or an interest in ideas that are abstract and not tied to specific people, or to real-world places, events, or times (108). Among these markers of detachment are use of the passive, which renders events abstract by focusing on action rather than agents, and use of generic adverbs (many of which act as sentential adverbs rather than verb phrase modifiers) such as *usually*, *normally*, or *primarily* (109). Biber finds general differences in markers of involvement and detachment and in explicitness of reference too, but his sample is much broader and more finely calibrated for distinctions of genre. Not surprisingly, he finds that personal letters and fiction show greater use of features of involvement and situation-dependent reference than other written genres (160-61).

On the syntactic level, there appear to be differences too, but there is less ostensible agreement among researchers as to their precise nature. Chafe and Danielewicz find that speakers in a variety of situations tend to rely on chaining together independent clauses to relate ideas, while writers in a variety of genres are more likely to use embedding (102-5). Halliday, by contrast, defines the language in his spoken sample as more grammatically intricate than the language in his written sample (63-68), but under his system of analysis hypotaxis (or chaining) is a more intricate operation than embedding, or parataxis. Biber, whose study is the most detailed and draws on the most extensive corpus, is able to make the finest distinctions, finding, for example, that embedded constructions such as nominal that-clauses and wh-clauses, and adverbial subordinators, which typically co-occur with markers of involvement such as first and second person pronouns, are characteristic of his spoken sample (229-30), while relative clauses formed with wh-pronouns (which, who), for example, are more common in written discourse.

Each of these studies has its limitations, especially those based on limited samples, and the linguists' conceptions of audiences for written discourse would probably strike many in composition as naive. The value for composition lies in the way these researchers regard their samples. It is significant, and perhaps a characteristically linguistic approach, that in accounting for differences between spoken and written language each researcher focuses on differences in production and processing. Simply by virtue of the anatomy of the human vocal tract, spoken language is temporally bound and organized linearly. Composition is performed on the fly, and revision is expressed in dysfluencies, hesitation, backtracking, and redundancy. Chafe and Danielewicz claim that some of the features associated with various types of spoken discourse, for example, restricted vocabulary, may reflect limitations in short-term memory. For Halliday, speech and writing can be considered forms of discourse associated (in our society) with extreme points on a continuum from most spontaneous to most self-monitored. Spoken language (at least casual conversation) is usually relatively unself-monitored, while writing is typically highly self-monitored. He claims that hesitations, false starts, and anacolutha monitored use of language (68-71).

If we can return to the idea that writing represents an intersection between thought, language, and technology, focus on the production aspects of speech and writing suggests that some of the "spoken" features of problematic student writing, for example, problems with pronoun reference, immature syntax, or inappropriate register, represent a failure to exploit the technology of writing in ways that are normally considered appropriate to an academic context. Some of these problems may simply reflect discourse that has not received the elaboration possible from and expected of writing in our culture: it is too close to speech for comfort because it has not been ground finely enough in the technological mill.

CONCLUSION

If I have seemed to lead the reader on an extended ramble through esoterica and then through a dull empirical wilderness to the mundane conclusion that student writers need to learn to revise and edit effectively, that is in some ways precisely my point about how linguistics can inform composition. It provides no revolutionary insights into the nature of invention, and although it provides terms for features of spoken and written discourse and empirical studies showing how these features occur in various genres, it provides neither a theory of style nor a theory of stylistic value; these are our jobs as composition researchers and teachers. What linguistics offers is warrants for productive attitudes toward writers and their work. It allows us to see our students (and, indeed, all writers) as competent users of language within particular social contexts, and it helps us to set goals for writers that are realistic. On the methodological level, if there is anything that linguistics has taught composition, it is that it is possible to temper the pedagogical imperative with reflective distance, to regard—at least temporarily—the product of writers as a subject of study rather than an object of intervention. Linguistics does not offer composition a free ride, but it may help us figure out where we are going.

NOTES

1. See Charney for an account of the effect of these attitudes on composition research.

2. See, for example, Newmeyer's account "The Opposition to Autonomous Linguistics," Chapter 5 in *The Politics of Linguistics*. Sociolinguistics emerged as a coherent subfield of linguistics during the 1950s through 1970s, drawing on traditions in

anthropological linguistics, sociology, and dialectology that had long been at odds with purely autonomous views of linguistics. Le Page provides a brief historical account of some of the major research strands within sociolinguistics.

3. See Nystrand et al. (285-93) for an account of the intellectual influence of social constructionist worldviews from sociolinguistics and functional linguistics.

4. Some knowledge of grammatical structures and terms provides a common vocabulary with which to talk about language, but any benefits for writing are probably indirect: they come from the ability of discussion to focus attention on language.

5. The technological aspects of writing are, of course, both physically embodied and situated within particular social and cultural contexts that determine both users' access to the technology and their attitudes toward it.

WORKS CITED

Bartholomae, David. "Released into Language: Errors, Expectations, and the Legacy of Mina Shaughnessy." *The Territory of Language. Linguistics, Stylistics, and the Teaching of Composition*. Ed. Donald A. McQuade. Carbondale: Southern Illinois UP, 1986. 65-88.

Biber, Douglas. *Variation Across Speech and Writing*. Cambridge, England: Cambridge UP, 1988.

Cahill, Aidan. "Psycholinguistics: The Study of Language Acquisition and Use." *Solving Language Problems*. Ed. R.R.K. Hartman. Devon, England: Exeter Press, 1987. 169-93.

Chafe, Wallace and Jane Danielewicz. "Properties of Spoken and Written Language." *Comprehending Oral and Written Language*. Eds. R. Horowitz and J. Samuels. New York: Academic Press, 1987. 83-111.

Charney, Davida. "From Logocentrism to Ethnocentrism. Historicizing Critiques of Writing Research." *Technical Communication Quarterly* 7 (1998): 9-32.

Chomsky, Noam, and Howard Lasnik "The Theory of Principles and Parameters." *Noam Chomsky, The Minimalist Program*. Cambridge: MIT Press, 1995. 13-127.

———. *Rules and Representations*. New York: Columbia University Press, 1980.

Cook, V. J. *Chomsky's Universal Grammar*. Oxford, England: Blackwell, 1988.

Crowley, Sharon. "Linguistics and Composition Instruction: 1950-1980." *Written Communication* 6 (October 1989): 480-505.

Elbow, Peter. "The Challenge for Sentence Combining." *Sentence Combining. A Rhetorical Perspective*. Eds. Donald A. Daiker, Andrew Kerek, and Max Morenberg. Carbondale: Southern Illinois UP, 1985. 232-45.

Faigley, Lester. *Fragments of Rationality. Postmodernity and the Subject of Composition*. Pittsburgh: U of Pittsburgh P, 1992.

Halliday, M. A. K. "Spoken and Written Modes of Meaning." *Comprehending Oral and Written Language*. Eds. R. Horowitz and J. Samuels. New York: Academic Press, 1987. 51-83.

Kempson, Ruth. "The Relation Between Language, Mind, and Reality." *Mental Representation: The Interface Between Language and Reality*. Ed. Ruth Kempson. Cambridge, England. Cambridge UP, 1988.

Labov, William. "The Logic of Non-Standard English." *Georgetown Monograph Series on Languages and Linguistics* 22. Ed. James E. Alatis. Washington, D.C.: Georgetown UP, 1970.

Lakoff, George. *Women, Fire, and Dangerous Things. What Categories Reveal about the Mind.* Chicago: U Chicago P, 1987.

Larson, Richard L. "Language Studies and Composing Processes." *Sentence Combining. A Rhetorical Perspective.* Eds. Donald A. Daiker, Andrew Kerek, and Max Morenberg. Carbondale: Southern Illinois UP, 1985. 213-23.

Le Page, R. B. "The Evolution of a Sociolinguistic Theory of Language." *The Handbook of Sociolinguistics.* Ed. Florian Coulmas. Oxford, England: Blackwell, 1997.

Montgomery, Michael. "Dialects and Basic Writers." *Research in Basic Writing: A Bibliographic Sourcebook.* Eds. Michael G. Moran and Martin J. Jacobi. Westport, CT: Greenwood Press, 1990. 95-115.

Newmeyer, Frederick J. and Stephen A. Weinberger. "The Otogenesis of the Field of Second Language Learning Research." Frederick J. Newmeyer, *Generative Linguistics. A History of Linguistic Thought.* New York and London: Routledge, 1996. 145-154.

⸺. *The Politics of Linguistics.* Chicago: U Chicago P, 1986.

North, Stephen. "The Death of Paradigm Hope, the End of Paradigm Guilt, and the Future of Research in Composition." *Composition in the 21st Century: Crisis and Change.* Eds. Lynn Z. Bloom, Donald A. Daiker, and Edward M. White. Carbondale: Southern Illinois U P, 1997. 194-207.

Nystrand, Martin, Stuart Green, and Jeffrey Wiemelt. "Where Did Composition Studies Come From? An Intellectual History." *Written Communication* 10 (July 1993): 267-333.

Olson, Gary A. and Lester Faigley. "Language, Politics, and Composition: A Conversation with Noam Chomsky." *Journal of Advanced Composition* 11 (Winter 1991): 1-35.

Parker, Frank and Kim Sydow Campbell. "Linguistics and Writing: A Reassessment." *College Composition and Communication* 44 (October 1993): 295-314.

Pinker, Stephen. *The Language Instinct.* New York: William Morrow, 1994.

Shaughnessy, Mina. *Errors and Expectations.* New York: Oxford UP, 1977.

Strong, William. "How Sentence Combining Works." *Sentence Combining. A Rhetorical Perspective.* Eds. Donald A. Daiker, Andrew Kerek, and Max Morenberg. Carbondale: Southern Illinois UP, 1985. 334-50.

Tobin, Lad. "Introduction: How the Writing Process Was Born—and Other Conversion Narratives." *The Writing Process Movement in the 90s.* Eds. Lad Tobin and Thomas Newkirk. Portsmouth, NH: Boynton/Cook, 1994. 1-14.

III

WRITING AND RIGHTING THE FUTURE: PREPARING NEW VOICES

15

Many a Slip Twixt the Cup and the Lip: Teaching and Learning with Graduate Instructors

Janice Witherspoon Neuleib and Maurice Scharton

Have computer classrooms become an obstacle to the new pedagogies of English studies? If new graduate teaching assistants and junior faculty have "post-process" ideas about writing courses, should programs move writing out of the computer classroom to accommodate innovation? Granted, the intellectual politics of English studies programs no longer foregrounds the discussion of writing processes that became the core of writing classes by the eighties. More humanistic pursuits, such as rhetoric, politics, and the philosophy of language have become the staple of discussion, and many writing programs have broadened their focus to encompass the interdisciplinary English studies model. Nevertheless, neither people nor their writing processes—if we may use those terms foundationally for a moment—have changed since the 1980s. Whatever media people work in, they still have to invent ideas, consider an audience, find language and form for their ideas, and revise the resultant unruly discourse to impose control over it. In consequence, many of the important values in a writing class have not changed. Controlling a sentence still matters, as do writing a paragraph, finding a reader, and listening to an editor. Experienced teachers-researchers, who themselves have seen many pieces of writing through to publication, know the details of handling those issues in a way that beginners who have written only for school have yet to experience. Quite conceivably, someone experienced in teaching and writing could employ any pedagogy to address a fundamental writing issue such as revision, but it is not reasonable to believe that every graduate student and junior faculty member can accomplish the same end. Thus, some form of infrastructure is required to keep new teachers on task or writing instruction itself might disappear from composition courses (Neuleib, "Revision"). The "limitations" of a computer classroom in fact represent the discipline of writing, and the struggles that students and teachers experience in accommodating their ideas to the status quo are evidence that the system is working.

THE IDEOLOGICAL IMPLICATIONS OF PHYSICAL SPACE

A classroom's physical layout signals some of the teacher's pedagogical assumptions. Given the ways that space controls interactions, it might be said that the classroom's configuration presents an argument about pedagogy, an argument that most students know how to read. Students know that rows of desks facing the blackboard signify a teacher's intention to pursue a lecture mode while desks in circles signify discussion, and long tables are meant to invite the collegiality of a seminar. Given the academic cultural assumptions about the space, clever or contrarian teachers can manipulate a classroom's configuration for effect. By choosing, for example, to lecture to a group sitting in a circle, the teacher can command more attentiveness. By setting up small groups and then joining one of them, the teacher can confer and withhold privilege. Both teacher and student are accustomed to the fact that the physical configuration literally establishes the grounds for their interaction. The space is protean, capable of being reconfigured to suit a number of purposes.

If all classrooms present assumptions that may be called arguments, computer rooms present a pedagogical argument that is in some ways irrefutable. For example, the computer rooms at Illinois State University argue for keeping the social units simple. In each of nine small computer rooms, eighteen to twenty-three students sit at computers placed on wall-mounted tables, not individual desks. Thus, primary attention is focused on the screen and secondary attention on the person at the next computer. Swivel chairs with casters make small groups feasible but awkward since a small group cannot effectively huddle over a single computer. Whole group discussion or lecture is difficult to sustain for more than a few minutes because the students must turn away from the computer and balance a notebook on a knee to take notes. Thus, an adaptive response to working in these rooms is for teachers to prefer writing to discussion, tutoring or collaboration to small group work, and group work to lectures. The syllabus for full-time work in these rooms naturally stresses drafting and revision with a tutorial emphasis.

AN ELITIST VIEW OF TIME

If the classroom argues for a pedagogy, the pedagogy must emerge from an ideology, and in this case it is one whose fundamental value is competence with language, particularly with the importance of learning to revise. Early studies like Shaughnessy's *Errors and Expectations*, Summers's "Revision Strategies," Emig's *Composing Processes of Twelfth Graders*, and Faigley and Witte's "Analyzing Revision" and others of their era framed the research agenda of composition with the idealistic assumption that people who were not of the socioeconomic brackets that had traditionally attended college could be shown how to produce writing that met the standards of academe (Brandt, Berthoff, Brannon, Emig, Faigley, Perl, Summers). Since those days, the very notion of competence has been subject to vigorous challenge in debates about testing, cultural difference, gender, and postmodern language philosophy. The senior faculty who constructed writing pedagogy and built the infrastructure to deliver it find that the poles of academic politics have shifted so that we are now the conservative forces. We have become the memory of a culture that has elected to move social justice and ideological purity ahead of competence and disciplinarity on its agenda (Bartholomae, Brodkey). We remember the struggles to move composition away from the literary mold in order to establish an identity for the field and to give some respectability to the enterprise of teaching people to write. We recall the moment when it was clear that we had won, that we had intellectual independence, better job prospects, and a set of problems far more interesting than those that literary study could present. We remember that we built the computer classrooms to focus attention on drafting and revision (Bruns, Fennick, Fortune, Scharton) and that the computer classroom became the infrastructure for a pedagogy of revision.

Although process pedagogy was idealistic, it was never liberal or egalitarian. The precise social inverse of the collectivist pedagogies that currently obtain in English studies, process pedagogy was anticipated by and in some instances borrowed from the Oxford dons who tutored the children of Britain's social elite (Gere and LeFevre). The basic premise of the Oxford tutorial method is to lavish resources on each student. It is extremely expensive to pay a highly educated person to listen to a student read a paper, to take each word of the paper seriously, to question meaning and appropriateness, and thereby to guide the student to produce more and more disciplined prose. Assuming that bright, committed students from various backgrounds were worth and could profit from that sort of attention constituted the idealism of process pedagogy. Building expensive computer classrooms in which to pursue individual, process-oriented instruction gave material form to that idealistic impulse and a vantage point from which to defend the ground composition gained in the sixties and the seventies.

In the nineties, writing courses at Illinois State University have continuously included perspectives and approaches that incorporate current research and evoke new thinking. The introductory course reiterates the received wisdom that students should read, write, revise, and create portfolios of their work. The goals for the course stress critical thinking and critical review of professional and student texts. It also asks students to perform a certain amount of meta-analysis of their own writing experiences. Graduate students who teach writing experience a variety of types of careful training, including week-long orientation sessions and a semester-long course that directs and coordinates new instructors' stints as co-teachers with experienced graduate instructors and as tutors in the learning center. These instructors also take a course in composition theory and research during the first semester and spend time visiting experienced teachers' classes, often those of their designated program assistants, experienced doctoral students who each attend to a group of six or seven new graduate instructors. This program receives constant personal attention from the Assistant Director of Writing and advanced doctoral students from the composition and rhetoric program, and also constant but less personal administrative attention from the Director of Writing Programs and the Coordinator of Writing Assessment.

PROBLEMS ON THE SPACE-TIME CONTINUUM

Of course, the graduate students and junior faculty who enter the teaching profession through the narrow straits of computer classrooms lack the memory of what computers represent to composition studies. To many of these instructors, political argument and ideological experimentation have a retro appeal, a hearkening to an era of social change, civil action, and educational reform that preceded the crass realities of Reagan's economics and Bush's militarism. The interdiscplinary eclecticism common to English graduate programs, particularly on the literature side, seems to some junior teachers to license experimentation in the classroom. Those who are relatively new to English may not notice that interdisciplinarity implies the existence of disciplines, or suspect that cynicism and intellectual imperialism might be among the motivations to reintegrate the elements of English departments. To give a familiar example of the sort of problem created when inexperienced people teach writing, we can consider Freirean pedagogy. In the abstract, liberatory pedagogy has both practical and idealistic appeals. If students can be shown how to assume control over their own education, then they will be better prepared to earn a place in the world and to make a positive difference (Shor). Freireans argue that in the classroom students will take responsibility for their own ideas, perhaps even collaborate with the teacher to help ease some of the administrative, evaluative, and clerical burden. However, in the concrete reality of the writing classroom, liberatory pedagogy's romantic appeal to certain teachers can persuade them to spend their time in direct pursuit of ideological ends. Thus "post-process" often ends up meaning "post-writing instruction" as social and political issues absorb all class time and most teacher attention.

The most susceptible writing teachers flatter themselves that daily discussions of intellectual issues punctuated at intervals with e-mail exchanges and a position paper will serve as a writing course. The most charitable interpretation of writing classes in which discussion predominates is that for these teachers, teaching a student how to control a text can be assumed to be a consequence of urging a student to take a position. The problem with this sort of thinking is that in teaching practice means and ends become reversed. If a politicized teacher must choose whether to spend classtime talking idealistically about social ills, teaching the postmodern textual realities of webpage design, or working on the practical details of student writing, spending time on student writing is the third choice. (See the order of essay choices and the argument in NCTE's new *Cross-Talk.*) Although society's ultimate ends may be to promote social justice or the university's ends may be to produce new knowledge, it does not follow that those are the immediate ends of a writing course, nor does it follow that those ends can become the means of teaching people to produce competent writing.

A STORY

An anecdote from recent experience illustrates the slip twixt the cup and the lip. It was a November afternoon. The setting was a computer classroom area, a group of nine networked rooms in which writing classes were meeting. A graduate instructor teaching in her computer classroom decided to run next door to ask a fellow doctoral student a question. She found a classroom of composition students busily writing away on their computers but no fellow instructor. When asked where their teacher was at the moment, the class responded that they had not seen him for a week and a half. The instructor asked the class what they had been doing in class while the teacher was gone, and they responded that they had been writing their papers, reading them, and revising. The instructor raced upstairs to report a miracle; Peter Elbow's vision of writing without teachers had spontaneously appeared in the writing classroom. The Writing Program sent out a search party and eventually found that the missing instructor had suffered the mild form of nervous collapse often attendant upon enrollment in graduate school. Amidst the dismay at this turn of events, it was impossible not to take some satisfaction that the syllabus and classrooms were designed well enough to support writing instruction in the absence of a teacher.

Although the course can function in a teacher-free mode, it is not teacher-proof, as the denouement of the anecdote will illustrate. Two advanced composition doctoral students, one our computer coordinator and the other an instructor on special assignment to the graduate director, took over the two orphan classes. These two had twelve days to decide on grades, but the portfolio requirements provided all the evidence an experienced instructor would need to assign grades. The portfolio requires six papers with all drafts, all teacher and peer suggestions for revision, a paper from another class with a discussion of its context, and a reflective essay that discusses how revision suggestions were used to revise the papers. Particularly important to grading, the reflective essay tells much about the nature of a student's progress in the class because unless the students understands the nature of revision, the reflective essay is impossible to write. These two advanced doctoral students, who were given the task of "finishing off" and giving grades in the orphan classes, both asked the writing program director what they should do about giving grades without the full experience of having taught the class for the entire semester. In response to the explanation that they could understand the nature of the class and of each student's experience from the reflective essay, both quickly said, "Oh yeah." Their confused and defensive responses suggested that even advanced standing in a graduate composition program had not equipped these teachers to draw what seemed to be an obvious pedagogical inference from the design of portfolios—that grades could be based on the written record, not their experience of class discussions.

A FEW FACTS

Some more empirical evidence supports the unhappy conclusion we draw from the anecdote. This evidence is drawn from student and instructor responses to the English Placement Test (freshman year) and the University Writing Examination (junior or senior year) at Illinois State University. In addition to the conventional holistically scored writing samples, both tests include a section that specifically prompts a writer to plan a second draft of the essay. Writers are required to "supply two good questions you would ask a reader to answer to help you improve the credibility of your essay," "rewrite two sentences from your essay to demonstrate how you might appeal to your reader's emotions," and "discuss ways you would plan to expand, rearrange, or shorten your essay." The second draft plan allows judges to estimate a writer's ability to evaluate and plan changes of a first draft. Before beginning the second-draft plan, students are prompted to demonstrate copy-editing skills by marking possible errors. With the popular concept of revision parsed to exclude copy-editing, student attention is thereby focused on changes in the form and content of the essay. Since students plan but are not required to execute revisions, students can offer suggestions from a lower level of certainty and commitment than would be required if the revisions were to be carried out. This allows for a greater range of freedom in imagining revisions.

The second-draft plans sort students who understand the nature of revision from those who do not. For example, say a student was responding to an essay on censorship of student newspapers. The student might write an essay that described a personal experience with censorship. Then in the revision section the student would ask a potential reader the appropriate (or inappropriate) questions. A useful reader question might be "In my second paragraph I discuss a fight with my high school principal over an article in our student newspaper; can you as a reader tell me about similar experiences so that I might enrich the essay with other perspectives?" Another useful request a writer might make of a reader could be "Please react to the importance of my experience by discussing whether you think my story is worth telling and why."

The exams are scored by three raters who use five-point scales in which five is the highest score. Two of the raters score the essay and the third scores only the second-draft plan. The rater who scores the second-draft plan uses a scoring guide that focuses attention on the specificity and strategic usefulness of the planned revisions, as the following excerpt from the scoring guide illustrates.

Plans Receiving a 3 (Suggesting Competence)

1. Pose questions that invite peer readers to make relevant substantive comments on the essay.

2. Identify at least one of the essay's substantive weaknesses and specify the appropriate changes.

3. Demonstrate the writer's ability to write in academic style.

Plans Receiving a 2 (Suggesting Incompetence)

1. Pose yes-or-no peer questions or highly abstract and general peer questions.

2. Repeat handbook advice about organization and development.

3. Display few or inappropriate changes in style

For this fall's Writing Exam scores (N=1717), nearly 62 percent of the writers scored a three for the essay. But only 37 percent of these advanced undergraduates, taking a test they must pass before graduation, scored a three; 58 percent scored a two or less, suggesting that they viewed revision as a diffuse random process of change.

We can present some reasonable speculations concerning the relationship between the writing curriculum and the test scores. In a teaching workshop, we asked graduate instructors to suggest questions in answer to sample tests and essays. Almost to a person, the instructors suggested peer questions such as "What else could I add to the essay?" and "Was the structure of the essay effective?" Many of these instructors had taught for a year or two, and all had been through orientation with the Language and Composition Guidebook that carefully describes revision question strategies, but had somehow emerged innocent of any information about how to pose effective peer questions.

We had stressed, or we thought we had stressed, two important aspects of asking reader questions.

1. Never ask a question that can be answered with a yes or no.

2. Never ask a question that could be asked of any essay.

Our strategy for teaching reader response to student (and professional) essays requires that all questions relate to the particular essay that the writer wants to improve. We found in our workshop that we had set a hard task not only for our students but also for our graduate instructors. We were asking them to apply standards for revision of the sort that professional journals set for reviewers.

When, in our capacities as reviewers in our field, we receive an essay or a book manuscript from a journal or publisher, the author or the editor has set specific questions about that particular text. We respond to those questions with answers meant to help the author revise the text, and we always have revision suggestions even when we suggest that an essay or book go to press. It is that criterion that we use when we set the standards for our student writers, and it is that standard that we expect from our graduate instructors. Unfortunately, such a skill in responding is hard to teach and equally hard to teach others to teach. Yet it is that skill that is the core of writing instruction (Kutz and Roskelly).

ANOTHER STORY

The complexity of the problem goes beyond the graduate instructors, of course. Why can they not teach these skills? Another anecdote of slippage will help to illustrate the problem. During a summer workshop for faculty instructors, the writing program director remarked offhandedly that it does no good to write on a paper if the student will not be revising the paper. A business professor responded that his life and his marriage were often in great stress because he spent so much time marking papers. He said that he marked everything he could find. Asked when these papers were turned in during the semester, he said that he gave them until the last week to complete the papers. Asked, "So do they pick up these papers the next semester?" He said that they mostly didn't.

Months later, at a winter workshop, the same business professor thanked the writing director for changing his life. He said he no longer wrote on papers if students were unlikely to read his comments. Asked casually whether he read drafts of his students' papers and whether he made suggestions for change early on in the semester, he looked crestfallen. He had operationalized the information that his comments came too late as permission to cease commenting altogether. The obvious strategy, moving the comments earlier in the process, did not present itself to him because he could not see the paper-marking enterprise in the larger system of writing instruction. Too many graduate instructors have been taught by teachers like this very able and hard-working business professor. Thus, their construct of writing instruction is, at its core, having plenty of time to write their papers, turn them in at the end of the semester, and receive comments that have no practical consequences. The "obvious" response to comments without consequences—revising a finished paper from one class to serve the requirements of another class—is viewed as immoral by many professors and departments.

Seeing individual pieces of revision advice as a cog in a much larger system and visualizing the teaching strategies implied by the system is easy only for the people who have designed, built, and experienced the system. New teachers who walk into a computer classroom fresh from a course in the postmodern novel or even a course in rhetorical theory are at any given moment probably operating from a completely different system, one in which they see themselves as public intellectuals or literary theorists or professors or graduate students in English studies: to those people at those moments, the machines are just machines and the course is only an introduction to something.

Because so many different people teach writing courses, the writing program must provide boundaries within which they can operate, boundaries that give their activities focus and meaning and that represent the hard-won disciplinary integrity of composition. Failing to maintain those boundaries signifies not broad-mindedness but benign neglect, an unwillingness to help new teachers see what the enterprise of writing instruction involves and how to integrate their own abilities and experiences into that enterprise.

WORKS CITED

Bartholomae, David, and Anthony Petrosky. *Facts, Artifacts, and Counterfacts*. Upper Montclair: Boynton/Cook, 1986.

Berthoff, Ann E. *The Making of Meaning*. Upper Montclair: Boynton/Cook, 1981.

Brandt, Deborah. "Toward an Understanding of Context in Composition." *Written Communication* 3 (1986): 139-57.

Brannon, Lil, and C. H. Knoblauch. "On Students' Rights to Their Own Texts: A Model of Teacher Response." *College Composition and Communication* 33 (1982): 157-66.

Brodkey, Linda. "On the Subjects of Class and Gender in 'The Literacy Letters.'" *College English* 51:2 (February 1989): 125-41 in Villanueva, Victor, ed. *Cross-Talk in Comp Theory*. Urbana: NCTE, 1997. 639-658.

Bruns, Gerald. *Inventions: Writing, Textuality, and Understanding in Literary History*. New Haven: Yale UP, 1982.

Emig, Janet. *The Composing Processes of Twelfth Graders*. NCTE Research Report No. 13. Urbana, IL.: NCTE, 1971.

Faigley, Lester, and Stephen Witte. "Analyzing Revision." *College Composition and Communication* 32 (1981): 400-14.

Fennick, Ruth. "The Creative Processes of Prose-Fiction Writers: What They Suggest for Teaching Composition." Diss. Illinois State, 1991.

Fortune, Ron. "Hypertext in a Manuscript Culture." *Illinois English Bulletin* 79:3 (Spring 1992): 3-10.

Gere, Anne Ruggles. *Writing Groups: History, Theory, and Implications*. Carbondale: Southern Illinois UP, 1980.

Kutz, Eleanor, and Hephzibah Roskelly. *An Unquiet Pedagogy*. Portsmouth: Heinemann, 1991.

LeFevre, Karen Burke. *Invention as a Social Act*. Carbondale: Southern Illinois UP, 1987.

Neuleib, Janice, et al. "Revision." *The Mercury Reader* (Illinois State University Fall 1998 Version). Needham Heights: Simon & Schuster, 1998. 25-42.

Perl, Sondra. "Understanding Composing." *College Composition and Communication* 31 (December 1980): 363-69.

Scharton, Maurice, and Janice Neuleib. *Inside Out: A Guide to Writing*. Needham Heights: Allyn & Bacon, 1993.

Shaughnessy, Mina P. *Errors and Expectations*. New York: Oxford UP, 1977.

Shor, Ira, ed. *Freire for the Classroom*. Portsmouth: Heinemann, 1987.

Summers, Nancy. "Revision Strategies of Student Writers and Experienced Adult Writers." *College Composition and Communication* 31:4 (December 1980): 378-88 in Villanueva, Victor, ed. *Cross-Talk in Comp Theory*. Urbana: NCTE, 1997. 43-54.

Villanueva, Victor. "Considerations for American Freireistas." *Cross-Talk in Comp Theory*. Urbana: NCTE, 1997. 621-37.

16

Obscured Agendas and Hidden Failures: Teaching Assistants, Graduate Education, and First-Year Writing Courses

Stuart C. Brown

A master's student comes into my office near the end of her first semester teaching. All semester I have watched her enthusiasm for teaching first-year writing grow; in her graduate seminars she has been relating what she is studying and learning to what her own students are encountering. But now she is in tears. Her advisor, a literature professor, has just informed her that minoring in rhetoric and composition is a bad idea, that the teaching of composition is "beneath" her, and that scholarly attention to it will assuredly hurt her chances for getting into a *real* Ph.D. program. Ours is one of the very few schools that has a Ph.D. in Rhetoric and not one in literature. I counsel. I explain. I bite my tongue.

I'm the Associate Department Head of the largest department in a middle-sized (15,000 students) Carnegie Class I research university and must be politic even when confronted with the pettiness of some of my so-called colleagues. English is the largest department because seventy some graduate assistants teach nearly 100 sections of five different General Education writing courses each semester. I am also the Writing Program Administrator. My program is larger than most departments on campus and offers courses that satisfy two universal undergraduate requirements. That literature professor owes her job to this program; if I thought it would actually make a difference, I would point out to her that she is able to teach her graduate seminar and her majors course because composition and its graduate student teachers carry the department. In fact, Robert

Scholes claims, many literature faculty have no incentive to change: "The more economically you can teach those writing courses—which is to say, the more students you can cram into them and the worse you pay the teachers—the better off the literature faculty is" (Schneider A14). Annette Kolodney, as Dean at the University of Arizona, once proposed that faculty could lecture on composition to hundreds of students and graduate-teaching assistants could grade the papers. Jeffrey Walker, on the other hand, offers a countering point of view. He notes on a listserv discussing the possible consequences of downplaying or abolishing the first year writing requirement: "English would become a backwater in the twenty-first century university organized around business, engineering and biotech. Where English has any status, it will have the sort of ornamental status that classics and philosophy have." Some days this seems a tempting scenario.

I have no say in who those seventy or so graduate student teachers are, although I am responsible for their teaching. The Graduate Studies Committee evaluates applications for each of our four emphases at the masters level (creative writing, literature, rhetoric, and technical communication) while another committee determines admittance into the Ph.D. program in Rhetoric and Professional Communication. Students are selected based on a committee's evaluation of a letter of intent, writing samples, transcripts, and letters of recommendation. The more favorable the impression of an applicant as a good student, the more likely the offer of an assistantship. It's not intentional, but student interest in and potential for teaching rarely come up in the discussions. The assistantship is seen as financial support for the student's graduate education. This is necessary to attract the best students. Once the student has arrived, teaching composition is seen as a by-product and, at times, an interference. I overstate the case to make a point, but I've been on those committees and have done the same thing. This was before I became responsible for the nearly 6,000 students each year who take the classes these graduate students teach.

In fairness to most of my colleagues, when I've raised the issue that I'd like justification for who will teach and who will not, they've been receptive. They wait for a proposal from me on what form it will take. I am still deliberating; I confess a reluctance to tinker with what, at least on first glance, seems to work. Every semester I read every student evaluation of those graduate-teaching assistants. Every semester I am startled at how positive they are, especially given the lack of training and supervision beyond the first semester we provide our teaching assistants. Our department offers the not uncommon week-long orientation followed by a semester-long required course in composition theory and pedagogy. I was trained in a similar fashion and perpetuate the same model now. Yet, in a recent Internet Colloquy, initiated by Robin Wilson's *Chronicle* article on shortages of composition teachers, the question was raised: What other profession would dream of allowing the untrained and uninitiated to teach fundamental—and purportedly essential—courses. Most professions, including some in English studies, require years of preparation before a teacher is assigned a class. Evidently, anyone can teach writing. Is it a wonder the teaching of composition is denigrated?

I won't analyze how we have gotten to this juncture of what I would call the *deprofessionalization* of composition. Robert Connors, Sharon Crowley, and Thomas Miller have each thoroughly explored the historical antecedents and have noted the relatively recent happenstance of surrendering the teaching of writing to novices. One has only to look at who was teaching writing before the enormous growth in graduate literature programs. One has only to note the implications of open admissions and the rise in college enrollments. The teaching of writing, one could argue, has been determined almost exclusively by expedience. Its disciplinary existence the result of exigence rather than any legitimate scholarly enterprise. Our very *service* orientation, while justifying our existence to the rest of the university and our constituent communities, relegates the profession to that of support staff. We might protest otherwise with our finger pointing at doctoral programs and research, conferences and academic journals, but are we talking only to ourselves?

As a sidebar, I will contest the use of the term *apprenticeship*. The Association of American Universities Committee on Graduate Education reports "Graduate students learn to teach and to conduct research by performing these activities under faculty mentorship. Apprenticeship teaching experiences at progressively more advanced levels, augmented by workshops and other pedagogical training programs, are extremely effective ways to teach prospective teachers how to teach" (12). Perhaps so. Is this a practice followed in the teaching of writing? Anywhere in English studies? The report also notes "Having graduate students serve as teaching assistants for extended periods without [their] advancing in pedagogical development is unfair to graduate students" (12). Obviously, it may also be unfair to the students these students teach. An apprentice cabinetmaker, for example, works with a master cabinetmaker learning to build cabinets, whereas composition teaching assistants rarely work with master teachers and rarely intend to teach composition for the rest of their lives.

I am not optimistic. I fear that even as composition develops as a discipline, its status will devolve further. I maintain a file of clippings and photocopies pertaining to graduate education in the humanities, mostly from *The Chronicle of Higher Education* and *The ADE Bulletin*. I pay close attention to articles portraying the dismal state of employment for Ph.D.s in English. These calls, such as the recent "The Final Report of the MLA Committee on Professional Employment," suggest "a new emphasis in graduate training on teaching" (3) (A60). Calls for reform in graduate education in English dominate these discussions. What I find disturbing, however, is that *teaching* (especially the so-called "service courses" of which first-year writing is by far the most common) has apparently been subsumed in favor of *getting a job* as the dominating construct in these suggested reforms.

Job market pressures, as Leonard Cassuto notes, have led to "the most highly professionalized and accomplished graduate students and incoming faculty members that anyone has ever seen" (B4). He proposes that English studies can be vastly improved by initiating the use of teaching portfolios and asserts that "those of us who teach graduate students need to set an example" by developing our own teaching (B5). The ironist in me wants to direct Professor Cassuto to some of what has been going on in composition studies for at least the last twenty years. But I will laud his effort because, after all, he is teaching at Fordham and he is referring to literary studies. Now that the Literary Studies component of the profession is officially acknowledging the job market in crisis again, the one predominant solution suggested is that overproduction of specialists will be cured if those "surplus" Ph.D.'s are construed as teachers rather than scholars. I have not seen any proposals on what training will actually take place or what students actually make of this. Sander Gilman has, for example, proposed in the 1995 Presidential Address to the MLA the creation of postdoctoral *teaching* fellowships that extend student subsidy to improve marketability (my emphasis). Doing is learning, we can assume. Elaine Showalter does call attention to teaching by raising the questions "Are great teachers born or made? How do we learn to teach, and how can we prepare graduate students to do it?" (3). She then goes on to profile her experience with a program in Great Britain as a possible model. She seems willing to import a training program of mentor teaching and ignore, it seems, the existence of a rich tradition of training in the teaching of composition at nearly every doctoral and most MA granting programs in America. Again, we presume she is referring to literary studies and the need to train graduate assistants in the teaching of literature. Perhaps she is also calling for a continuing training and one that is preparing graduate assistants for their lives after graduation.

I am troubled by how graduate education in English and the proposed reforms ignore the role of graduate assistants in the teaching of undergraduates, especially those in first-year writing courses. In fact, I see a number of issues around this topic with which I am uncomfortable, although in all honesty, I have no real solutions for any of them. These concerns stem from the facts that:

1. The training of graduate students in the teaching of composition is done primarily at universities where student populations often do not mirror the students and courses these teachers will actually encounter (provided they obtain academic employment at all).

2. Many graduate students rarely receive training beyond an introductory course or a few days of orientation before entering the classroom.

3. Formal and effective evaluation/assessment of graduate teaching assistants is problematic, as is any sort of remediation for ineffectual teaching. We seem to embrace a strident skepticism toward standards, on one hand, while professing the need for exemplary teaching on the other with little attention on how to get to this point.

4. Most programs rely on graduate student teachers who often are not pursuing studies in

the teaching of writing, and who primarily view this teaching as an economic subsidy for their studies; these students are too often "mentored" by faculty who directly or indirectly further this attitude. This situation is not unlike training a future plumber in auto mechanics, with the difference that both of these trades are highly employable.

5. Trained compositionists, even as graduate students, are likely to spend much more professional time as administrators than as teachers. Given the scope and funding levels of most of the first-year writing programs, graduate assistants who express any interest in administrative work are quickly co-opted and are consumed as cheap resources (see Fontaine, for example, on the ethical implications of this practice).

6. There is increasing schism amongst composition people themselves (the theorists, practitioners, and historians of writing) that is reflected in the graduate education that writing specialists receive. It is not uncommon for graduate programs in rhetoric to offer few, if any, actual course work in pedagogy as their faculty present more history, theory, and faculty research-oriented curriculums (see Brown, Enos, and Lauer; Brown, Meyer, and Enos). If this is not enough, then consider adding to these issues that affect the teaching of writing: the use and abuse of part-time instructors and adjuncts; the difficulties of many entry-level composition faculty in getting tenure recognition for teaching and/or administering the "service" level courses; and the failure of the academy to justify, or at least to explain, its use of resources. That is, do we, in fact educate our students? Do our students write better than they have in the past? "Things," as one American sage is reputed to have said, "are more like they are now than they have ever been."

My intention here is to provoke. The points I've raised aim to question fundamental assumptions underlying graduate education, not only in English studies at large, but specifically within the discipline of rhetoric and composition. What I wish to generate is a discussion of how graduate studies are formulated, the costs of that formulation (economic and scholarly among others) to beginning college writers, and some considerations for rectifying these problems. In doing so, I would caution the profession to consider Crowley's observation that "if you work in a corrupt system, you have to face the fact that making things better for people working in one part of the system may make things worse for people who work in another part of it" (240). Fine cabinets, after all, usually represent deforestation.

Lil Brannon argues that we must "challenge the skills model—the idea that writing is essentially a technology rather than a social practice, that is 'comes' in discrete mechanical parts that people learn to assemble" (241). This model essentially mirrors the idea that if one can write, one can teach writing. Or, as Ed White notes on a listserv discussion, an obstetrician friend claims that 90 percent of what he does could be done by most anyone with rudimentary medical training; it is the other 10 percent of his work time where the years of training and experience come into play. If we are to follow Brannon's model, we will need to make a similar argument for teaching, especially the teaching of writing.

We might also better represent both our own professional attitudes and our own practices in our teaching of the teachers of those courses. Our designation of those teachers, for example, as graduate assistant or *graduate teaching assistant* or *teaching assistant* sends a strong signal to the teachers themselves, their students, their administrators, their teachers, those who fund them, and the public at large. How very unpostmodern of us not to attend to the obvious here. How, for example, are we using the term *assistant*? Most graduate students teaching writing courses are very much on their own in the classroom, especially beyond whatever initial training they might have received. The designation of *assistant* is, by implication, demeaning, and inaccurate—particularly if there are no actual professors available to be assisted. TAs are signified not by what they do, but how they are named. Administrators are delighted because graduate assistant teaching credits accrue to a department while the graduate students themselves generate credits from their own course work as a condition of employment. And status-conscious faculty are kept complacent because there is a large population of teachers with lower status than they themselves have. As Crowley notes, the teaching of composition in an English department makes for an interesting use of metaphors. She extracts terms from our literature and our lore that colonial studies has so effectively problematized: "children, serfs, prisoners, and slaves" (127).

Justifiably, we bemoan the plight of part-timers and adjuncts as described by Joseph Berger in *The New York Times*, when he chronicles the travails of Wendy Scribner, an adjunct writing teacher, who teaches sixteen credits a semester, has no office, no benefits, and a minimal income. This is an unfortunate commonplace with which most of us already are too familiar. But I am also disturbed by the lead to this article: "Wendy Scribner spent ten years writing her dissertation, typing it at night in a railroad flat on East Ninth Street while her two small boys were growing up in a windowless middle room. It was the pinched, obsessed life of an underground character in a novel by Dostoevsky." During this time, I want to know who her students were and how she was teaching them. What was the effect of this kind of life on her teaching? How has it carried over to her current situation? *The Chronicle of Higher Education* creates another flurry of electronic buzz on my e-mail lists by publishing "Universities Scramble to Find Teachers of Composition" (Wilson). In this article, the author finds one Mark R. Kelley, incoming president of the Graduate Student Caucus of the Modern Language Association, who puts the question bluntly: "If *anyone* can teach writing, why have an English Department?" (my emphasis, 2). Why, indeed, when it has never been formally established that people in English studies know how to teach—or to write for that matter—any better than anyone else? The article chronicles the commonplace: "Many graduate students who teach composition at Illinois say they feel qualified to do so because they are good writers themselves, a skill many of them say they learned as undergraduates. None of the TAs interviewed for this story, however, had received any formal training in how to teach writing beyond what Illinois offers. And some hadn't even had that" (3). I would like a nickel for every undergraduate student who denied a need for first-year composition because "I'm already a good writer."

David Bartholomae recognizes that "growth in composition has been accompanied by a growth in the size of graduate programs, programs of literature and theory and cultural studies. It is not unusual to find a department, at least in large universities, where the faculty teaches only majors and graduate students . . . turning introductory courses and general education over to teaching assistants" (20). Michael Bérubé notes that "By AAUP's most recent count, part-time faculty now make up approximately 45 percent of the American professoriate; and at many large American universities, graduate students teach more than half the introductory undergraduate courses in all fields" (62). "In 1996-97," Phyllis Franklin of the MLA reports, "of first-year writing sections in the average English Program, 61% were taught by graduate-student teaching assistants, 20% were taught by part-time teachers, 14% were taught by full-time non-tenure-track faculty members, and 5% were taught by tenured or tenure-track teachers;" she proposes acceptable "Possible Standards" to raise the ratio of full-time faculty teaching to 70 percent in BA-granting colleges and 55 percent in Ph.D.-granting institutes (6). Maureen Goggin claims that " despite decades of scholarly focus on first-year composition, the institution has not been changed in any significant way during this century" (41). Again, there is little wonder that composition is dismissed by our colleagues, both within and outside English studies, and that our graduate students most commonly voice the desire to "anything but."

As a profession, we ask continually for better writing teachers. And we should. Crowley, Miller, Brereton, Connors, and others scrutinize our past and complicate our views of the present. As in other disciplines, we propose reforms in our teaching because of our research and consequent theorizing. We have dramatically constructed a discipline in the last twenty years as evidenced by the growth in doctoral programs and number of Ph.D.s produced by those programs (Brown, Meyer, and Enos; Miller, Brueggemann, Blue, and Shepard) and, we have reconceptualized the study of the teaching of writing, developing training programs, and supporting course work (see Raymond, for example). As Crowley observes, we posit a value for composition because everyone requires it, but we then staff it with graduate assistants (i.e., inexperienced teachers) or with part-time or temporary faculty because costs preclude doing otherwise (118). She recognizes some of the reasons why people are interested in teaching composition: they want to teach, they enjoy the intimacy and immediacy of teaching writing, and they recognize its value—both in the educational and the public sphere (119). As Joseph Harris suggests, *public* needs to become a keyword in the teaching of writing. Or does it? Do we want the public looking at who is teaching writing in America's colleges and universities?

We often scrutinize "the student," but how often do we look at "the student teacher," other than in their role as the subjects of initial, intensive (and too often minimal) teacher training? It is already frightening enough to recognize that the field of composition probably leads every other discipline on campus in preparing its graduate students to teach. How do we articulate our training of those teachers to the various stakeholders mentioned above? Despite recent strides in developing program evaluation and outcomes assessment, we remain vague about teaching evaluations. We reinforce Crowley's observation that "comp teachers speak of 'the classroom' as though this space is similarly constructed at Yale and at San Jose Community College" (221). Ray Wallace suggests that most composition graduate programs "do a fairly ineffective job in preparing graduates for the low and middle-to-low students most colleges and universities admit these days." He sees an increasing number of rhetoric and composition graduate students entering the field with strong theoretical and historical training in rhetoric and in literature. But he asks, "How will this get thirty badly prepared students from S. Texas and C. Louisiana through even the most basic developmental course, never mind English 101?" (e-mail).

What are our alternatives? Michael Bérubé, in support of graduate teaching assistant unionization, notes "As long as people are working as instructors or as teaching assistants and being paid for their work, I think it makes sense to consider them 'employed,' to consider their work 'employment,' and to admit, therefore, that they are in some sense 'employees'" (37-38). Bérubé argues for assigning an actual value to the work these people do. But as sympathetic as I am to this proposal, I wonder whether this movement does not spell the end for graduate assistantships in teaching. If graduate assistants should be treated as employees, then they must, of necessity, have the credentials to be employed. We may be left with the College of Education model that requires a series of pedagogy courses *before* allowing a student to teach, *before* allowing certification, and *before* providing a classroom full of beginning writers.

Others, including Connors ("New Abolitionism"), Crowley, and Charles Schuster, have suggested completely abolishing composition as a requirement. On too many days I can easily concur with Schuster's comment that either the required writing course needs "to matter to our departments, or we have to get rid of it, or get rid of our colleagues" (6). This proposal needs further scrutiny as does the trend toward separating writing courses from English departments. As composition studies becomes a more dominant discipline and begins to assert itself as that maturation takes place, we may find that just as we have chafed under the hegemony of literary studies, we are in danger of creating our own. On a more positive note, perhaps we will follow James Slevin's suggestion that we might "come at the notion of discipline as a system of instruction—a discipline not as the knowledge of a particular area of inquiry and not as the professional conversation about that knowledge but rather a discipline as the act of inviting and enabling others to join that conversation" (156). I would like to think so. I would like to capture the enthusiasm and energy I see in my training program every semester poured into first year-writing classrooms by brand new graduate assistants. They are excited and challenged and alive to possibilities. And something happens. By their third or fourth semester teaching, I hear "I get to go teach" replaced by "I have to go teach."

Personally, I am haunted by an incident from my adolescence in which my father, a career military officer, was inquiring about my "plans for the future." His questions concerned whether I intended to finish high school or not. After mumbling that high school didn't seem to be providing for my future, I stated—rather arrogantly—that I could "always join the Army." I have never asked him about that incident, but I can still see the surprise and the hurt in his face this comment caused. I suspect we may have created the same attitude in many of our graduate programs—"I can always teach composition."

NOTE

I would like to recognize the contributions that Leslie Coutant, Rebecca Jackson, Amanda Cobb, Ray Wallace, and the 1998 Tucson WPA Workshop participants have had on my thinking about these issues. They, of course, should in no way be held accountable for what is portrayed.

WORKS CITED

Association of American Universities Committee on Graduate Education. *Report and Recommendations*. Online. Oct. 1998. http://www.tulane.edu/~aau/GradEdRpt.html.

Bartholomae, David. "What Is Composition and (if you know what it is) Why Do We Teach It?" *Composition in the Twenty-First Century: Crisis and Change*. Ed. Lynn Z. Bloom, Donald A. Daiker, and Edward M. White. Carbondale and Edwardsville: Southern Illinois UP, 1996. 11-28.

Berger, Thomas. "Trying to Turn a Patchwork of Part-Time Jobs into an Academic Career." *New York Times* 8 Mar 1998, late ed.

Bérubé, Michael. *The Employment of English: Theory, Jobs and the Future of Literary Studies*. New York: New York UP, 1998.

Brannon, Lil. "(Dis)Missing Compulsory First-Year Composition." *Reconceiving Writing, Rethinking Writing Instruction*. Ed. Joseph Petraglia. Mahway, NJ: Lawrence Erlbaum, 1995. 239-48.

Brereton, John C., ed. *The Origin of Composition Studies in the American College, 1875-1925: A Documentary History*. Pittsburgh: U of Pittsburgh P, 1995.

Brown, Stuart C., Theresa Enos, and Janice Lauer. Unpublished survey results, 1996.

Brown, Stuart C., Paul R. Meyer, and Theresa Enos. "Doctoral Programs in Rhetoric and Composition: A Catalog of the Profession." *Rhetoric Review* 12 (Spring 1994): 240-389.

Cassuto, Leonard. "Pressures to Publish Fuel the Professionalization of Today's Graduate Students." *The Chronicle of Higher Education*. 27 Nov. 1998: B4-5.

Connors, Robert J. *Composition-Rhetoric: Backgrounds, Theory, and Pedagogy*. Pittsburgh: U of Pittsburgh P, 1997.

———. "The New Abolitionism: Toward a Historical Background." *Reconceiving Writing, Rethinking Writing Instruction*. Ed. Joseph Petraglia. Mahwah, NJ: Lawrence Erlbaum, 1995. 3-26.

Crowley, Sharon. *Composition in the University: Historical and Polemical Essays*.

Pittsburgh: U of Pittsburgh P, 1998.

Fontaine, Sheryl I. "Revising Administrative Models and Questioning the Value of Appointing Graduate Student WPAs." *Foregrounding Ethical Awareness in Composition and English Studies*. Ed. Sheryl I. Fontaine and Susan M. Hunter. Portsmouth, NH: Boynton/Cook, 1998. 83-92.

Franklin, Phyllis. Editor's Column. "Setting Standards: Acceptable Ratios of Full- to Part-Time Faculty Members." *MLA-Newsletter* 30.3 (Fall 1998): 5-6.

Gilman, Sander. "*Habent Sua Fata Libelli*; or Books, Jobs, and the MLA." *PMLA* 111 (1996): 390-94.

Goggin, Maureen. "The Disciplinary Instability of Composition." *Reconceiving Writing, Rethinking Writing Instruction*. Ed. Joseph Petraglia. Mahway, NJ: Lawrence Erlbaum, 1995. 27-48.

Harris, Joseph. *A Teaching Subject: Composition Since 1966*. Upper Saddle River, NJ: Prentice-Hall, 1997.

Miller, Scott L., Brenda Jo Brueggemann, Bennis Blue, and Deneen M. Shepherd. "Present Perfect and Future Imperfect: Results of a National Survey of Graduate Students in Rhetoric and Composition Programs." *College Composition and Communication* 48 (1997): 392-409.

Miller, Thomas P. *The Formation of College English: Rhetoric and Belles Lettres in the British Cultural Provinces*. Pittsburgh: U of Pittsburgh P, 1997.

Modern Languages Association. *The Final Report of the MLA Committee on Professional Employment*. Delegate Assembly Meeting 29 December 1997 Toronto Item No. 5 (a) 41 pages.

Raymond, Rich. "Preparing Writing Professionals for the Classroom: TAs and the Practice of Composition Theory." *Composition Forum* 9.2 (Fall 1998): 20-37.

Schneider, Alison. "Bad Blood in the English Department: The Rift Between Composition and Literature." *The Chronicle of Higher Education* 13 Feb. 1998: A14-A15.

Schuster, Charles. "Toward Abolishing Composition." (Dis)Missing Freshman English: Alternatives to the Universal Requirement. Conf. on Coll. Composition and Composition Convention. Sheraton Hotel, San Diego. 2 Apr. 1993.

Showalter, Elaine. "A Teacher Prepares." *MLA Newsletter* 30.3 (Fall 1998): 3-4.

Slevin, James F. "Disciplining Students: Whom Should Composition Teach and What Should They Know?" *Composition in the Twenty-First Century: Crisis and Change*. Eds. Lynn Z. Bloom, Donald A. Daiker, and Edward M. White. Carbondale and Edwardsville: Southern Illinois UP, 1996. 153-65.

Walker, Jeffrey. Jswl@psu.edu. "Scholarly Book Review List." 16 Nov. 1998. PRETEXT@LISTSERV.UTA.EDU.

Wallace, Ray. E-mail to author. 27 Aug. 1998.

White, Ed. Ewhite@csusb.edu. "Who should teach freshman comp?" 27 Oct 1998. WPAL@ASUVM.INRE.ASU.EDU.

Wilson, Robin. "Universities Scramble to Find Teachers of Freshman Composition." *Chronicle of Higher Education* Online. 26 Oct. 1998 http://www.chronicle.com/colloquy/98/froshcomp/background.htm.

The Preparation of Graduate Writing Teachers: Creating Substance Out of Shadows

Beth Maxfield

As a new teaching assistant at a small university in the early 1980s, I was handed a textbook, a class roster, a room number, and the best wishes of my mentor. As I approached the classroom for the first time, I was filled with trepidation. What had I gotten myself into? How was I supposed to teach these students to write? The only experience I had to rely on was my own experiences in composition classes: freshman composition and advanced composition. I had been assigned a mentor by the English department, but this professor was also the mentor for every other teaching assistant in the department; he told us in our group preservice meeting that he only wanted to see our first examination and/or writing assignment. After that, we were on our own. This "preparation" left me feeling less than adequate as I entered the classroom for the first time as a writing teacher.

Fifteen years later in the late 1990s, most graduate programs in English have evolved to include some training in composition theory and the teaching of writing. In fact, Richard Fulkerson has asserted that "English students who hold teaching assistantships are receiving effective, sometimes extensive, training for teaching college writing" (3) and, more recently, Catherine Latterall has observed that "GTA education programs are doing more and are doing a better job" (7). I recently completed a project in which I compared the instructional practices of writing teachers at the secondary and post-secondary levels within a limited geographic region. As a part of this project, I explored the graduate program of a research university, a university at which only graduate students teach the first-year composition sequence. I looked at both the training program of graduate students and the practices those graduate students employ in the writing classroom. I would argue that the training program I discovered in this case study is indicative of a general trend among contemporary graduate programs and graduate students.

At this research university, a one-week preservice workshop is required of all graduate students; this workshop is planned and largely run by veteran teaching assistants, who lead "teams" of assistants through their tenure at the university. The workshop lasts 3 to 5 days when stipends are not available and 5 to 6 days when they are available, and teachers attend sessions for the better part of every day, 9-4:30. One six-year veteran of this program had the following remarks to make about the workshop:

The workshops are essential for first-year graduate students, especially since they must follow a required syllabus for the first 6 weeks of class. However, the returns diminish after several years, because the same topics are rehashed every year. Too, the money for stipends is always tight. [The program's director] had to fight hard for money to pay for training this year. The university wants excellent graduate teachers and effective writing instruction, but it doesn't want to spend $40,000 for a training program to achieve that goal. (Interview)

During this workshop, new graduate teachers are placed in groups; one experienced graduate teacher is assigned to lead each group and to mentor the newer assistants. These groups offer new teaching assistants an opportunity to discuss fears and problems with someone who has experience in the writing classroom but is a step below the full-time faculty in department hierarchy. Such a system has the advantage of bonding the graduate students while creating a venue for discussion without the intimidation many graduate students feel toward their professors.

Graduate teaching assistants in this program must also complete a course in theory and practice of writing instruction before entering the classroom, but one teacher who was interviewed observed that this course may contain little or no theory, depending on who teaches it. This observation, naturally, could be made about almost any training course. Furthermore, as is often the case, some graduate training takes place in the writing center. A considerable body of research points to the merits of tutoring as an excellent method by which graduate writing teachers learn to put theory into practice while learning about individual composing processes. Writing centers represent a valuable aspect of training because they can help theory and practice converge; they can help teachers "understand the practical implications of student-centered theory and [may make] them significantly more committed to practicing it in the classroom"(Cogil 80). Thus, it is not unusual that at a research university the writing center poses one avenue for teacher training.

If this university's training program for graduate writing teachers is similar to many others across the country and therefore indicative of current trends in graduate education in English, it would seem that new generations of writing teachers are wellversed in composition theory and how to apply it in the classroom. But is this scenario complete? Have modern composition theories, in fact, infiltrated the modern writing classroom, or are they are merely abstractions that sound good on paper? Once graduate students leave the theoretical seminars, the discussion groups, the mentors, the writing center, and enter their individual writing classrooms, how do they teach writing? Do they apply practices that align with current composition theory? Are they aware of what theoretical schools they are applying with any given practice? Has current-traditional rhetoric been in fact replaced in first-year writing classrooms? If so, by what theory or theories? The answers to these questions, we often like to assume—even assert—are yes. But all too often, they are not. All too often, the writing classroom is quite a different place from that which we envision as we train these teachers. As in our own classrooms, theory and practice are often at odds with one another, and they often collide. Many graduate writing teachers may find, upon serious reflection, that they profess an emphasis on process but evaluate with an emphasis on product, as noted by Appleman and Green. The project I conducted was guided by the ultimate purpose of surveying closely the realities of writing instruction in first-year writing classrooms in order to discover, in a limited manner, some of the ways writing is really taught today. An important part of the project was to determine whether contemporary theory is relevant to instructional practice in contemporary classrooms and, if so, to what extent. As composition scholars and teachers, seeking out the ways in which theory and practice diverge and finding ways to bridge the gap between the two should be an important part of our work.

One significant finding of my survey was that modern composition theory is not of great interest to many graduate writing teachers. One graduate assistant teacher observed in a telephone interview that many of his colleagues at the research university "are blissfully ignorant" of theory; in fact, he said, "Not only is there no reflective writing going on in the classroom; there's no reflective teaching going on, either." He went on to explain that many of his colleagues simply do not have the time to think about how theory informs their practice. Quite simply, graduate writing teachers generally believe that they do not have the time for such reflection; rather, they are caught up in a race to juggle responsibilities and keep pace with the dual demands of being both a teacher and a student.

Despite these findings about theory, all of the graduate writing teachers surveyed said that formal training is necessary for one to become an effective writing teacher. And a third of them reported being first exposed in graduate school—probably because many of them have liberal arts undergraduate degrees. However, even liberal arts graduates are introduced to teaching methods in undergraduate school, albeit indirectly through their teachers' methods (a concept

I will discuss later); their answers reflect their first formal instruction in methodology. Furthermore, research such as Arthur Applebee's suggests that all teachers tend to teach—at least in some ways—the way they were taught, and the responses reported here do not take that factor into account.

Thus, several classroom instructional methods used by these graduate writing teachers do not appear to be guided by any specific theoretical foundation; rather, the results of my survey bear out my earlier observation that theory and practice often find themselves in direct opposition in what is presumably the most academic setting—the university. In fact, some of these conflicts may be found in areas that are commonly considered to be the most significant issues in modern composition studies:

A. Process versus Product

B. Structure of Writing Assignments

C. Revision

D. Writing Practice

PROCESS VS. PRODUCT

Although almost every theory and fashion of composition instruction currently espouses the process model of writing instruction over the product model, many of the graduate writing teachers I surveyed continue to evaluate papers with an emphasis on the final product—almost half of them proclaim they are product-oriented teachers of writing. The data show, however, that teachers with fewer years' experience seem to be more process-oriented than more experienced teachers; therefore, as the more experienced teachers retire, more process-oriented writing instruction may be expected. And this is in spite of the emphasis on process engendered by the portfolio program used by the research university. The final portfolio even includes "an appendix exhibiting the multiple draft, writing process the writer used in developing an essay"[sic] (Internet). This conflict may be the result of these writing teachers' efforts to achieve a balance between process and product, as Corbett has called for teachers to do. Such an assumption is a dangerous one to make, however. Training programs need to address directly these divergent ends and provide some practical means for achieving and supporting a balance between the two.

STRUCTURE OF WRITING ASSIGNMENTS

The graduate writing teachers in this survey are probably no different from many of their counterparts across the country; they like organizational structure in their students' papers. One example of this reliance on structure is the use of the modes of discourse as a primary framework for teaching writing. One assignment trend found in these writing classrooms is an emphasis on the modes as a primary method of writing instruction; 90 percent of respondents reported favoring modal essay assignments. The modes are usually associated with current-traditional rhetoric, but North connects them with what he calls lore (29). This difference in theoretical association presents some possibilities to explain the college teachers' use of the modes. For example, many of the textbooks from which these teachers teach writing are organized modally, and North claims that textbooks are the most widely disseminated form of written lore (30). This most obvious departure from contemporary composition theory is also one that deserves attention in composition theory courses. Faculty teaching these courses should address the controversy over the modal assignment, for only after entering this conversation can graduate writing teachers make informed decisions about the structure of their own classroom assignments.

REVISION

As may be expected, the word revision conjures a variety of meanings for this group of graduate writing instructors, and no meaning seems to be guided by one clearly delineated theoretical approach. The university's portfolio program relies on extensive revision by students, but one instructor remarked that the majority of students in this program do not treat revision any more seriously or learn any more from the process than students in a more traditional classroom do. He contended that most first-year composition students simply cannot or will not think reflectively about their writing. This observation implies that student attitudes about revision (i.e., that revision and editing are synonymous terms) are deep-seated and cannot be undone by one teacher, one course, one semester, or one year. The concept of revision as a complete rethinking and rewriting process is one that graduate writing teachers should be taught in their graduate seminars; as students, they should be encouraged to practice revision in this manner, not merely, as teachers, to impose it on their students.

WRITING PRACTICE

Both Corbett and Sizer have commented on the tendency of many writing teachers to spend too much classroom time talking about writing and too little time giving students the opportunity to write, but this does not seem to apply to the graduate writing teachers at this university. They have expressed the conviction that students must write often if they are to learn to write well. Every teacher in this survey indicated that she assigns some form of writing on a weekly basis at minimum, and many indicated that they have students write something every class period. The use of journals also points to teachers' interest in writing practice, but it also reflects the philosophy of the freshman writing program at this school. The university makes systematic use of journaling; all students in the freshman writing program are required to keep a journal, which is described as follows: "Through journal writing you will draft (1) responses to class activities,

(2) summaries, observations, and questions about reading assignments, and (3) information pertinent to your longer writing assignments. In addition, you will write journal entries in class. An entry is generally one or two pages long"(Internet). Thus, the graduate writing teachers in this survey seem to have put into practice the philosophy that students learn to write best by practicing their writing. However, only if this dictate is reinforced with discussion and use of journals in graduate seminars and in the training program will the next generations of writing teachers understand the value and the theoretical underpinnings of journaling.

THE GAP BETWEEN THEORY AND PRACTICE

The instructional gaps noted among these graduate writing teachers are often the result of a subtle but powerful gap, that between theory and practice. Daniel Dietrich has argued that today's teachers of composition are much like their counterparts in 1912, all too frequently basing their decisions about teaching methods and course content on personal intuition, trends, or tradition. However, where the teachers of sixty years ago had no research findings available to them, today's teachers can call upon any of the abundance of research findings that are now being disseminated. There are several possible reasons for this gap between theory and practice, and there are several ways training programs can be used to bridge the gap.

One aspect of theory and practice, alluded to earlier, has tremendous influence on how writing teachers teach their discipline. Because this aspect of theory is practice-based, it may be considered more a body of knowledge than a theory; Stephen North has labeled this type of knowledge "lore"(22). Lore is quite different from a clearly articulated theory with associated practices. Composition's lore is a unique combination of all manner of practices, knowledge, and literature and is as old as the teaching of writing. North defines lore as "the accumulated body of traditions, practices, and beliefs in terms of which Practitioners understand how writing is done, learned, and taught"(22). The term "practitioners" as used by North means, essentially, classroom teachers, writing lab or writing center consultants, and others whose main job is to teach writing—those people whose main mode of inquiry is their teaching of composition. For these people, lore is pragmatic, "concerned with what has worked, is working, or might work in teaching, doing, or learning writing," and it is "essentially experiential"(23) in nature.

According to North, lore takes three primary forms: ritual, writing, and talk. Rituals are "those patterns of practice which acquire what amounts to a ceremonial status, and which get passed along mostly by example"(29) and include the red pen for grading, the green gradebook, the use of modal assignments, and the codes used to respond to student papers. North explains the practical function of rituals as follows: "Writing and the teaching of writing are activities as complex as any human beings undertake. All of what is involved cannot be articulated, let alone codified. Thus, a great deal of what one knows must not only be held but passed on as ritual knowledge: Nobody could ever explain all that there is to know or do, so we simply do as those before us have done. It is the way"(30). Writing lore is included in some professional journals such as *Exercise Exchange, Language Arts*, and *The Writing Instructor* (North 31-32); textbooks; lesson plans; syllabi; handouts; and even commentary on student papers. Talk is the most widely used, most powerful form that lore takes (32) and is shared in conference presentations, classroom lectures, conferences with students, even hallway, office, and faculty lounge conversations.

As a credible venue of knowledge, lore's value has diminished in the thirty-five years since Albert Kitzhaber and Wayne Booth issued their famous calls for a new rhetoric; those calls in themselves devalued lore as a valid theoretical framework from which writing should be taught. North ironically states that lore "is now a second-class sort of knowledge, rapidly approaching the status of superstition—to be held or voiced only apologetically, with deference to the better, new knowledges"(328) created by scholars and researchers. Too, those who practice lore have come to be considered by many to be mere purveyors of knowledge rather than makers of knowledge (North 23).

However, if it is true that students learn to teach by example, then we who are already in the ranks have the opportunity to influence the next generations of writing teachers simply by what we do and do not do in the first-year writing classroom. Furthermore, since no theory was overtly demonstrated in my own survey, it may be that lore's ritual and talk forms are the most common methods by which teachers in that survey arrive at their instructional methodologies. Indeed, it may be that this tradition of teaching is by far the most powerful. As a colleague recently observed, the model students internalize from their own experiences—good or bad—is extremely difficult to displace when they become teachers. She offered an example from a recent methods class: "We spent all semester experiencing new, participatory, interactive ways of teaching writing and literature and of doing evaluation. On the final exam, when asked to explain how they would teach a given body of material (and they had choices), almost everyone reverted to the ways in which they had been taught"(Dobie). This observation illustrates the powerful influence of example on teacher practice. It also highlights the importance of attitude toward composition that faculty present to students, undergraduate and graduate. There are other reasons for student failure to transfer theory into practice, however. These reasons should be addressed if true reform in the composition classroom is to be achieved.

First, many graduate writing teachers who responded to this survey seem to be uninterested in current composition theory in part because they generally do not see it as having any real or practical application in the classroom. Hashimoto has noted that

it's a telling fact that most of the famous people in "composition studies" are famous not because they are good teachers (although some of them might be), but because they advocate popular or accepted *visions* of the writing "process" or have staked out territories and become "experts" on a respectable aspect of theory or history of rhetoric. . . . [But] we sometimes forget that this knowledge ought to make us better *teachers*. (15-16)

Perhaps one issue those involved with training graduate writing teachers need to address, then, is how to make theory more practical and less abstract. Another reason theory and practice remain separate for a number of graduate teachers of first-year composition is that they have little time to think reflectively about the scholarship they are required to read for classes, for they must balance the roles of student and teacher. This balance is often a tenuous one at best, and almost inevitably one role or the other is given short shrift at any given time. The issues of relevance and accessibility of theoretical research should be addressed by the those who train graduate writing teachers so that more of them make the time to inform themselves on the diverse theoretical and practical perspectives.

A second, more important, problem is the focus of most graduate programs in English. Many of these programs still spend more time teaching their students how to do research than how to teach the various aspects of the discipline. This is one characteristic of the graduate curriculum that should be altered. Therefore, I maintain, as Harold A. Hellwig did at the annual NCTE meeting in 1992, that graduate programs in English should focus specifically on the teaching of writing—and literature—and not merely research methods of these disciplines, for almost all of these master and doctoral candidates will spend a much more substantial portion of their careers teaching, not conducting research.

To achieve that end, the administrators of graduate programs in English should begin to rethink their aims and purposes for those programs. As the job market shrinks and educational economic pressures increase, graduate programs in English are, more than ever, obligated to serve their graduate students, their institutions, the profession, and the society in general well—the overwhelming ethical reasons for doing so aside. The MLA Committee on Professional Employment recently prepared and released a guide for evaluating graduate programs in English; among the guidelines suggested for departments are several that directly affect the way graduate writing teachers learn to teach composition to undergraduates.

5.1.1.1 How are teaching assistants introduced to, prepared for, and supported in their assignments? Does the department offer . . . seminars in appropriate areas, such as the teaching of composition? If so, how effective are they? Do faculty members actively and consistently provide teaching assistants ongoing the ongoing supervision and support that allow teaching assistantships to be vital parts of graduate students' education? How often are teaching assistants more or less left on their own to sink or swim? (1182)

The question regarding the effectiveness of graduate seminars emphasizes the need for English departments not only to offer these classes but also to evaluate them and to modify them when and where necessary. Just as first-year composition teachers must realize they don't teach in a vacuum and that they must open themselves to new practices, so must the trainers of new composition teachers realize their parallel obligation to these new teachers.

5.1.1.4 What opportunities do graduate students have to talk about, practice, and receive comment on activities like leading discussions, lecturing, constructing a syllabus, creating assignments, reading and responding to student writing, having students discuss and edit class work in groups and teaching with audiovisual and computer-based materials? Are graduate students informed of the obligations and rights that inhere in the institutional and professional position of the classroom teacher? (1182)

These questions deal with practical aspects of teaching writing, but they allude back to the questions about leaving graduate students to "sink or swim" and they foreshadow the questions about models and messages faculty send graduate writing teachers. New teachers of composition must see how theory informs each of these mundane details that do not occur inside the writing classroom, and they can do so in a much better fashion through discussion and individual attempts to mesh theory and practice in these media.

5.1.1.8 What models and messages about teaching do the faculty members demonstrate in their teaching, directly in graduate seminars and indirectly in their participation in the department's undergraduate program? (1183)

This final area is a most important one. How much of what students do when autonomous in the classroom is resistance to their graduate programs', their seminar professors', and/or their training supervisors' beliefs about composition theory and its application in the classroom?   Do we teach them to think independently and form their own teaching style? Do we want to indoctrinate or educate our graduate students? The latter allows for differences of opinion and fosters dialogue among those differences. As Nancy Welch has argued, "When the voices of other Institutions and Inclinations are banned [either implicitly or explicitly] in a seminar room, it becomes virtually impossible for participants to doubt and debate, question and revise, and find ways of working within a culture without being dominated and enslaved by it"(400). If only one perspective prevails, students learn only to follow that path, or they are forced to resist or to subvert that path in any number of ways. When one single "correct" theory and methodology are imposed on graduate writing teachers, the opportunity is lost to teach the reflection, questioning, and discovery that is so important to both graduate and undergraduate writing and to education in general. After all, each of us has a particular set of assumptions, "historically situated and politically informed ways of constructing and understanding teaching and learning"(Welch 399). These assumptions have merit; they cannot be dismissed out of hand because they are "wrong" or simply not in vogue at the moment.

In conclusion, there are many competing—and conflicting—notions of how writing instruction should proceed at any given level. There are a number of ways writing can be taught effectively in any of the various epistemologies. Good writing teachers employ eclectic approaches; they remain open to trying new or different strategies of writing instruction. How can universities design writing programs that facilitate learning the art of teaching composition and help graduate students remain open to a variety of approaches? This chapter is certainly not the final word on the subject. Now we must discover other ways in which we can reconcile our ideas about how writing should be taught with how writing is taught and apply that knowledge to training the next generations of writing teachers.

WORKS CITED

Applebee, Arthur N. *Tradition and Reform in the Teaching of English: A History*. Urbana: NCTE, 1974.

Appleman, Deborah, and Douglas E. Green. "Mapping the Elusive Boundary Between High School and College Writing." *CCC* 44 (1993): 191-99.

Cogil, Jane. "Theory Made Visible: How Tutoring May Effect Development of Student-Centered Teachers." *WPA: Writing Program Administration* 21.1 (1997): 76-84.

Corbett, Edward P. J.. "Teaching Composition: Where We've Been and Where We're Going." *CCC* 38 (1987): 444-52.

Dieterich, Daniel. "Teaching High School Composition." ERIC/RCS Report. *English Journal* 62 (1973): 1291-92.

Dobie, Ann B. E-mail to the author. 9 Dec. 1998. "Evaluating the Mission, Size, and Composition of Your Doctoral Programs." MLA Committee on Professional Employment. *PMLA* 113 (1998): 1178-87.

Fulkerson, Richard, ed. "On Preparing College Composition Teachers: An Annotated List of Relevant Sources." Prepared by the CCCC Committee on Preparation of College Teachers of Writing. Urbana: CCCC, 1993. ERIC ED 355 536.

Hashimoto, Irvin Y. *Thirteen Weeks: A Guide to Teaching College Writing*. Portsmouth, NH: Boynton/Cook, 1991.

Hellwig, Harold A. "The New Breed of Graduate Programs: Preparing for the Changing Market." Paper presented at the Annual Meeting of the National Council of Teachers of English (82nd, Louisville, KY, November 18-23, 1992). ERIC ED 354 533.

Latterall, Catherine G. "Training the Workforce: An Overview of GTA Education Curricula." *WPA: Writing Program Administration* 19.3 (1996): 7-23.

Maxfield, Beth Ann May. Rhetorical Competence and Performance: A Case Study of High School and College Writing Instruction. Diss. Univ. Southwestern LA, 1998. Ann Arbor: UMI, 1998. 9903386.

North, Stephen. *The Making of Knowledge in Composition: Portrait of an Emerging Field*. Portsmouth, NH: Boynton/Cook, 1987.

Sizer, Theodore R. *Horace's Compromise: The Dilemma of the American High School*. Boston: Houghton Mifflin, 1984.

Welch, Nancy "Resisting the Faith: Conversion, Resistance, and the Training of

Teachers." *College English.* 55 (1993): 287-401.

Winterowd, W. Ross, with Jack Blum. *A Teacher's Introduction to Composition in the Rhetorical Tradition.* NCTE Teacher's Introduction Series. Urbana: NCTE, 1994.

Cognition and Culture: Addressing the Needs of Student-Writers

Alan Jackson

The study of composition has passed through many phases and resulted in an assortment of teaching styles and approaches. Yet, after the thousands of books and tens of thousands of essays written in the field (and hundreds of thousands of students with college credit in composition courses), certain essential questions remain unanswered and seldom addressed:

1. What do (and should) we know about how cognition and culture affects writers?

2. What aspect of cognition and/or culture influence influences writers?

3. How can writing instruction influence cognition and/or culture in order to improve the quality and quantity of writing a person produces?

In short, what do we really know about writers?

The sad truth is that Composition Studies has focused far too much on ourselves, a narcissistic act that has left our students with no better writing instruction than thirty years ago while we stare at our reflection in a pool. Evidence of this can be found in two areas: first, on our concern for texts rather than process, a holdover from literature departments where, unfortunately, composition remains; second, in our handwringing over the politics of academia, a silly exercise that has accomplished nothing toward the goal of understanding where and how writers produce their texts.

Many experts on basic and freshman writers, from Rose to Bartholomae, talk about the need to introduce students to academic discourse or academic writing. But what is academic writing or discourse? The academic community as I know it does not have one single style or voice or language. Consider the field of composition: James Berlin, Linda Flower, and Victor Villanueva all hold a place in the academic discourse of composition, yet no one would suggest that these three write with the same rhetorical style, same purposes, or same assumptions. In fact, these three, as well as many others, engage in academic discourse without ever imitating the other.

Moreover, scholars such as Mike Rose, though advancing proposed changes that lead toward academic writing courses, acknowledge that academic writing can be alienating, limiting, and confusing. Often, the abundance of jargon, along with a series of assumptions that the reader will discover the meaning and recognize the veiled references, prevent many insiders, not to mention the outsiders, from gleaning the text's value. One might wonder why anyone would direct his or her students to such restrictive discourse. The paradox lies in an academy that does not seek to embrace its apprentices or expand its scope, or clarify its ideas, yet demands that others pass through its labyrinth and pass by its Minotaur in order to acquire a discourse that owns so many oppressive qualities. Rose may not like the discourse, but he knows that a certain social, political, and economic acceptance awaits those who can use it.

But the solution to helping writers enter the academy and use the academy's discourse should not be in recruiting writers into an elitist, oppressive band, especially if the student merely wants an undergraduate degree that leads him or her to a nice career and one step up the socioeconomic ladder, but not into the world of the academy. Instead, the academy should change by recognizing that our discourse is often embracing, expansive, and clear, and that most composition scholars and teachers prefer this kind of writing. After all, no writing course, basic or other, immediately awards membership to the academic community to students who pass through it, but it can let them see the borders and visit the residents on the edges (Murray, Carl Sagan, and Stephen Gould). When the time comes to read and synthesize the alienating, limiting, and confusing texts of academic discourse, the students can move into the particular academic neighborhood he or she wishes to know.

This problem, then, for students results in confusion over what style they are to imitate. As Bartholomae points out in "The Study of Error," errors may result from a student's attempt to imitate the perceived academic discourse he or she wishes to enter; however, because no one has defined academic writing or discourse, the student may well imitate a form that represents a small, narrow, and devalued academic style. Not surprisingly, the problem for teachers of basic writers is no less complicated. For teachers, defining academic discourse is quite difficult because we interact daily with its different levels, styles, and content.

We may know what it is, but we often cannot define it or communicate it to our students. Unfortunately, unless we can articulate some definition for academic writing, few of our students, especially those in first-year writing courses, will acquire the skills needed to enter the academic world. Without some ability to illustrate academic writing standards, academic discourse becomes as intangible as our concepts of learning and teaching. Nevertheless, we must arrive at some basic definition or means to introduce academic discourse into our classrooms if we intend to demand it of our students.

In fact, the academy itself has not decided upon what the academic discourse should include. Even in our field of Composition, scholars argue about what academic discourse entails. Consider the infamous issues of *College English*, which pitted Maxine Hairston and John Trimbur in a discussion over recent articles (discourse) in *College English*. Maxine Hairston asserts that many recent articles do not have a place in a major writing journal. She says:

I find the magazine dominated by name-dropping, unreadable, fashionably radical articles that I feel have little to do with the concerns of most college English teachers . . . I'm also concerned about the image of the profession I think the magazine would convey to the public if they read it (thank goodness they don't!): that of low-risk Marxists who write very badly, are politically naive, and seem more concerned about converting their students from capitalism than in helping them to enjoy writing and reading. (695)

She goes on to lament the recent articles to be "as opaque and dull as anything in *PMLA* or *Critical Inquiry*." (Obviously, the problem that Mike Rose finds in academic discourse is not merely confined to any single academic source.) All this shows a real problem within one academic field, notably the one field most interested in and diverse in its approach to writing. If Hairston is right, then the alienation begins at the top, with publishers and publishing scholars, then filters down to "the writing and thinking of graduate students who then teach freshman English"(696). In addition, if she is right, bad writing is given a revered place and becomes the standard to which our composition students should aspire. As Hairston says, "It's not a happy prospect." And, whether she is right or not about the clarity and quality of those articles, her protest against them proves that we in composition have yet to determine our own scholarly boundaries for academic discourse. If we cannot draw the borders, how can we expect to point our students to an academic writing style that will be embraced by the academy?

Trimbur, in his response to Hairston, complicates the issue of academic discourse even further when he says, "What this means, moreover, is that the 'mainstream' Maxine refers to isn't quite there anymore . . . . Composition studies have grown, have discovered new lines of intellectual affiliation, and have differentiated internally" (700). In essence, Trimbur has placed most of academic discourse on the fringes in pockets of like-minded thinkers. However right he is, the problem for freshman composition teachers is magnified. Which pocket on which fringe do we direct our students? What models do we choose for them? If we choose the mainstream, will our students not be entering academic discourse? More important, if there is no mainstream, only a series of stagnant pools, is a real academic discourse, an exchange of ideas taking place, or are we merely talking to our own kind? If we are, then our students (not to say ourselves) are doomed to failure in entering the kingdom of academic discourse and writing.

(RE)SOLVING COMPOSITIONS' CULTURE(S)

Although the debate between Hairston and Trimbur began ten years ago, it has never been resolved; nonetheless, it stands as a seminal moment in composition studies when narcissistic self-interest, not student-writers, became the dominant force in scholarship. We had, as composition professionals, become more concerned with ourselves than our students, with our politics than our teaching responsibilities. Yet, our composition courses remain divided between vague notions of academic discourse and cultural studies.

Cultural Studies seems to breed the worse of this self-interest and to advocate the least-desirable learning environments. None of this would seem harmful if its proponents wanted to situate their studies in advanced specialty courses, not in a compulsory skills course like first-year composition. Yet, composition courses are where many want to teachers "to resist pragmatism and commodity capitalism and commit themselves to neo-Marxism and cultural materialism" (Severino 74). Instead of discussion about invention and audience, style, language, organization, one finds conversations (monologues?) about writing as "an active means to transform the existing social inequities of commodity capitalism" (France 2) or as a way "to bring about more personally humane and socially equitable economic and political arrangements" (Berlin 50). In nearly every example one finds of cultural studies and composition, the *professors' desires* for change, *not the students'* are addressed and, more important, the intellectual questions of student-writers are discarded in order to provide answers to narrow political concerns.

Furthermore, students do not have problems of issues of power—they don't have much and they know it. They also know that to succeed in the endeavors they choose, which is rarely the life of a Marxist college professor, their discourse must be adaptable—one will not last long as a worker (or a student) if one merely resists the powerful employer (or professor). And students also recognize that cultural hierarchies exist and want to know what they are in order to find acceptance among whatever group they join. To accept the idea of Henry Giroux, that teachers should "abandon the goal of giving students access to that which represents a culture" (478), is to deprive students of essential cultural information.

What students do want is to learn how to write better in order to achieve their goals and to negotiate the world. Students, by the time they arrive in a college classroom, understand that writing and speaking ability will gain them access to places they wish to enter; what they need to learn is how to expand the knowledge and skills that will make them better writers in order to succeed in academics and beyond.

Where Cultural Studies goes wrong is in its desire to impose views on students, or at least a view of the world that is not theirs, and in reading most cultural studies advocates, a view held by a small group of people. But culture is important and we can include the study of culture in composition classes, but we must keep the focus on student-writers.

A better approach is to encourage students to observe both the general culture from which they come and the academic culture into which they have entered. The academic world is complicated enough for many students who are first-generation college students, but by encouraging students to pay attention to that which anthropologists define as culture's primary components—tools, customs, institutions, beliefs, rituals, games, works of art, and language—and to recognize that their own learning has been shaped by a myriad of sources in infinite ways, they should begin to understand how culture works and how language represents culture. Such an approach should also allow them to negotiate, even though they may not fully understand or want to become a member, the academic culture, and one hopes the larger culture.

Teachers, at the same time, should bring ethnographic methodology to study students and the classroom. In some ways, composition has done this in studies of writers (Emig, Shaughnessy, Rose) and in essays laced with anecdotal evidence; however, we have not done enough to investigate what assumptions students make about writing before they compose.

How do our students write? In what environments do they write best? How do classroom social, intellectual, and cultural interactions influence students and their texts? We need to study our students in order to identify their cultures, both their personal and academic ones. We need to recognize that our academic culture and discourse as instructors is not theirs—they are outsiders in our academic world and we are outsiders in their academic world. And we need to learn how student assumptions about writing instructors and about writing instruction impact their discourse. The composition classroom must become a place of study about writing and about writers. We have not seriously addressed these vital issues. Nor have composition professionals acknowledged the vast differences in students' background and in academic cultures.

In the Atlanta area, where I live, different academic cultures abound. I teach at a multi-campus two-year college with many older, working students, all of whom commute to the college. Within thirty miles of my college, one can find a small, elite college in Emory University; a large, urban, mostly commuter university in Georgia State; a selective, state university in Georgia Tech; several black colleges in Spelman (all-female), Morehouse (all-male), and Clark Atlanta; and several commuter state four-year institutions. To suggest that these schools are alike is folly; not only do they serve different student populations, they vary greatly in budgets, missions, and histories.

For the most part, students in classrooms at these colleges share some common culture, but even individual classrooms place students with different backgrounds together. Nontraditional students, often with full-time jobs and families, may never really enter the academic world, only play at its margins—college education is a luxury, a way to better the life they currently have, not a transformational experience. These students also alter the dynamics of classroom activities because of their age, experiences, and view of the world. At present, we have no tools to ensure that each student gets what he or she wants.

COGNITION REVISITED

Another area where composition can refocus attention on the student-writer is to reawaken our study of cognition. Beginning in the early 1970s, composition professionals began to incorporate cognitive psychology into writing instruction. Janice Lauer and Richard Larson found in cognitive psychology a strong connection with invention and the creative process. From their work, particularly Lauer who bore the brunt of much of the early criticism, came an onslaught of interest in cognition. The work of Linda Flower and John Hayes, Sondra Perl, Mina Shaughnessy, and Nancy Sommers brought a serious investigation of the behavior of writers and the benefits for student-writers who learned problem-solving strategies as part of their writing processes.

And others offered vital studies to the relationship of cognition and composition. James Britton and James Moffett recognized the importance of cognition to language development. Barry Kroll designed a different way of looking at audience. Mike Rose gave valuable insight into writer's block. David Bartholomae provided a better understanding of errors.

By the late-1980s, cognition held a popular, if not always respected, place in composition studies. Yet even in the heydey of the union of cognitive psychology and composition, the relationship for teachers was often covert and misunderstood and for scholars focused more on the production of text than on the intellectual development of the student. By this time, much of the scholarly interest in cognition investigated text-production, as found in the work of Lester Faigley, Joseph Williams, and Lee Odell, along with a host of other scholars.

Ten years later, cognitive studies have diminished—in part because of the attacks by anti-empiricists and in part because cognitive studies has relied upon the same old ideas of cognition. Cognition began to become associated only with problem-solving, as if cognition is a method (i.e., mapping) rather than a subject to be studied. Also, the rise of cultural studies in composition usurped much of the role of cognition as a means to understand student-writers and their behavior. So too, many of the most influential cognition and composition scholars—Linda Flower, James Moffett, Mike Rose—have faded away from college composition journals and/or moved on to other matters, which left a void that has not been filled.

One area that does seem to hold great promise in reviving cognition in

Composition Studies is "emergents." Emergents, as defined by Duane Rumbaugh, are "novel patterns of responding or choosing between alternatives" that cannot be predicted by and often appear "with some element of surprise to the observer" (7). Emergents are complex and the choices one makes indicate hierarchical integration and creativity, not merely random or trained responses.

This new category in psychological research, which connects the behavioral and cognitivist camps, could prove quite valuable when applied to the study of student-writers for several reasons. First, emergents researchers have discovered that one "might progress with no obvious manifestation," then exhibit one's new knowledge in complex ways in new contexts (3), which would explain how and why student-writers seem to develop in spurts. Second, the choices one makes are not simply experiential or taught, but "reflect upon past experiences and events projected in the future" (2), which offers us a chance to learn more about how expectations alter student writing.

If applied to writing, the study of emergents may help us answer Britton's speculation about student-writers shaping at the point of utterance. We can begin to understand the deep sources that influence the choices student-writers make about words and phrases, about organization, about invention and audience, even about errors.

The most important contribution emergents can make to composition is to remind us to focus our attention on the individual student. Student experiences inside and out of academics have a great influence on their writing. Student experiences, knowledge (perhaps knowledge he or she has yet to manifest in his or her writing), and expectations influence all the choices student-writers make. Rather than dwell on generic assumptions about academic discourse and writing instruction, writing instructors must concentrate on the student's individual progress. Rather than expect particular responses to instruction, instructors must accept that some lessons are learned but not reflected immediately. And rather than think only in terms of instructional strategy, we must address learning strategies.

By moving away from the generic perspective on student-writers and to the individual understanding of each student-writer, instructors will be able to design courses that allow for personal progress, to offer new and novel assignments that encourage emergent responses, and to bring to students greater awareness of their own learning processes. Emergents, unlike traditional concepts of cognition, lead to a closer relationship between culture and cognition. As emergents researchers have shown, choices are influenced by "silent learning," which would include the components of culture. Both the larger culture and the academic one will play a role in the student-writers cognitive development. So too, an investigation of a subculture like academics would focus on cognitive advances, since they are a central feature of academic culture. Until now, we have separated the inner and outer world of the student-writer by continuing to define cognition and culture as incompatible, but, with emergents, we can join cognition and culture to gain more insight than ever into the student-writer.

CONCLUSION

By incorporating cognition and culture into the way we answer questions about student writers, composition professionals will focus more attention on the student writer, where it belongs, and less on ourselves. We do not need to buy into new theories—composition is cluttered with theoretical junk—or dwell on interdisciplinary matters—composition is a disciplinary mongrel; instead, we need to study our students, their writing processes, their cultural influences, and their cognitive changes.

The narcissism of the past decade must end. We cannot simply define academic or nonacademic discourse to suit ourselves and we cannot force a cultural view on students to satisfy narrow political agendas. We must become the ethnographers of the academic culture to truly understand how students learn about writing and about discourse communities. And we must become the observers of their cognitive development to maximize their learning processes. As I noted in the beginning, we have seen many years pass and many thousands of students exit our composition courses without knowing if or how we made them better writers.

Because writing is an individual cognitive experience that interacts with the culture around the writer, writing instructors are wrong to dwell on our selfish concerns or insist that student-writers stare at our reflection in the pool. Instead, we should look at student-writers, their cultures and their cognition, to understand the value and meaning of ourselves and of composition.

WORKS CITED

Berlin, James A. "Composition and Cultural Studies." *Composition and Resistance*. Eds. C. Mark Hurlbert and Michael Blitz. Portsmouth, NH: Boynton/Cook, 1991: 47-55.

France, Alan W. *Composition as Cultural Practice*. Westport, CT: Bergin and Garvey, 1994.

Giroux, Henry, David Shumway, Peter Smith, and James Sosnoski. "The Need for Cultural Studies: Resisting Intellectuals and Oppositional Public Spheres." *Dalhousie Review* 64 (2): 472-86.

Hairston, Maxine. Letter to Editor. *College English* 52.6 (October 1990): 694-96.

Rumbaugh, Duane M., David A. Washburn, and William A. Hillix. "Respondents, Operants, and Emergents: Toward an Integrated Perspective in Behavior." *Learning as Self Organization*. Eds. Karl Pribram and Joseph King. Hillsdale: Erlbaum, 1996.1-8

Severino, Carol. "Teaching and Writing 'up Against the Mall.'" *College English* 59.1 (January 1997): 74-82.

Trimbur, John. Response. *College English* 52.6 (October 1990): 696-700.

Breaking the Learning Monopoly: Acknowledging and Accommodating Students' Diverse Learning Styles

Eric H. Hobson

The invitation to "write/right the wrongs" in college composition is seductive. Admittedly, when asked to participate in this project, I leaned toward polemic—the invitation seemed to beg, "Say what you've always wanted to say about college composition." The invitation offered free space in which to articulate the Solution that rallies everyone to produce the high levels of student communicative ability that our institutional mission statements allude to and that our course catalogues and outcome statements promise. That offer is hard to refuse. Equally hard was determining what about college composition I wished to focus on. Thankfully, my colleagues' chapters cover many topics about which I have an opinion. Also, their chapters' comprehensiveness—along with my chapter's position at the end of the collection—allows me to shift the discussion somewhat.

I offer no cure-all prescription for what's ailing college composition. Instead, this chapter flirts with the issue of what it will *really* take for college writing teachers to deliver the outcomes that we have promised to our stakeholders: students, colleagues, administrations, parents, boards, alumni, legislatures, regulators, and accreditation agencies. What is needed, I believe, already exists; we really don't need new theories, or worse, new paradigms. Theory building and paradigm shifting often are activities of convenience: they make a minority group in the process of higher education (e.g., composition specialists) feel productive, even profound; they provide excuses to forego hard, down-n-dirty work in the trenches of writing classes found across post-secondary education. As authors in the preceding chapters have pointed out, too often those positing theories about writing instruction teach decidedly few students, especially student writers in the first-year composition sequence—the location drawing the most institutional and external fire.

Working from studies of student learning styles and learning preferences, I suggest that for any fix-it plan to reform writing instruction—from the 1st year writing sequence on—we must redirect our theory-building, curriculum-generating, teacher-training gaze. Most revision agendas for composition are articulated from a perspective that views students predominately as composite groups, wholes comprised of subsets often differentiated along racial, gender, and socioeconomic lines. While the nod is given to these differences—differences that do affect educational opportunities—scant attention is given to how these students learn and how that situation differs from student to student. Implicit in this lack of consideration are two unwarranted assumption:

1. Students, for the most part, learn best in ways condoned or defined by the academy.

2. Students share (or, should adopt) their instructors' learning preferences and biases.

To make the types of learning gains that reformers have heralded will result from the ascendancy of X or Y change to composition instruction, the crafters of and apologists for these projects must focus their gaze on the needs of the individual students who will sit in the writing classes offered as a result of their curricular revisions.[1] Then, the teachers who teach the resulting writing classes must acknowledge and work with these students' individual needs in ways that enable students to use their specific learning styles to succeed in each course, while also helping them to develop a broader range of learning strategies that require students to use less comfortable ways of knowing.[2] Gains of the type long claimed by compositionists and long demanded by outside stakeholders will happen only when writing instruction works in concert with the variety and diversity of learning systems on which students rely in any given classroom. Put simply, most writing instruction at the college level ignores what is known about how students learn. From this chapter's outset, however, I must state that I have my doubts about how willing are college composition teachers (me included) to meet the challenges I describe. If we are willing, great; however, there will be costs, many of which could disrupt our routines and programs. If not, we must reconsider the promises we make to our many constituents.

WHERE I'M COMING FROM

The 1980s and 1990s have been particularly boisterous within composition studies as composition theorists, critics, researchers, and practitioner communities championed any number of "correctives" to the dominant philosophical and instructional paradigms on which writing programs (most often first-year writing programs) are based.[3] We've witnessed the rise, fall, reclamation, and reformulation of many models: Current Traditional Rhetoric, Expressivism, The Process Movement, Social Constructivism, Cultural Studies—some of which now sport "Neo" prefixes to symbolize their re-emergent status in the community. Expressivist and neo-expressivist theorists have argued that a continued focus on the individual experience is an important part of a writer's developing sense of self and actual discursive ability as an individual within a social and cultural context. Proponents of cultural studies have argued that writing courses benefit from having an informed critical center that enables students to examine such thematic issues as race, power, politics, and economics. This position links their corrective plan to similar calls for reform that would have first-year writing courses center around critical thinking/problem-solving foci. Responding to Writing Across the Curriculum's (WAC) success, others (see Sampson, this volume) see a remedy to the traditional paradigm in a writing sequence with a distinctly disciplinary focus, often spread over several years of study.

Regardless of each proposal's logic, merit, and consistency with the best of both liberal arts and professional education, a fundamental flaw allows their corrective measures limited hopes for success. Most of the existing "correctives" cannot achieve the student learning outcomes expected (realistically or not) of required college-level writing courses—courses considered essential for academic and social/citizenry success—at least not at the programmatic level. Reflecting a systemic problem in U.S. higher education, each is predicated on an uncritical, uninformed, and unrealistic understanding of their clientele, students. Even when they congratulate themselves on crafting classrooms that are in the students' best interests, and, thus, seem to have given close scrutiny to the needs of *each* student in the class, or course, or program, they don't. For the most part, the correctives presented in the past two decades paint students taking writing courses—first year or beyond—with too broad a brush. These plans fail to consider the students in the classes as distinct individuals, not homogenous groups of 20 to 30. For the most part, these reform plans treat students as institutional amalgams, undifferentiated blocks of registration numbers making up specific segments of the institution's student body. Consider the sheer number of students in some type of post-secondary education at any one moment, however, and it is not surprising that individual student needs get lost in the crowd. Colleges are bureaucracies, and in most respects curricula are designed to meet needs other than student needs. These plans do not acknowledge (because they fail to even consider them) the variety of learning styles and preferences that students bring to the composition classroom—as well as to their every academic and nonacademic learning experience. As individuals who negotiate their way through the world each day, these students bring with them learning algorithms through which they make sense of the world at-large and of immediate classroom instruction.

STUDENT DEMOGRAPHICS

What most college-level teachers know about their students comes from surface markers that provide somewhat reliable predictors about students' ethnicity, gender, socioeconomic backgrounds, and so on. This information is easy to gather and is often supplied, unasked for, in one form or another by the academic institution. There also exists a readily accessible, but consistently ignored, literature coming out of research into the ways that people go about learning. Faculty developers, teaching and learning specialists, and other academicians have worked to make this information an integral part of curricular planning, class structures, and assessment across the curriculum, as well as part of institutional academic support activities. Little of this information, however, has shaped the correctives offered for teaching college-level writing classes, even though it should.[4]

The demographic information available paints a complex picture of students and their teachers. Studies of college student populations have produced findings that can help teachers understand important things about how students develop during their time on college campuses. The development studied ranges from emotional and intellectual maturation (Bloom, Perry, Kolb), to moral development (Belenky et al:, Gilligan), to personality definition (Myers and Myers; Lawrence), to gender-influence within all these developmental domains (Belenky, et.al., Gilligan). A cursory review of several frequently cited developmental models provides a glimpse into the rich data available to writing teachers who wish to know more about who are their students as thinkers and learners.

INTELLECTUAL AND ETHICAL DEVELOPMENT

Most comprehensively presented in *Forms of Intellectual and Ethical Development in the College Years: A Scheme* (1970), William Perry's model of intellectual and ethical development is the most widely applied model of such development for traditional undergraduate students.[5] His comprehensive model presents a nine stage process of achieving cognitive maturity; however, the simpler four stage model is the version most frequently referred to in the literature.[6] Typical undergraduate students progress ideally through the following stages of development during their collegiate lives, too: dualism, multiplicity, relativism, commitment. Each stage is marked by fairly typical attitudes, worldviews, and behavior.

1. *Dualism*: Students view the world and knowledge in black-and-white terms; their actions and beliefs are governed by absolute standards of right and wrong; teachers are authorities who provide the correct answers.

2. *Multiplicity*: Students acknowledge that uncertainty exists; however, they don't like it and believe that if they find the competent/right authority, they will find the right answer. Ambiguity suggests incompetence.

3. *Relativism*: Students no longer look to authority figures for truth, because they now believe that all answers/interpretations are equally valid. They embrace a "whatever works for you" perspective toward knowledge.

4. *Commitment*: Students begin to create criteria that they can use to help them make decisions that they can stand by within a relativistic knowledge framework. They rely on articulated criteria to make decisions and to justify their choices.

Within the composition community's literature, one of the few recent (1993) discussions of Perry's model and its uses for teaching writing is *The Critical Writing Workshop*, edited by Toni-Lee Campossela. This text illustrates my earlier comment that most discussions of composition courses maintain a programmatic, institutional gaze; their details and planning focus less on individual student needs than on other issues. Even in this collection of essays, where the discussion's stated focus on instructional strategies for developing students' critical thinking skills, only three (two by Campossela) of this collection's twelve chapters place the instructional design advocated within a cognitive development framework that acknowledges the individualized nature of students' critical thinking development. In the chapter, "Using William Perry's Scheme to Encourage Critical Writing," Campossela lends her assessment to the point made by a range of authors in the teaching and learning/faculty development community (e.g., Bonwell & Sutherland; Grasha; Miller, Groccia, & Wilkes) that carefully planned and articulated course and program structure is essential to help students move from one cognitive position to another. To assist students as they develop as critical thinkers and writers, teachers must plan activities with students' current cognitive developmental levels in mind. Campossela states:

If the demands of the course are pitched more than one stage beyond a student's current cognitive level, she is likely to become alienated and baffled. In particular, dualistic students who fear that they are in over their heads become even more reliant on authorities' opinions and less likely to take risks in their writing. To reduce the potential for alienation, support is required in assorted forms and lavish amounts: a nothreatening classroom atmosphere, many ungraded forms of writing, various kinds of collaboration and feedback, discussion of sample essays, and multiple opportunities to re-draft and revise. (60)

Partially in reaction to Perry's exclusively use of male examples to illustrate the steps in his model, Mary Belenky, Blythe Clinchy, Nancy Goldberger, and Jill Tarule interviewed 135 women in an attempt to identify the processes that women use to make decisions, interact with others, and accept/reject knowledge.[7] Labeling the resulting themes "ways of knowing," Belenky et al. produced a model of cognitive development in women that can be best summarized in a tripartite manner:

1. *Received Knowledge*: Information is either correct or not; there are fixed ways of looking at the world; and, authorities are there to tell one what to think and how to (inter)act in the presence of ambiguous information/situations.

2. *Subjective Knowledge*: Ambiguity is a fact of life and leads naturally to many points of view. These different perspectives are equally valuable.

3. *Procedural Knowledge*: There are differences between opinions and available options: some sources and opinions are better than others. Best decisions are arrived at by balancing external criteria (logic, data, evidence) with internal criteria (feelings, relationships, beliefs).

In *Teaching with Style: A Practical Guide to Enhancing Learning by Understanding Teaching and Learning Styles* (1996), Anthony Grasha demonstrates that the Perry and Belenky et al. models are quite compatible. Although based on research conducted with decidedly different study populations, yet using the similar research protocol of in-depth interviews, both models posit three common stages of cognitive and moral development: dualism/received knowledge, "seeking the "right" point of view"; multiplism/subjective knowledge, "developing multiple points of view"; relativism/procedural knowledge, "using criteria to evaluate multiple points of view" (217-19).

David A. Kolb's book *Experiential Learning: Experience as The Source of Learning and Development* (1984) presents a model of learning that attempts to categorize the learning styles that students prefer to use; it also can provide fluidity to the (sometimes interpreted as rigid) stage models of development presented in the preceding models. Meaningful learning, Kolb argues, is a series of events that integrates feeling, perceiving, thinking and acting, and consists of four phases that learners cycle through: concrete experience, reflective observation, abstract conceptualization, and active experimentation. The full description of the learning cycle presented in this model is quite complex; however, that surface complexity belies the model's pedagogical usefulness. Nilson's summary of this cycles provides a particularly useful distillation of Kolb's model. She writes:

The *concrete experience* mode is characterized by a reliance more on feeling than on thinking to solve problems. In this mode, people interpret human situations in a very personal way and focus on the tangible here and now. Intuitive, open-minded, social, and artistic in their information processing, these learners center on knowledge that demonstrates the complex and the unique vs. the systematic, scientifically derived theories and generalizations.

The *reflective observation* mode is similarly marked by intuitive thinking, but as applied to observing and understanding situations, not solving and manipulating them. Using this mode, a learner is quick to grasp the meanings and implications of ideas and situations and can examine situations and phenomena "empathetically" from different points of view. Patience, objectivity, and good judgement flourish in this mode.

Reliance on logical thinking and conceptual reasoning characterizes the *abstract conceptualization* mode. It focuses on theory building, systematic planning, manipulation of abstract symbols, and quantitative analysis. This mode can generate personality traits such as precision, discipline, rigor, and an appreciation for elegant, parsimonious models.

Finally, the *active experimentation* mode is directed towards the practical and concrete and rational thinking. But its orientation is towards results: influencing people's opinions, changing situations, and getting things accomplished—purely pragmatic applications. This mode fosters strong organizational skills, goal-direction, and considerable tolerance for risk. (63-64)

For the purposes of college-level writing instruction, the frameworks presented by Perry, by Belenky et al., and by Kolb should warrant careful consideration. The vast majority of the students taking required writing courses are in the earliest stages of their post-secondary education and research findings from studies of first- and second- year college students argue strongly that most of these students operate almost exclusively within a dualist/received knowledge model of knowledge (Grasha 219). These are students who fundamentally believe that Truth is available unconditionally and that the teacher's job is to give them the answers/knowledge they need to bring closure to their current task of completing a course. These are students who value structure in their learning environments combined with clear explanations of what they are to do in the activities they will take part in (Miller, Groccia and Wilkes).

Often, however, the writing courses they take have course objectives that state that for students to succeed in the course, they need to be much further along than they probably are in their cognitive development. In *Taxonomy of Educational Objectives (Handbook 1: Cognitive Domain)* (1956) Benjamin Bloom and colleagues present a taxonomy of six levels of critical thinking that many educators find provides a useful framework for illustrating the mismatch that often exists between where college students are in their cognitive ability and what they are asked to demonstrate the ability to do in their courses. This hierarchical taxonomy presents six levels of thought that increase in complexity:

(most complex) evaluation
synthesis
analysis
application
comprehension

(least complex) knowledge (recall)

Students who view the world and knowledge using Perry's and Belenky's dualistic/received knowledge frames of reference are most comfortable and effective when working in the two least complex levels of thinking, knowledge/recall and application. They can easily call up "correct" answers to straightforward questions and apply a prescribed formula to given situations. The agendas that fuel writing programs with a cultural studies influenced focus of engaging close reading and critique of ideological cultural frameworks, for example, often encounter stiff student resistance, admittedly because they intentionally challenge these students' ideologically determined frames of reference. However, student resistance is also a by-product of course objectives that ask students to make rapid, possibly unrealistic cognitive and ethical growth. It is not too much of a stretch (and I put the bull's eye on my forehead first) to suggest that many composition teachers ask students to work effectively at the upper reaches of Bloom's taxonomy (synthesis and evaluation) without providing students the overt explanation they need to understand what's going on and what's expected of them, or providing them the structured and carefully crafted support they need to move from one "way of knowing" to another. More to the point that I am making in this chapter about the need for composition program planners to focus on how students learn and what types of support and structure best assist students in achieving the levels of intellectual development that are implicit in most writing sequences, in "Thinking and Writing: A Sequential Curriculum for Composition," one of the few articles to directly address the issue of applications of Bloom's taxonomy to teaching college composition, Karen Spear writes that

The research on cognitive development in young adults makes a strong case for the cognitive needs of college writers, needs that have probably never been marginally satisfied or perhaps considered in designing and organizing writing courses. Bloom's taxonomy provides one model of thought structures and their relationships; there are others. Their value lies in evoking questions about cognitive sequences, about the effect of a curriculum in stimulating development, and about alternative curriculum designs. (60)

Given the methods through which many post-expressivist/social constructivist influenced composition theories seem to be enacted in the college writing classroom, one would think the theories themselves are predicated on the assumption that most undergraduate students are not firmly egocentric in their worldview, that they are not extremely uncomfortable in the face of ambiguity, and that they are facile playing with (and recognizing the presence of) the types of higher-order thinking that their teachers value, are comfortable with themselves, and have as (unstated) goals for their writing courses. Student demographic data challenge these assumptions, although not the overall educational outcomes aimed at by these projects. Available data about the intellectual and ethical development of traditional undergraduates (such as that glossed above) argue persuasively that it is probably unrealistic for composition programs to claim to achieve the higher-order critical gains they frequently advertise with typical undergraduate populations within the framework of traditional course schedules (ten to sixteen weeks of instruction). Such gains probably only stand a chance of being realized in carefully constructed, closely administered WAC-based writing programs in which direct writing instruction spans years, not weeks. Programmatic success in this context requires a phenomenal amount of commitment on the parts of teachers and students. Given staffing and support patterns for writing courses in most post-secondary institutions (heavy reliance on nonfaculty teaching staff who receive little sustained training, oversight, or the financial security and resources to encourage innovation), the teachers' side of the equation will rarely balance. Given the students' lack of tolerance for the types of (perceived) ambiguity in most writing classes, it is doubtful that this side of the equation will balance either.[8] The individual writing courses, as well as the overall composition curricula that many "corrective" composition agendas endorse are suited better—a better developmental "fit"—for nontraditional/mature undergraduates, upper-division undergraduates, and graduate students than for most lower-division undergraduates. As Spear notes, "From a cognitive perspective, most writing instruction in higher education is consistent with that in secondary education: what Stephen Judy described as 'Advanced Hodgepodge' in the high school gives way to 'Arrogant Hodgepodge' in college" (47).

PERSONALITY PROFILES AND LEARNING PREFERENCES

Just as the works of Perry, Kolb, and Belenky et al. provide a revealing portrait of the stages of intellectual development that traditional undergraduate students progress through on their way to cognitive maturity, there exists a substantial body of research into the personality differences that students exhibit and the implications of such difference for teaching and learning.

The Myers-Briggs Type Indicator (MBTI) is one of the most widely recognized and implemented personality style inventories and it has been used extensively in education circles for the past two decades. Working from Carl Jung's theory of psychological "types" (Myers and Myers, Lawrence), a model that explains how people take in information and make decisions, MBTI uses an extensive questionnaire to chart an individual's preferences in each of four binary domains:

1. Sources of energy/Interaction with the outside world

> Extraversion: Attitudes and interests oriented toward the external world of actions, people, objects, and events.

Introversion: Inner subjective orientation toward life. Attitudes and interests are directed toward concepts, ideas, theories, and modes of reality.

2. Information gathering/Perceptive processes

Sensing: Obtaining information from sensory input associated with the immediate, real, and practical facts of experience and everyday life.

Intuition: Gathering information by going beyond the immediate experiences of life to consider possibilities, probabilities, and other aspects of people, objects, relationships, and events that are not immediately available to our senses.

3. Judgment

Thinking: Becoming objective, impersonal, logical, looking for causes of events, and the pros and cons of various approaches.

Feeling: Subjectively and personally weighing the values of choices and how points of view and decisions affect other people.

4. Style of living

Judgment: Living in a decisive, planned, and orderly manner with strong needs to regulate and control events.

Perception: Living in a spontaneous, flexible manner, aiming to understand life and to adapt to the changes that occur in as efficient a manner as possible. (Grasha 24)

From the pairs within the four domains are derived sixteen possible types that represent an individual's preferred way of doing things. Although everyone will use strategies that are more closely associated with type preferences other than the four considered dominant for them, particularly as they mature and work from greater stores of life experiences, we retain a preference for particular ways of interacting with the world, ideas, and other people.

MBTI has received more attention in composition studies than have other lines of research into personality or learning styles (although that attention itself can hardly be described as overwhelming).[9] The most thorough, research-based, and well-received discussion of how MBTI can apply to the teaching of writing is *Personality and the Teaching of Composition* by George H. Jensen and John K. DiTiberio.[10] In addition to providing an introduction to Jung's psychological theories, a careful review of the history of the MBTI's development, and a detailed accounting of the eight personality dimensions covered by the MBTI,

Jensen and DiTiberio draw clear connections between different type preferences and the writing processes that individuals with specific preferences most often rely on. Their analysis of type-specific composing strategies and overall composing processes attracted much attention in the late 1980s and early 1990s. Their analysis helped to explain many of the frustrations writing teachers faced working with the wide range of students found in developmental and first-year composition courses and it also elided well with emerging research on such issues as writer's block and rhythms of the composing process.

A look at the composition community's literature, however, demonstrates that available information about personality type preferences and the connections that have been drawn to writer's composing processes has not achieved wide integration into the discipline's discussions about writing in general and its teaching or the implications that such information carries for new teacher training and for ongoing faculty and curricular development. In addition to the negligible coverage of issues related to cognitive development and personality types in the composition community's most prestigious journals, these issues get almost no mention in the most frequently adopted texts used in the training of composition teachers. The following five books (some newer than others) are ones that I have encountered in a large number of composition teacher training programs: *Training the New Teacher of Composition; The St. Martin's Guide to Teaching Writing; Rhetoric and Composition: A Sourcebook for Teachers and Writers; Nuts and Bolts: A Practical Guide to Teaching College Composition;* and *The Writing Teacher's Sourcebook.* Spanning a period from 1981 to 1993, a time of almost frenetic activity in the development of composition theory and methodology, these books offer a revealing angle into the themes dominating the discipline's discussions. Only one of the five, Graves's *Rhetoric and Composition,* devotes any space to discussions of how students learn within a cognitive framework or to the presence of personality type and learning style preferences in the academic performance of writers. These two articles are reprinted versions of arguments made elsewhere, and thus do not add much weight of discussions about these issues and their consideration in the design of writing curricula, in the teaching of writing, or in the training of writing teachers.

The reasons for the absence of strong application of the findings from the personality type research in the typical composition sequence are many, and they range from absence due to ignorance, to absence based on daunting logistical hurdles. MBTI, although the most popular and widely used of several available personality type indicators, is quite a complex tool and comes in several administration forms (e.g., a short form and a standard form). This inventory is also proprietary property: programs that wish to use the inventory must work through copyright holders to have a local administrator properly trained and certified in the inventory's administration, scoring, and interpretation; copies of the inventory must also be purchased through the copyright holder's publisher/agent. For large composition programs and for smaller ones also, instructional or faculty support budgets cannot absorb these costs. Successful use of the inventory is further complicated by the tendency of many inventory administrators and inventory takers either to oversimplify or reify the inventory results. The personality profiles generated by MBTI are metaphors, not yardsticks; however, these profiles are frequently discussed and applied to teaching situations as givens, and doing so dilutes their effectiveness in helping teachers and students develop a shared understanding and language for discussing and anticipating individuals' responses to different types of situations and activities.

One of the most useful findings to emerge from MBTI-based research is in the dissimilarities that exist between students and their teachers. In terms of their dominant personality types, most faculty interact with the world, information, and others in ways that are quite different from how most of the population do. Summarizing data from a number of studies of type profiles among academic populations, Grasha, like Lawrence, shows that faculty exhibit a disproportionate preference for introversion and intuition in relation to their students and the general population (43):

	Faculty	Students
Extraverted	46%	70%
Introverted	54%	30%
Sensing	36%	70%
Intuitive	64%	30%

In articulating the implications of these differences for how teachers and students interact in the classroom, Grasha writes,

I typically find that the discrepancies between faculty and their students on the dimension of introversion and intuition are particularly problematic for faculty . . . . [C]ompared to the average college student, college faculty are overrepresented on these two types. In effect faculty interests and energy are largely captured by the inner world of ideas and they are more willing to consider possibilities for things that are not immediately apparent or available to the senses. Most college teachers also have the capacity to formulate hypotheses, to anticipate expected outcomes, and to formulate the implications of existing ideas and data from their disciplines. While such qualities are ideal for scholarship, they often clash with the more extraverted and sensing qualities of students. Unlike many of their instructors, most students get their energy from the world of people, objects and events. They prefer to see, touch, and feel things in order to gather information. Their orientation is more to the hands-on experiences and the practical implications of issues. Theoretical concerns and analysis is not typically one of their strong points.[11]

Thus, when faculty become excited about theoretical and conceptual issues, most students are looking for concrete and clear examples of terms and concepts. While some faculty may be satisfied with a rich verbal description of a point, many students want to see, hear, or touch something that is a representation of the conceptual point. When teachers become too theoretical and conceptual, the majority of their students are often lost. Deep intellectual analysis is not their strong suit. (43-44)

In a nutshell, the research on differences exhibited between teachers and students suggests that, more often than not, classroom activities that make perfect sense to teachers can easily be interpreted by students in almost diametrically opposite ways (Lawrence; Jensen and DiTiberio).

PRAGMATIC RESPONSE TO LEARNING STYLE AND PERSONALITY TYPE DIVERSITY

A more accessible inventory than MBTI is the VARK learning styles inventory, developed by New Zealand educators Neil Fleming and Colleen Mills (1992). Rather than focus on personality preferences as a means of gaining insight on how students prefer to learn, Fleming and Mills focused on the "sensory modalities as a learning style dimension" (138). Their sensory-based learning styles model, VARK, derives it name from the following four "perceptual modes" that individuals gravitate toward as they deal with day-to-day activities and with formal learning situations:

Visual: preference for graphical and symbolic ways of representing information.
Aural: preference for "heard" information.
Read/Write: preference for information printed as words.
Kinesthetic: preference for the use of experience and practice (simulated or real). (140)

This inventory is much more accessible than MBTI is. The "How Do I Learn Best" questionnaire consists of thirteen items, is easily self-scored, and requires little to no administrative training. The strategies presented for helping teachers understand how their learning style preferences influence their choice of teaching activities are straightforward and intuitively appealing. The same can be said for the guides for students that provide strategies for note taking, study activities, and exam preparation. Additionally, the tool is free and easily obtained.

Where Fleming and Mills differ from educators like Jensen and DiTiberio and other proponents of MBTI for instructional planning is in their pragmatic response to the real issue of the daunting number of different learning style preferences a teacher can expect to encounter in any given group of students. While they believe, like Grasha and Nilson, that teachers should accommodate students' learning styles somewhat in each course they teach, Fleming and Mills are realistic enough to know that students cannot count on such altruism as a matter of course (138). Explaining the observations that led them to develop the VARK inventory and its attendant support materials for students, they write:

If we assume that the matching of presentational style and learner styles is a desirable objective, teachers face an incredibly demanding task. The range of style dimensions and therefore the combinations that might occur in one particular student group are likely to be so extensive that teachers are unable to extend their repertoire of teaching methods toencompass all of them. . . . [I]t is simply not realistic to expect teachers to provide programs that accommodate the learning style diversity present in their classes, even if they can establish the nature and extent of that diversity. We have come to the conclusion that the most realistic approach to the accommodation of learning styles in teaching programs should involve empowering students through knowledge of their own learning styles to adjust their learning behavior to the learning programs they encounter. (138)

THE OUTLOOK FOR POST-SECONDARY WRITING INSTRUCTION

By this point, it should be clear that it is no easy task to create writing sequences that take into careful consideration where each student enters the course stream as learners, how they prefer to learn and to interact with the world and others, and how the courses we offer to them can be structured to ensure that these students achieve levels of development on target with course and curricular goals. Yes, in the brave new world of writing instruction, all writing courses would be created and taught in a multimodal manner, with the entire sequence choreographed to support students' cognitive development while also making instruction methods commensurate with as many separate learning styles and personality profiles as possible. I am not holding my breath till this particular wind of change blows through the composition community, however.

Like Fleming and Mills, I do not expect to see most composition faculty extending themselves in this manner, particularly given that historical precedence does not bode well for a sudden raise in interest about student learning processes among the members of the composition community who most often chart the course that the community's discussions will take. And so, it is tempting to assuage the guilt that results from not doing all that we might do as concerned and informed educators by reaching for the VARK learning styles inventory, including it in the writing course's first-day activities, and congratulating ourselves for the accommodation we have shown to our students. This is certainly a less demanding commitment than trying to use MBTI or Kolb's learning cycles as a foundation for a writing course, or developing assignment sequences and instructional activities that intersect smoothly with the variety of all students' learning preferences. Yet composition is such an odd duck swimming in the academic course pond that Fleming and Mill's pragmatic strategy of helping students deal with dissonance between the ways that they prefer to intake and process information and the ways that many teachers structure their presentation of course material does not offer writing teachers the easy rhetorical out that it offers faculty in other disciplines. Fleming and Mills notetaking, study, and exam strategies work best in courses that have the defined course "content" and regular tests that many writing courses do not. These aids are crafted within the overriding gestalt of the traditional lecture/discussion-based, content-based curriculum. And so, we are back where we started, faced with several unappealing choices.

As I see it, writing teachers have three choices for reacting to what is known about the cognitive development patterns, learning and personality profiles typically found among lower-division undergraduate students: do nothing, dive in, change the course outcomes.

Option 1: Do Nothing

Given the inertia that defines academe, Option 1 is the most likely choice, although it will most likely be dressed up in the language of deflection of responsibility, "We can't do that because the institution won't fund it," and so on. We will probably cling to this choice until calls for accountability and programmatic assessment get too intense to ignore, until funding for curricular programs is tied to meaningful outcomes assessment, or until internal and external stakeholders mandate some combination of the two. At that point, we can all raise our voices in moral indignation and decry the injustice of whatever system is imposed on us and our programs.

The other two choices offer more complex alternatives and, regardless how unlikely it is that either will surface as the course of action chosen by the composition community, each warrants a bit of speculation about its merits, shortcomings, and logistics.

Option 2. Dive In: Put the Best Available Information Into Practice

It might seem natural that given the composition community's long-standing sales pitch that this is a community more concerned about student growth than other disciplinary communities we would be willing to jump in and create curricula and courses that strive to put into practice material along the lines of that presented in this chapter. I doubt such action will happen, however. The project would be a massive undertaking for one thing. It would also disrupt comfortable academic routines. Specifically, to strive for the goal of creating a multimodal learning environment in each writing course on a campus, a number of thorny, currently unresolved issues must be addressed. None of these issues is new. Yet they are ones that the composition community has not been successful in resolving, even in the face of continuing advocacy for change coming from the grassroots and national organizational levels.

Staffing: Many writing programs are of a size that they must offer anywhere from thirty to 200+ sections of just first-year writing courses each term. Such course demands mean that these programs need anywhere from ten to 75 teachers to adequately staff these classes. To date, in many programs these teachers are members of a peripatetic part-time, adjunct, graduate student pool. However, constancy of one's teaching staff is a necessity for a program that tries to institute a curriculum that strives to meet the individualized learning needs of each student enrolled. This need for a stable, full-time teaching staff is not only pedagogically and programmatically desirable, it is also an economic necessity.

Faculty Training and Ongoing Development: Because of the novelty of this approach to teaching, an extensive and ongoing training program is needed to educate current faculty in the methods advocated by the available research on student learning, but also to continually educate needed replacement faculty and to re-educate and refocus continuously. Such activity is never cheap and a stable instructional force will be one of the key elements in making the overall program, as described, cost effective—even before considering the types of salary and benefits adjustments needed to stabilize this labor pool. One other issue that will come to the forefront during workshops and seminars about students' learning cycles is the time needed for most individuals to make cognitive gains of the kind implied in most writing courses.

Course Placement and Time Lines: The ten- week quarter and the sixteen-week semester are not ideal time frames within which to make substantive cognitive growth, particularly when one's attention is spread thin between four or five competing academic demands—not to mention nonacademic demands. Realistically, upper-division students are better prepared cognitively to achieve with many of the course outcomes found in many writing courses. They are better able to analyze complex arguments and situations, synthesize responses to them, and to be able to justify and articulate the validity of their choices than are first-year students. Therefore, one option is to move the writing courses into later years of the curriculum. Doing so, however, would be a disadvantage to lower-division students who do benefit from the cognitive push they feel in writing classes and so another option to explore is taking the writing course out of the standard academic term boundaries and making written competence an exit ability outcome of the student's entire educational experience, spreading instruction across every step of the curriculum.

The Writing Center: Actually, a logical model for achieving a highly individualized learning environment designed to meet the specific needs of students at every step of their development as learners and writers exists in the form of writing center pedagogy. By working with students through their entire post-secondary experience, writing center staff could almost guarantee that demonstrable gains would be made—assuming of course that students share the desire to achieve those gains and are willing to work in the comparatively unstructured situation of the one-to-one or small-group tutorial. Working in this type of setup, students' entry-level learning styles, personality profiles, and levels of cognitive development could be assessed, learning goals and schedules established, and achievement of learning outcomes demonstrated. However, such a program, even on small campuses, would be expensive (not to mention the extent to which its existence would force college registrars and other administrators to think outside the familiar box of the academic term).

For all the reasons stated above, and for others as yet unarticulated, I cannot see the needed critical mass of compositionists opting for this plan anytime soon. Thus, there remains one other option to consider.

Option 3: Revise the Course and Program Outcomes for College-Level Composition Sequences

Although this third option might strike any number of writing teachers as unthinkable, I disagree. Rather, I think that revising the goals for the writing course, restating the course outcomes to reflect learning gains that can be achieved with the large majority of students in the tight confines of the academic term, is an honest response to a less-than-desirable situation that has been allowed to run unchecked for too long. Most writing classes—even entire writing programs—rarely state clearly the outcomes for the course and then match the course structure, assignment, and texts for the achievement of those outcomes. Most of the statements that pass for outcome measures for these courses are global, vague, poorly defined, unrealistic statements along the lines of making students critically engaged thinkers and adept manipulators of academic prose. In reality, when working with lower-division students who see the world in black-and-white terms, who view the teacher as the sole voice of authority, and who probably interact with information and experiences in decidedly different ways from the teacher, the honest and achievable course goals are to try to get students somewhat comfortable with the reality of ambiguity in the world, somewhat adept at summarizing and analyzing texts and arguments, and aware of their ability to accurately self-assess the larger elements that define the strengths and weaknesses of their written communicative activities.

While these goals are attainable in a fifteen-week semester—as long as everyone works hard—they are not glamorous. Nor are they all that mysterious and evocative: the goods they promise to deliver are rather mundane, especially compared to the tenor of the previous promises about the results of college-level writing courses on student learning. I believe too that many compositionists will consider course outcomes such at these too low a goal for a college-level writing course? Yet, if we come back to the issue of where do our students come into these writing courses as learners, then consider how are they likely to go about learning in these courses, and finally assess how much time it will take for most of them to demonstrate proficiency with the types of performances we choose to use as evaluation instruments, these goals gain some redemption.

Composition as a required part of a college education is not going to disappear. However, it should, and can, be more honest to its many stakeholders than it has been historically. Our community has often colluded with our institutions and the larger culture to hold out the writing sequence as the key to academic success and social mobility, even when we put students in courses whose structure, instructors, and activities offer beneficial learning environments for a proportionately small number of these very students. The ultimate redemption for college writing courses and programs will not be found in some yet-to-be-found new theory or paradigm but, rather when these courses deliver on their promises and each student is afforded the same opportunity to develop as a thinker, individual, and a writer. That is a type of redemption to which the composition community should strive.

NOTES

1. An argument in a similar vein is made by Kate Ronald and Jon Volkmer in their *JAC* article "Another Competing Theory of Process: The Student's." They ask "researchers and teachers of composition to resist elevating writing instruction to some lofty abstract perch and to pay attention to the context of students' lives as they write and learn" (84).

2. Henson and Borthwick (1984) review long-standing assumptions about student performance as indicators of intelligence and note a surprising change in study findings. They question the findings of influential studies early in the century that indicated that student achievement correlated with intelligence because these studies were structured so that "all students were given the same type of instruction and the same amount of time to learn" (4). When the question of performance and intelligence was seriously reconsidered later in the century, in studies in which students had unlimited time to learn and were exposed to many types of teaching, results differed markedly. "Under these conditions the findings were totally different. . . . given the time and the correct teaching methods almost any students can learn or master the material set before them" (4). Like other researchers, Henson and Borthwick see "that individual learners have their own preferred learning styles and that teachers have some responsibility for gearing up their teaching style to 'fit' the preferred learning style of the learners" (4).

3. For widely cited summaries of this process, see Berlin, *Rhetoric and Reality*, and Faigley, "Competing Theories of Process: A Critique and a Proposal."

4. *College English* and *College Composition and Communication*, the field's flagship journals, have printed nothing dealing directly with individuals' learning styles and personality preferences, or their cognitive or intellectual development within the past decade. *The Journal of Advanced Composition* has printed two articles that apply, one in 1983, the other in 1989. To find more discussion of these issues within the context of college-level writing instruction, one must look to more outlying, fringe journals such as *JAEPL: Journal of the Association of Expanded Perspectives on Learning*, *Writing Center Journal*, *Writing Lab Newsletter*, and *Writing on the Edge*.

5. Although rightly critiqued for the less-than-representative nature of his initial study population (all white males from affluent East Coast backgrounds), Perry's findings have held up to repeated replication studies.

6. For accessible syntheses of Perry's model, see Grasha 1996 and Nilson 1998.

7. Belenky et al. is widely cited in the composition literature; however, among those articles drawing on this research, few use the developmental model presented to articulate instructional scaffolding beyond advocating the use of collaborative situations as fitting in well with women's needs for consensus building, or for presenting nonargumentative writing tasks as allowing women space to express themselves in

nonaggressive, decidedly masculine discourse patterns. Carol Gilligan's work is similarly thinly applied in the composition literature, when it is used.

8. Add to this equation the dissonance that lower-division college students perceive between the obvious levels of ambiguity they deal with in their writing classes and the seeming certainty presented in other introductory courses across the curriculum and it is easy to see why students who operate largely from a dualist world view can easily discount much of the "instruction" they face in the composition course.

9. Noted art education scholar and teacher educator Janet L. Olson (1992) reports that in most elementary, middle, and secondary school classrooms, one will find four basic types of students, each type representing approximately 25 percent of the class. They can be described as follows: A. High visual and high verbal skills; B. High visual and low verbal skills; C. Low visual and high verbal skills; and D. Low visual and low verbal skills. (45) Her work stresses the need to link visual and verbal instruction if teachers are to help *all* students develop the range of communication and problem-solving skills they need in order to succeed in today's information-rich economy and culture.

10. Other books and articles about MBTI use in teaching writing exist; many of them are more recent than *Personality and the Teaching of Composition*. Such useful book as *Writing and Personality: Finding Your Voice, Your Style, and Your Way,* by DiTiberio and Jensen, and Tom Thompson's edited collection, *Most Excellent Differences: Essays on Using Type Theory in the English Classroom,* have received no attention in the mainstream composition literature.

11. The "not" in this sentence was inadvertently deleted in the published text. I have replaced the missing word in my quotation with the author's permission.

WORKS CITED

Belenky, Mary F., Blythe M. Clinchy, Nancy R. Goldberger, and Jill Tarule. *Women's Ways of Knowing: The Development of Self, Voice, and Mind.* New York: Basic Books, 1986.

Berlin, James A. *Rhetoric and Reality: Writing Instruction in American Colleges, 1900-1985.* Carbondale and Edwardsville: Southern Illinois UP, 1987.

Bloom, Benjamin S., and others. *Taxomony of Educational Objectives, Vol. 1: The Cognitive Domain.* New York: McKay, 1956.

Bonwell, Charles C. "Active Learning and Learning Styles: Making the Connection." Albany College of Pharmacy, Albany, NY, 25 October 1998.

————. and Tracey E. Sutherland. "The Active Learning Continuum: Choosing Activities to Engage Students in the Classroom." In Sutherland and Bonwell, 3-16.

Brand, Alice G. "The Why of Cognition: Emotion and the Writing Process." *College Composition and Communication,* 38 (Dec. 1987): 436-443.

Campossela, Toni-Lee. Ed. *The Critical Writing Workshop: Designing Writing Assignments to Foster Critical Thinking.* Portsmouth, NH: Boynton/Cook, 1993.

————. "Using William Perry's Scheme to Encourage Critical Writing." In Campossela, 52-70.

Childers, Pamela B., Eric H. Hobson, and Joan A. Mullin. *ARTiculating: Teaching Writing in a Visual World*. Portsmouth, NH: Boynton/Cook, 1998.

Connors, Robert, and Cheryl Glenn. *The St. Martin's Guide to Teaching Writing*, 2nd ed. New York: St. Martin's, 1992.

DiTiberio, John K., and George H. Jensen. *Writing and Personality: Finding Your Voice, Your Style, Your Way*.Palo Alto, CA: Consulting Psychologists Press, 1995.

Faigley, Lester. "Competing Theories of Process: A Critique and a Proposal." *College English* 48 (1986): 527-42.

Fleming, Neil D., and Colleen Mills. "Not Another Inventory, Rather a Catalyst for Reflection." *To Improve the Academy* 11 (1992): 137-55.

Flynn, Elizabeth A. "Composing as a Woman." *College Composition and Communication* 39 (December 1988): 423-35.

Gardner, Howard. *Frames of Mind: The Theory of Multiple Intelligences*. New York: Basic Books, 1983.

Gilligan, Carol. *In a Different Voice: Psychological Theory and Women's Development*. Cambridge: Harvard UP, 1982.

Grasha, Anthony F. *Teaching with Style: A Practical Guide to Enhancing Teaching by Understanding Teaching & Learning Styles*. Pittsburgh: Alliance Publishers, 1996.

Graves, Richard L., ed. *Rhetoric and Composition: A Sourcebook for Teachers and Writers*. 3rd ed., Portsmouth, NH: Boynton/Cook, 1990.

Henson, Kenneth T. and Paul Borthwick. "Matching Styles: A Historical Look." *Theory into Practice*; 23,1: Win 1984: 3-9.

Jensen, George H., and John K. DiTiberio. *Personality and the Teaching of Composition*. Norwood, NJ: Ablex, 1989.

Kolb, David A. *Experiential Learning: Experience as the Source of Learning and Development*. Englewood Cliffs, NJ: Prentice-Hall, 1984.

Lawrence, G. *People Types and Tiger Stripes*, 2nd ed. Gainsville, FL: Center for the Application of Psychological Type, 1982.

Miller, Judith E., James E. Groccia, and John M. Wilkes. "Providing Structure: The Critical Element." In Sutherland and Bonwell, 17-30.

Myers, I.B. *Introduction to Type*. Palo Alto: Consulting Psychologists Press, 1987.

Myers, Isabel B., and P. B. Myers. *Gifts Differing*. Palo Alto: Consulting Psychologists Press, 1980.

Newkirk, Thomas. Ed. *Nuts & Bolts: A Practical Guide to Teaching College Composition*. Portsmouth, NH: Boynton/Cook, 1993.

Nilson, Linda B. *Teaching at Its Best: A Research-Based Resource for College Instructors*. Bolton, MA: Anker, 1998.

Olson, Janet, L. *Envisioning Writing: Toward an Integration of Drawing and Writing*. Portsmouth, NH: Heinemann, 1992.

Perry, William G. *Forms of Intellectual and Ethical Development in the College Years: A Scheme*. New York: Holt, Rinehart & Winston, 1970.

Ronald, Kate, and Jon Volkmer. "Another Competing Theory of Process: The Student's." *Journal of Advanced Composition* 9 (1989): 83-96.

Spear, Karen. "Thinking and Writing: A Sequential Curriculum for Composition." *Journal of Advanced Composition* 4 (1983): 47-63.

Sutherland, Tracey E., and Charles C. Bonwell, eds. *Using Active Learning in College Classes: A Range of Options for Faculty. New Directions for Teaching and Learning*, no. 67. San Francisco: Jossey-Bass, 1996.

Tate, Gary, and Edward P. J.. Corbett, Eds. *The Writing Teacher's Sourcebook.* New York: Oxford UP, 1981.

Thompson, Thomas C. (Ed.). *Most Excellent Differences: Essays on Using Type Theory in the English Classroom.* Gainsville, FL: Center for Applications of Psychological Type, 1996.

Selected Bibliography

Anson, Chris M. "Distant Voices: Teaching and Writing in a Culture of Technology." *College English* 61 (1999): 261-80.

Astin, Alexander. *What Matters in College? Four Critical Years Revisited.* San Fancisco: Jossey-Bass, 1991.

Bartholomae, David. "What Is Composition and (if you know what it is) Why Do We Teach It?" *Composition in the Twenty-First Century: Crisis and Change.* Eds. Lynn Z. Bloom, Donald A. Daiker, and Edward M. White. Carbondale: Southern Iliinois UP, 1996. 11-28.

Berlin, James. *Rhetoric and Reality: Writing Instruction in American Colleges, 1900-1985.* Carbondale: Southern Illinois UP, 1987.

Berlin, James. Rhetorics, Poetics, and Cultures: *Refiguring College English Studies.* Urbana, IL: NCTE, 1996.

Berube, Michael. *The Employment of English: Theory, Jobs and the Future of Literary Studies.* New York: New York UP, 1998.

Bishop, Wendy. "Students' Stories and the Variable Gaze of Composition Research." *Writing Ourselves into the Story: Unheard Voices from Composition Studies.* Eds. Sheryl Fontaine and Susan Hunter, Carbondale: Southern Illinois UP, 1993.

Bizzell, Patricia. *Academic Discourse and Critical Consciousness.* Pittsburgh: U of Pittsburgh P, 1992.

Brannon, Lil, "(Dis)Missing Compulsory First-Year Composition." *Reconceiving Writing, Rethinking Writing Instruction.* Ed. Joseph Petraglia. Mahwah, NJ: Lawrence Erlbaum, 1995. 239-48.

Brereton, John C. (ed.). *The Origin of Composition Studies in the American College, 1875-1925: A Documentary History.* Pittsburgh: U of Pittsburgh P, 1995.

Brodkey, Linda. *Writing Permitted in Designated Areas Only*. Minneapolis: U of Minnesota P, 1996.

Brown Stuart C., Paul R. Meyer, and Theresa Enos. "Doctoral Programs in Rhetoric and Composition: A Catalog of the Profession." *Rhetoric Review* 12 (Spring 1994): 240-389.

Burnham, Christopher C. "Expressive Rhetoric: A Source Study." *Defining the New Rhetorics*. Theresa Enos and Stuart C. Brown (eds). Newbury Park, CA: Sage, 1993. 154-70.

Campossela, Toni-Lee, ed. *The Critical Writing Workshop: Designing Writing Assignments to Foster Critical Thinking*. Portsmouth, NH: Boynton/Cook, 1993.

Charney, Davida. "From Logocentrism to Ethnocentrism: Hisoricizing Critiques of Writing Research." *Technical Communication Quarterly* 7 (1998): 9-32.

Childers, Pamela B., Eric H. Hobson, and Joan A. Mullin. *ARTiculating: Teaching Writing in a Visual World*. Portsmouth, NH: Boynton/Cook, 1998.

Connors, Robert J. *Composition-Rhetoric: Backgrounds, Theory, and Pedagogy*. Pittsburgh: U of Pittsburgh P, 1997.

Crowley, Sharon. *Composition in the University: Historical and Polemical Essays*. Pittsburgh: U of Pittsburgh P, 1998.

David, Denise, et al. "Seeking Common Ground." *College Composition and Communication* 46 (December 1995): 522-32.

Dobrin, Sidney I. *Constructing Knowledges: The Politics of Theory-Building and Pedagogy in Composition*. New York: State U of New York P, 1997.

Dobrin, Sid. "The Politics of Theory-Building and Anti-Intellectualism in Composition." *Composition Forum* 6 (Summer 1995): 90-99.

Faigley, Lester. *Fragments of Rationality: Postmodernity and the Subject of Composition*. Pittsburgh: U of Pittsburgh P, 1992.

Fleming, David. "Rhetoric as a Course of Study." *College English* 61 (November 1998): 169-91.

Flower, Linda. *The Construction of Negotiated Meaning: A Social Cognitive Theory of Writing*. Carbondale: Southern Illinois UP, 1994.

Fontaine, Sheryl I. "Revising Administrative Models and Questioning the Value of Appointing Graduate Student WPAs." *Foregrounding Ethical Awareness in Composition and English Studies*. Eds. Sheryl I. Fontaine and Susan M. Hunter. Portsmouth, NH: Boynton/Cook, 1998. 83-92.

Giroux, Henry. "Where Have All the Public Intellectuals Gone? Racial Politics, Pedagogy, and Disposable Youth." *Journal of Advanced Composition* 17.2 (Spring, 1997): 191-205.

Gradin, Sherrie. *Romancing Rhetorics: Social Expressivist Perspectives on the Teaching of Writing*. Portsmouth, NH: Boynton/Cook, 1995.

Grazian, Frank. "Who Really Cares About Grammar and Usage?" *Public Relations Quarterly* 42.3 (1997): 5-6.

Grego, Rhonda and Nancy Thompson. "Repositioning Remediation: Renegotiating Composition's Work in the Academy." *College Composition and Communication* 47 (February 1996): 62-84.

Gregory, Marshall. "The Many-Headed Hydra of Theory vs. The Unifying Mission of Teaching." *College English* 59.1 (Jan. 1997): 41-58.

Hairston, Maxine. "Diversity, Ideology, and Teaching Writing." *College Composition and Communication* 43 (1992): 179-93.

Harding, Julia, "Writing in Business." Toby Fulwiler and Art Young (eds.), *Programs That Work: Models and Methods for Writing Across the Curriculum*. Portsmouth, NH: Boynton/Cook 1990. 83-113.

Harris, Joseph. *A Teaching Subject: Composition Since 1966*. Upper Saddle River, NJ: Prentice-Hall, 1997.

Harris, Muriel. "Collaboration Is Not Collaboration Is Not Collaboration: Writing Center Tutorials Vs. Peer Response Groups." *College Composition and Communication* 43.3 (1992): 369-83.

Hawisher, Gail E., et al. *Computers and the Teaching of Writing in American Higher Education, 1974-94: A History*. Norwood, NJ: Ablex, 1996.

Hunter, Susan M., and Ray Wallace. (eds.). *The Place of Grammar in Writing Instruction: Past, Present, Future*. Portsmouth, NH: Boynton/Cook, 1995.

Kutz, Elanor, and Hephzibah Roskelly. *An Unquiet Pedagogy*. Portsmouth, NH: Heinemann, 1991.

Latterall, Catherine G. "Training the Workforce: An Overview of GTA Educational Curricula." *WPA: Writing Program Administration* 19.3 (1996): 7-23.

MacDonald, Susan Peck. "Voices of Research: Methodological Choices of a Disciplinary Community." Eds. Christine Farris and Chris M. Anson, *Under Construction: Working at the Intersections of Composition Theory, Research, and Practice*. Logan: Utah State UP, 1998. 111-23.

Marius, Richard. "Composition Studies." *Redrawing the Boundaries*. New York: MLA, 1992. 466-81.

McCormick, Kathleen. *The Culture of Reading and the Teaching of English*. New York: Manchester UP, 1994.

Miller, Scott L., Brenda Jo Brueggermann, Bennis Blue, and Deneen M. Shepard. "Present Perfect and Future Imperfect: Results of a National Survey of Graduate Students in Rhetoric and Composition Programs." *College Composition and Communication* 48 (1997): 392-409.

Miller, Susan. *Textual Carnivals: The Politics of Composition*. Carbondale: Southern Illinois UP, 1991.

Miller, Thomas P. *The Formation of College English: Rhetoric and Belles Lettres in the British Cultural Provinces*. Pittsburgh: U of Pittsburgh P, 1997.

Mullin, Joan A., and Ray Wallace. (eds.). *Intersections: Theory-Practice in the Writing Center*. Urbana, IL: NCTE, 1994.

Newkirk, Thomas. *The Performance of Self in Student Writing*. Portsmouth, NH: Heinemann, 1997.

North, Stephen M. *The Making of Knowledge in Composition: Portrait of an Emerging Field*. Portsmouth, NH: Boynton/Cook, 1987.

Nystrand, Martin, Stuart Green, and Jeffrey Wiemelt. "Where Did Composition Studies Come From? An Intellectual History." *Written Communication* 10 (July 1993): 267-333.

Olson, Gary. "Writing Literacy and Technology: Toward a Cyborg Writing." *Journal of Advanced Composition* (Winter 1996): 1-16.

Olson Gary A. and Lester Faigly. "Language, Politics, and Composition: A Conversation with Noam Chomsky." *Journal of Advanced Composition* 11 (Winter 1991): 1-35.

Phelps, Louise Wetherbee. "The Dance of Discourse." *Pre/Text: The First Decade.* Ed. Victor Vitanza. Pittsburgh: U of Pittsburgh P, 1993. 31-64.

Qualley, Donna. *Turns of Thought: Teaching Composition as Reflexive Inquiry.* Portsmouth, NH: Boynton/Cook, 1997.

Raymond, Rich. "Preparing Writing Professionals for the Classroom: TAs and the Practice of Composition Theory." *Composition Forum* 9.2 (Fall 1998): 20-37.

Roskelly, Hephzibah, and Kate Ronald. *Reason to Believe: Romanticism, Pragmatism, and the Teaching of Writing.* Albany: State U of New York P, 1998.

Russell, David R. *Writing in the Academic Disciplines, 1870-1990: A Curricular History.* Carbondale: Southern Illinois UP, 1991.

Schilb, John "Histories of Pedagogy." Review of *Feminist Accused of Sexual Harassment,* by Jane Gallop, *Pedagogy, Democracy, and Feminism: Rethinking the Public Sphere,* by Adriana Hernandez, *The Formation of College English: Rhetoric and Belles Lettres in the British Cultural Provinces,* by Thomas P. Miller, *Writing in an Alien World: Basic Writing and the Struggle for Equality in Higher Education,* by Deborah Mutnick, and *Pedagogy: Disturbing History,* 1819-1929, Ed. Mariolina Rizzi Salvatori. *College English* 61 (1999): 240-46.

Severino, Carol. "Teaching and Writing 'up Against the Mall.'" *College English* 59.1 (January 1997): 74-82.

Shaughnessy, Mina P. *Errors and Expectations: A Guide for the Teacher of Basic Writing.* New York: Oxford UP, 1977.

Sidle, Michelle and Richard Morris. "Writing in a Post-Berlinian Landscape: Cultural Composition in the Classroom." *Journal of Advanced Composition* 18.2 (Spring 1998): 275-91.

Slevin, James F. "Disciplining Students: Whom Should Composition Teach and What Should They Know?" *Composition in the Twenty-First Century: Crisis and Change.* Eds. Lynn Z. Bloom, Donald A. Daiker, and Edward M. White. Carbondale: Southern Illinois UP, 1996. 153-65.

Sosnoski, James. "Postmodern Teachers in Their Postmodern Classrooms: Socrates Begone!" *Contending with Words: Composition and Rhetoric in a Postmodern Age.* Eds. Patricia Harkin and John Schilb. New York: MLA, 1991. 198-219.

Strickland, James. *From Disk to Hard Copy: Teaching Writing With Computers.* Portsmouth, NH: Heinemann-Boynton/Cook, 1997.

Thompson, Thomas C. (ed.). *Most Excellent Differences: Essays on Using Type Theory in the English Classroom.* Gainesville, FL: Center for Applications of Psychological Type, 1996.

Tobin, Lad. "How the Writing Process Was Born–And Other Conversation Narratives." *Taking Stock: The Writing Process Movement in the 90's*. Eds. Lad Tobin and Thomas Newkirk. Portsmouth, NH: Boynton/Cook, 1994. 1-16.

Trainor, Jennifer Seibel and Amanda Godley. "After Wyoming: Labor Practices in Two University Writing Programs." *College Composition and Communication* 50.2 (December 1998): 153-81.

Villanueva, Victor (ed.). *Cross-Talk in Comp Theory*. Urbana, IL: NCTE, 1997.

Wallace, Ray and Jeanne Simpson (eds.). *The Writing Center: New Directions*. New York: Garland, 1991.

Yagelski, Robert. "Who's Afraid of Subjectivity? The Composing Process and Postmodernism or a Student of Donald Murray Enters the Age of Postmodernism." Eds. Lad Tobin and Thomas Newkirk, *Taking Stock: The Writing Process in the 90's*. Portsmouth, NH: Boynton/Cook, 1994. 203-18.

§

Index

—————————— § ——————————

About the Contributors

LYNNE BELCHER is an Associate Professor of English at Southern Arkansas University. Among her publications are articles on CAI in the teaching of literature and composition and preparing international graduate students to teach university classes. She has served as an editorial reader and as a textbook reviewer for many years.

WENDY BISHOP is a Professor of English at Florida State University. She completed a Ph.D. in English/Rhetoric at Indiana University of Pennsylvania. Her most recent publications include: *Released into Language: Options for Teaching Creative Writing* (National Council of Teachers of English/2nd edition, Calendar Islands P, 1998); *Working Words: The Process of Creative Writing* (Mayfield 1993). *The Subject Is Writing: Essays by Teachers and Students* (Boynton/Cook Heinemann, 1992; 2nd edition, 1999); *Ethnographic Writing Research–Writing It Down, Writing It Up, and Reading It* (Boynton/Cook Heinemann 1999), and a co-edited volume–with Hans Ostrom–*Colors of a Different Horse: Rethinking How We Teach Creative Writing* (National Council of Teachers of English, 1994).

STUART C. BROWN is Associate Professor of Rhetoric and Professional Communication in the English Department at New Mexico State University. His publications include *Defining the New Rhetorics* (Sage, 1993) and *Professing the New Rhetorics* (Blair, 1994), both coedited with Theresa Enos; *Green Culture: Rhetorical Analyses of Environmental Discourse* (U of Wisconsin P, 1996), coedited with Carl Herndl; the advanced composition textbook *The Writer's Toolbox* (with Robert Mittan and Duane Roen, Allyn & Bacon, 1997) and *Living*

Rhetoric and Composition: Stories of the Discipline with Duane Roen and Theresa Enos (Lawrence Erlbaum, 1999).

DON BUSHMAN is an Associate Professor of English at the University of North Carolina at Wilmington. His published work has appeared in *Rhetoric Review*, *Writing Lab Newsletter*, and numerous other journals and edited collections.

GINA S. CLAYWELL is an Assistant Professor and Director of Freshman Composition at Murray State University in Murray, Kentucky. Her publications include "Redefining Research: Finding Authority in Unexpected Places" in *Oklahoma English Journal* (1997); "Re-righting Grammar: Reasserting Grammar's Position in the Trivium in American College Composition" in *The Place of Grammar in Writing Instruction: Past, Present, Future*, Ray Wallace and Susan Hunter, eds. (Boynton/Cook 1995); *Recreating Realities: An Ethnographic/Case Study Approach to the Historic Composition Classroom* ERIC Clearinghouse on Reading and Communication Skills (ED 372 397); and "Nonverbal Communication and Writing Lab Tutorials" *Writing Lab Newsletter* (1994), as well as several reviews and conference proceedings.

J. ROCKY COLAVITO received his Ph.D. in Rhetoric, composition, and the Teaching of English at the University of Arizona. He is currently teaching at Northwestern State University of Louisiana.

ERIC H. HOBSON, Associate Professor of Humanities at the Albany College of Pharmacy, is the founding Director of the ACP Center for Teaching and Learning. His most recent book, *Wiring the Writing Center* (Utah State UP, 1998) was awarded the National Writing Centers Association 1999 Scholarship Award for best book on writing center theory and practice.

ALAN JACKSON is an Associate Professor of Humanities at Georgia Perimeter College in Atlanta. He is editor-in-chief of *Humanities in the South*.

SARA KIMBALL is an Associate Professor and Director of the Undergraduate Writing Center at the University of Texas at Austin. Her publications include "Using the World Wide Web for Outreach to WAC Faculty." (Eric Hobson, ed., *Wiring the Writing Center*, Utah State U P, 1998); "Cybertexts/Cyberspeech: Writing Centers and Online Magic" (*Writing Center Journal* Fall, 1997), and numerous linguistics articles.

JOE LAW is Associate Professor of English and Coordinator of Writing Across the Curriculum at Wright State University in Dayton, Ohio. With Christina Murphy, he co-edited *Landmark Essays on Writing Centers* (Hermagoras, 1995) and was one of the compilers of *Writing Centers: An Annotated Bibliography* (Greenwood, 1996).

KELLY LOWE is an Assistant Professor of English and Director of Writing Programs at Mount Union College in Alliance, Ohio. He has published essays and reviews in *The Writing Lab Newsletter* and has a chapter (with Eric Hobson) in the forthcoming collection *The Politics of Writing Centers*.

BRUCE McCOMISKEY is an Assistant Professor of English at the University of Alabama at Birmingham (UAB). McComiskey has published articles on classical and neo-sophistic rhetoric in *Rhetoric Review* and the *Rhetoric Society Quarterly*, and a translation of the sophist Gorgias's On Non-Existence in *Philosophy and Rhetoric*. His essay in *Teaching English in the Two-Year College*, "Postmodern Cultural Studies and the Politics of Writing Instruction," was a runner-up for the 1998 article of the year award, and his *Journal of Advanced Composition essay,* "Social-Process Rhetorical Inquiry" won the 1997 James L. Kinneavy Award.

JAMES C. McDONALD is an Associate Professor of English at the University of Louisiana at Lafayette. His publications include *The Allyn & Bacon Sourcebook for College Writing Teachers* and chapters in *Teaching the Research Paper: From Theory to Practice, From Research to Writing; Visions of Rhetoric: History, Theory and Criticism*; and *Realms Of Rhetoric: Phonic, Graphic, Electronic*. He has published articles and reviews in *The Writing Center Journal, The Journal of Advanced Composition, English Journal, Composition Chronicle, Focuses, The Louisiana English Journal*, and *Bulletin of Bibliography*.

BETH MAXFIELD is currently an instructor at Northwest Mississippi Community College, DeSoto Center, in Mississippi. She has served as a contributing bibliographer for the annual *CCC Bibliography* and has written commissioned reviews for Mayfield Publishing and for *Dialogue: A Journal for Writing Specialists*.

KERRI MORRIS is a member of the Department of English at the University of Alaska, Anchorage. With colleage Dana Gulling Mead, she has recently published in *Writing on the Edge* and the *Journal of Advanced Composition*.

CHRISTINA MURPHY is Assistant Dean of the College of Humanities and Social Sciences and Professor of English at William Paterson University in New Jersey. Her books include *Writing Centers: An Annotated Bibliography, Landmark Essays on Writing Centers, The St. Martin's Sourcebook for Writing Tutors, Writing Center Perspectives, Critical Thinking Skills Journal, Ann Beattie*, and *The Theory and Criticism of Virtual Texts: An Annotated Bibliography*.

LINDA MYERS-BRESLIN is an Assistant Professor at Texas Tech University. Breslin has articles and book reviews in journals such as the *Journal of Advanced*

Composition, Computers and Writing, Freshman English News, and *Research in the Teaching of English*; most recently, her chapter "Computer Based Composition: Classrooms in Search of Transformative Curricula" was included in *Complexity in the Classroom*, edited John Harmon (NCTE, 1998).

JANICE WITHERSPOON NEULEIB is Professor of English and Director of Writing Programs, Illinois State University. Her book publications include: *Things Your Grammar Never Told You* (Allyn and Bacon, 1999) with Maurice Scharton; *The Mercury Reader*, (Simon and Schuster, 1998) with Kathy Kain, Stephen Rufus, and Maurice Scharton; and *Inside/Out: A Guide to Writing*, (Allyn and Bacon, 1993) with Maurice Scharton.

DONALD SAMSON teaches at Radford University, a state-supported school of 8,000 students in southwestern Virginia. He is the author of *Editing Technical Writing* (Oxford University Press, 1993) and co-author of *Professional Writing in Context: Lessons from Teaching and Consulting in Worlds of Work* (Erlbaum, 1995).

MAURICE SCHARTON is Professor of English and Coordinator of Writing Assessment at Illinois State University. He has published articles on writing assessment, teaching, and tutoring in various journals and has published three textbooks.

RAY WALLACE is Dean of Arts and Sciences at Troy State University Montgomery. Two books, *The Writing Center: New Directions* (Garland, 1991), with Jeanne Simpson, and *Intersections: Theory/Practice in the Writing Center* (NCTE, 1994), with Joan Mullin, have won book-of-the-year awards in national educational organizations. His third volume is *The Place of Grammar in Writing Instruction: Past, Present, Future* (Boynton/Cook, 1995), with Susan Hunter.

SUSAN LEWIS WALLACE, formerly an Instructor of Writing and Reading at Northwestern State University of Louisiana, teaches college writing in Alabama.

ISBN 0-313-31093-9

EAN

9 780313 310935

HARDCOVER BAR CODE